Modeling Semantic Web Services

Jos de Bruijn · Dieter Fensel · Mick Kerrigan
Uwe Keller · Holger Lausen · James Scicluna

Modeling Semantic Web Services

The Web Service Modeling Language

 Springer

Jos de Bruijn
Free University of Bozen-Bolzano
Faculty of Computer Science
KRDB Research Centre
Piazza Domenicani, 3
39100 Bozen-Bolzano BZ
Italy
debruijn@inf.unibz.it

Dieter Fensel
Mick Kerrigan
Uwe Keller
Holger Lausen
James Scicluna

STI Innsbruck
ICT - Technologiepark
Technikerstr. 21a
6020 Innsbruck
Austria
dieter.fensel@sti2.at
mick.kerrigan@sti2.at
uwe.keller@sti2.at
holger.lausen@seekda.com
james.scicluna@sti2.at

ISBN: 978-3-642-08785-1   e-ISBN: 978-3-540-68172-4

ACM Computing Classification: H.3.5, K.4.4, I.2.4, D.2.12

© 2010 Springer-Verlag Berlin Heidelberg

Cover design: KünkelLopka GmbH, Heidelberg

Printed on acid-free paper

9 8 7 6 5 4 3 2 1

springer.com

Preface

Motivation

Semantic Web services promise to automate tasks such as discovery, mediation, selection, composition, and invocation of services, enabling fully flexible automated e-business. The description of Web services plays an important role in the realization of his vision. The Web Service Modeling Ontology (WSMO) identifies the conceptual elements that are required for such descriptions, thereby providing the means for Web service description from a user point of view. However, the automation of Web service-related tasks requires a suitable concrete formal language. The formal description of Web services, as well as user goals, has three major aspects: static background knowledge in the form of ontologies, the functional description of the service (suitable for discovery and high-level composition), and the behavioral description of the service (suitable for selection, mediation, composition, and invocation). In this book we present a language framework addressing all three aspects. To address the problem of ontology description we present a language framework incorporating the Description Logic and Logic Programming formal language paradigms and the RDF Schema and OWL Semantic Web ontology languages. For the functional description of services we present a flexible framework based on Abstract State Spaces, which can be combined with a number of logical languages. Finally, we address the problem of behavioral description by presenting a flexible expressive language that has its conceptual roots in Abstract State Machines.

Goal

The usage of Web services requires a significant amount of human intervention due to the lack of support for the automation of tasks such as discovery, composition, and invocation. Key to the automation of such tasks is the availability of a means to describe user goals, Web services, and their interrelationships in a formal, machine-processable way. This book lays the foundations for understanding the requirements on the description of the various aspects related to Semantic Web services. It introduces the Web Service Modeling Language (WSML), which provides means for describing the functionality and behavior of Web services, as well as the underlying business knowledge in the form of ontologies, with a conceptual grounding in the Web Service Modeling Ontology (WSMO).

Target Audience

This book is suitable for professionals, as well as academic and industrial researchers, who have an interest in Semantic Web services. The book is aimed at providing insight into the area of Semantic Web services, and especially the Web Service Modeling Language to persons with various levels of knowledge. On the one hand, the book gives a comprehensive overview of the concepts and challenges in the area of Semantic Web services, gives an overview of the Web Service Modeling Ontology, introduces the concepts behind and syntax of the Web Service Modeling Language WSML, and describes the enabling technologies. On the other hand, the book provides an in-depth treatment of the semantic foundations and logical grounding of the ontology, functional, and behavioral descriptions in WSML.

Acknowledgments

The work presented in this book has been funded in part by the European Commission under the Knowledge Web (FP6-507482) and DIP (FP6-507483) projects.

We would like to thank all members of the WSML working group, and Axel Polleres in particular, for their invaluable contribution to the development of the WSML language. Thanks to Stefan Grimm and Gabor Nagypal for their contributions to Section 8.3 and Nathalie Steinmetz for her contribution to Section 8.4, as well as her ongoing efforts in editing the WSML language reference.

The authors, March 2008

Contents

List of Figures

List of Tables

List of Listings

1

Introduction

The Semantic Web [18, 128] aims to make the vast amount of information on the Web accessible to machines through the annotation of Web content using machine-understandable formats such as RDF,[1] and enable comprehension and integration of this information through the use of ontologies [55], which may be specified using the Web Ontology Language OWL [103]. However, these annotations refer only to static knowledge, and ontologies are – generally speaking – static descriptions of background knowledge in a particular domain. Web services [4] are concerned with providing functionality over the Web, and are thus more than chunks of static information; an example of such functionality is the sale of books over the Web, e.g., Amazon.[2] Mainstream Web service technologies such as SOAP[3] and WSDL[4] provide means for the structured XML-based annotation of, and interaction with, Web services. However, the description of the functionality of services using these technologies is limited to natural language text and a description of the structure of input and output messages. These limitations make it hard – especially for a machine – to understand the functionality of a service, let alone automatically discover, combine, and execute Web services. Consequently, the location, selection, combination, and usage of Web services requires considerable human effort [57, Section 4.5].

There is a conjecture that the combination of Semantic Web and Web service technologies, called *Semantic Web services*, has the potential to overcome these limitations [104]. To facilitate combining these technologies, several approaches to Semantic Web service description have arisen. They range from bottom-up approaches that extend existing technologies, such as WSDL-S [2] and SAWSDL [54], to top-down approaches that introduce new languages for the semantic description of Web services and subsequently "ground" such

---

[1] http://www.w3.org/RDF; see also Section 2.2.1
[2] http://www.amazon.com
[3] http://www.w3.org/TR/soap/
[4] http://www.w3.org/TR/wsdl

descriptions in existing technologies. The two most prominent top-down approaches are OWL-S (OWL-Services) [102, 8] and the Web Service Modeling Ontology (WSMO) [121, 57]. The former is tied in with the DL (Description Logic) sub-language (*species*) of the Web Ontology Language OWL [46, 77], and requires the use of OWL DL for the description of services.[5] WSMO provides a language-independent conceptual model for the description of services; it does not require using specific language, but requires languages that implement WSMO to follow the structure of the conceptual model.

The Web Service Modeling Language WSML [68, 29] (pronounced *wiss-mill*), which is the topic of this book, is a language implementing the conceptual model of WSMO (pronounced *wiss-mow*). In particular, WSML provides:

- a concrete language for writing WSMO ontologies, goals, Web services, and mediators;
- three concrete syntaxes for editing, representing, and exchanging WSML descriptions: a (1) BNF-style surface syntax for use by authors of descriptions and examples and (2) XML and (3) RDF representations for automated exchange of descriptions and integration with other data on the (semantic) Web;
- a choice in knowledge representation paradigm: the user can choose either Description Logics [11] or Logic Programming [96, 13, 61] as the underlying paradigm for ontology and Web service description;
- three sub-languages for describing the key aspects of services:
  1. ontologies, which provide the terminology and background knowledge for service description,
  2. functional service descriptions, which comprise the requested functionality of a goal or the provided functionality of a Web service, and are primarily used for automating Web service discovery, and
  3. behavioral service descriptions, which are descriptions of service interfaces in terms of their possible interactions, and are primarily used for automating Web service execution; and
- the possibility to use RDF Schema [28] and OWL DL [46] ontologies for Web service description, thereby enabling the reuse of existing ontologies on the Semantic Web in Web service descriptions.

In this book we describe the language and show how the above-mentioned aspects of WSML are realized. Although this book does contain a brief introduction to WSMO, we refer the reader to a book written by Fensel et al. [57] for a more elaborate description of the conceptual model itself, as well as possible uses thereof.

Besides technical aspects of the language, we describe two software applications that work with WSML. The first, WSML2Reasoner, exploits the fact that WSML is based on the Description Logic and Logic Programming knowledge representation paradigms. It takes as input WSML descriptions

---

[5] For a more elaborate comparison of OWL-S and WSMO see [91].

and translates them to formats internal to Description Logic and Logic Programming reasoners, thereby providing reasoning support; see Chapter 8. The second tool, the Web Service Modeling Toolkit (WSMT), is an Integrated Development Environment (IDE) for Semantic Web services and provides comprehensive support for the full life cycle – creation, management, and usage – of WSML descriptions; see Chapter 9. For more details around the implementation of Semantic Web services in the context of WSMO and WSML we refer the reader to a book edited by Fensel, Kerrigan, and Zaremba [56].

In Section 1.1 we introduce the running example used for illustration of the concepts throughout the book. We describe the outline of the book in Section 1.2.

1.1 Running Example

To illustrate the use of WSML we use a running example throughout the book. The example is a scenario concerned with a media shop – that is, a shop that sells media products such as books, CDs, and DVDs. We proceed with a description of the scenario.

The company Media Sales International (MSI), a reseller of media products such as books, CDs, and DVDs, wants to sell its products online, using Web service technology. The company has warehouses where the media products are stored, and from where the products are dispatched to the customers. However, the products are shipped by other companies, e.g., the Postal Service or an express shipping company.

MSI currently uses the express shipping company FHS for the delivery of all goods. However, FHS is not always the cheapest or fastest delivery service. Depending on the destination, there are other express shipping companies that are cheaper or faster. Using these other shipping services would require adaptation of the business processes and IT infrastructure at MSI, for each additional shipping service which is being used. MSI hopes that with the migration to Web service technology, it will be easier to choose different shipping services, always selecting the cheapest or fastest service, depending on the customer's preference.

Finally, MSI outsources payments of goods to the company CheapC-CProcessing, which does validation of credit card information, and takes care of payment processing. MSI has had only positive experiences with CheapC-CProcessing; the company is cheap, and payments are processed in a timely manner. Thus, MSI wants to continue exclusively using the services of Cheap-CCProcessing for credit card payments. However, MSI would also like to give its customers the possibility of directly paying using their bank accounts; MSI does not have any experiences with companies providing such services.

Figure 1.1 illustrates the services MSI wants to offer to its customers using a Web service interface and the services it requires from other organizations.

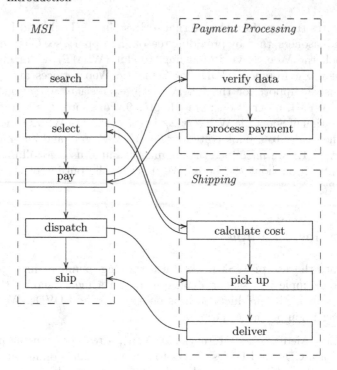

Fig. 1.1. Scenario of the running example

MSI wants to offer the following functionality to its customers, as illustrated in Figure 1.1. The figure also illustrates the services MSI requires from other organizations.

- MSI allows the customer to *search* the product catalog.
- When the customer has *select*ed a product from the catalog, he/she can add the item to the shopping basket, view and update the basket, and, after providing shipping information, view the shipping cost. The shipping cost is provided by the selected shipping company.
- After providing payment details and billing information, the customer can *pay* for the products and shipping. A payment processing service validates the payment details and processes the payment.
- After payment has been received, the product(s) is/are *dispatch*ed, which means that the shipping company does the *pick up* of the goods.
- Finally, the goods are *ship*ped, i.e., they are *deliver*ed at the address provided by the customer.

The challenges addressed in this book are concerned with both the description and usage of services such as those in Figure 1.1. Specific challenges are the description of the functionality of the services as a whole (i.e., *MSI*, *Payment Processing*, and *Shipping*; see Chapter 6), the description of their individual components (e.g., *select, pick up*) and the interaction between these individual components, i.e., the behavior of the services (see Chapter 7), as well as the description of the terminology, in the form of ontologies, used in Web service descriptions (see Chapter 5).

1.2 Outline of the Book

The main content of the book is structured into three parts:

Part I Basics

This part contains a description of the background technologies and an overview of the WSML language. A brief overview of the Web, Semantic Web, and Web service technologies, as well as challenges facing these technologies, is presented in Chapter 2. Chapter 3 contains an overview of the Web Service Modeling Ontology and describes its components on an intuitive level. Chapter 4 describes some of the underlying principles of WSML, introduces the WSML language through its surface syntax, gives an overview of the exchange syntaxes, and describes how RDF and OWL ontologies can be used in WSML.

Part II The WSML Description Components

This part describes the main components of WSML descriptions, namely ontologies and functional and behavioral Web service descriptions, in detail. Chapter 5 addresses WSML ontologies, and their combination with RDFS and OWL DL ontologies. The chapter gives an overview of the semantics of all WSML variants, which are based on the knowledge representation paradigms of Description Logics and Logic Programming. Functional description of services is addressed in Chapter 6, in which two means for describing the functionality of WSML services – set-theoretic relations and abstract state spaces – are discussed in detail. Chapter 7 presents a language for the behavioral description of services – the WSML choreography language.

Part III Enabling Technologies for WSML

In this final part two applications for processing and managing WSML descriptions are described. Chapter 8 describes a generic software framework for reasoning with WSML descriptions, and the use of this framework with existing Description Logic and Logic Programming reasoners. The Web Service Modeling Toolkit (WSMT), a comprehensive management environment for WSML descriptions, is described in Chapter 9. The chapter describes how to edit, browse, validate, and test WSML ontologies, Web services, and goals.

Finally, conclusions are presented in Chapter 10.

Part I

Basics

2

Semantic Web Services

In this chapter we briefly review the current Web, Web service, and Semantic Web technologies, in the Sections 2.1, 2.3, and 2.2, respectively. We then review the typical usage patterns for Web services, and show the shortcomings of current technologies with respect to these usage patterns, motivating the need for adding semantics to Web services, in the Sections 2.4 and 2.5.

For a more detailed description of Web technologies we refer the reader to [57, Chapter 2]. For a detailed description of the concepts underlying Web services, as well as Web service technologies, we refer the reader to [4].

For more comprehensive surveys on Semantic Web technologies we refer to [57, Chapter 3], [3], and [9].

2.1 Web Technologies

The *World Wide Web* (WWW, or simply *Web*) is a collection of interlinked documents, which might be written using the (X)HTML [67] format, accessible over a standardized protocol (e.g., HTTP [64]), and each document is identified by a Uniform Resource Identifier (URI) [49, 17]. The *Web* character of the World Wide Web comes from the interlinked nature of the documents; HTML documents contain links to other documents.

HTTP (HyperText Transfer Protocol) is the primary protocol for the transfer of documents on the Web, and HTML (HyperText Markup Language) is the format for representing documents and their inter-linkage on the Web. However, one may also use other protocols (than HTTP) for the exchange of information over the Web. Examples of such protocols are FTP (File Transfer Protocol), SMTP (Simple Message Transfer Protocol), and, indeed, SOAP (see the next section). Although HTML has been, and still is, the dominant format for the representation of Web documents, recently more and more formats for the representation of data on the Web have arisen. Examples are PNG (for images), CSS (style sheets), and XML (described in more detail below), as well as numerous XML-based formats such as XHTML (the

```
<books xmlns="http://example.org/msi#" >
  <book isbn="0684803356">
    <title>For Whom the Bell Tolls</title>
    <author>Ernest Hemingway</author>
  </book>
  <book isbn="0553211757">
    <title>Crime and Punishment</title>
    <author>Fyodor Dostoevsky</author>
  </book>
    ⋮
</books>
```

Listing 2.1. Example XML document

successor of HTML), SMIL (Synchronized Multimedia Integration Language), and RDF/XML (see Section 2.2).

Of all the Web standards, URI is seen as most central to the Web. In fact, the World Wide Web Consortium (W3C) recommendation *Architecture of the World Wide Web* [80] defines the Web as "an information space in which the items of interest, referred to as *resources*, are identified by global identifiers called Uniform Resource Identifiers (URI)."

URI

Uniform Resource Identifiers (URIs) are globally unique identifiers of resources. These resources *may or may not* correspond to documents on the Web. For example, the URI http://www.w3.org corresponds to the homepage of the W3C, which is an HTML document on the Web, whereas http://www.w3.org/1999/02/22-rdf-syntax-ns#type is the identifier of a particular RDF constructs (see also Section 2.2). Note that if you enter the URI http://www.w3.org/1999/02/22-rdf-syntax-ns#type in your browser, you will retrieve a document which describes RDF using RDF/XML. However, http://www.w3.org/1999/02/22-rdf-syntax-ns#type does not refer to these documents, or any part of this document. Rather, the document at the location http://www.w3.org/1999/02/22-rdf-syntax-ns gives additional information about http://www.w3.org/1999/02/22-rdf-syntax-ns#type.

XML

The eXtensible Markup Language (XML) [27] is a language for the representation of (semi-)structured data. The data in an XML document is organized in a tree structure. The basic building block of XML is the *element*, which has a number of associated *attributes*. Each element may contain text, and the elements may be nested inside other elements, thereby obtaining a tree data structure; each XML document must contain exactly one root element. Listing 2.1 contains an example XML document.

In the example, the root element is books. This element consists of a number of a book elements. Each book has an attribute isbn, and has two elements: title and author. That xmlns attribute of the books element is a standard "built-in" attribute of the XML, and stands for "XML Namespace":
The *namespace* [26], which is a URI, plays a key role in XML. In fact, every (expanded) name in XML is a pair $< namespace, localname >$. For example, the expanded name of the root element in Listing 2.1 is <http://example.org/msi#, books>. It is possible to use different namespaces in the same document; in this way, one can combine data whose formats are defined in different locations in a single XML file. A typical usage for namespaces is referring to a description of the document structure, possibly in the form of an *XML schema* [53], which is an XML-based format for defining the structure of XML documents.

XML has widely been adopted as a format for exchanging structured data over the Web. In fact, it forms the basis for the formats typically used in the context of Web services (see the next section) as well as the Semantic Web (see Section 2.2). Several languages have been developed for XML such as schema languages (XML Schema [53]), query languages (XPath[1], XQuery[2]), a linking language (XLink[3]), and a transformation language (XSLT [81]). Furthermore, there are numerous formats which are based on XML, including the Web service and Semantic Web formats described in the following section.

2.2 Semantic Web Technologies

A major drawback of the use of XML as a data model is that XML documents do not convey the meaning of the data contained in the document. Schema languages such as XML schema allow constraining the *format*, but not the *meaning* of XML data. Exchange of XML documents over the Web is only possible if the parties participating in the exchange agree beforehand on the exact syntactical format (possibly expressed using XML Schema) of the data and the meaning of the terms and structures into XML documents. The Semantic Web [18] allows the representation and exchange of information in a meaningful way, facilitating automated processing of descriptions on the Web.

Annotations on the Semantic Web express links between information resources on the Web and connect information resources to formal terminologies – these connective structures are called ontologies [55], which form the backbone of the Semantic Web. They allow machine understanding of information through the links between the information resources and the terms in the ontologies. Furthermore, ontologies facilitate interoperation between information resources through links to the same ontology or links between ontologies.

---

[1] http://www.w3.org/TR/xpath20

[2] http://www.w3.org/TR/xquery/

[3] http://www.w3.org/TR/xlink11/

The language for creating links between resources and annotating resources with connections to ontologies on the Semantic Web is RDF. There are two Semantic Web ontology languages recommended by W3C, namely RDF schema and the Web Ontology Language OWL. The latter is an extension of the former.

2.2.1 The Resource Description Framework

The Resource Description Framework (RDF) [90] is the first language developed especially for the Semantic Web. RDF was developed as a language for adding machine-readable metadata to existing data on the Web. RDF uses XML for its serialization [14]. RDF Schema [28] extends RDF with some basic (frame-based) ontological modeling primitives. There are primitives such as classes, properties, and instances. Also, the instance-of, subclass-of, and subproperty-of relationships have been introduced, allowing structured class and property hierarchies.

RDF has the subject–predicate–object triple, commonly written as s p o, as its basic data model. An object of a triple can, in turn, function as the subject of another triple, yielding a directed labeled graph, where resources (subjects and objects) correspond to nodes, and predicates correspond to edges. Furthermore, RDF allows a form of reification (a statement about a statement), which means that any RDF statement can be used as a subject in a triple. Finally, RDF has a notion of *blank node* (bNode), which is essentially a node that does not have a name.

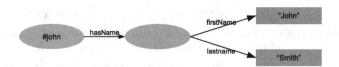

Fig. 2.1. Example RDF graph

Figure 2.1 illustrates the main concepts of RDF. The node labeled #john depicts a particular *resource*. This resource is linked to another resource with the property hasName – this resource does not have a name and is thus depicted using a blank node. In turn, the unnamed resource is linked to two *literals*, which are essentially strings; literals are depicted by rectangles in the figure. Besides illustrating some of the concepts of RDF, the figure shows how structured objects – in this case a name consisting of a first name and a last name – can be written in RDF.

In some sense, RDF is built on top of XML. RDF does not extend XML, but XML can be used for writing down and exchanging RDF statements. RDF/XML [14], as the XML-based serialization of RDF is called, can be seen as an XML language. In fact, RDF/XML is the standard syntax for

RDF. There are other syntaxes for RDF that are more suitable for human consumption – an example is Turtle [15] – but these are not recommended for exchanging RDF.

RDF Schema

RDF Schema (RDFS) is a lightweight ontology language for defining vocabularies that can be used with RDF. Unlike XML Schema, which prescribes the order and combinations of tags (the structure) in an XML document, RDF Schema only provides information about the interpretation of the statements given in an RDF data model. RDF Schema does not say anything about the syntactical appearance of the RDF description. RDFS can in fact be seen as an extension of RDF with a vocabulary for defining classes, class hierarchies, properties (binary relations), property hierarchies, and property restrictions. RDFS classes and properties can be instantiated in RDF. For a more detailed comparison of XML Schema and RDF Schema we refer the reader to [89]. Figure 2.2 shows an RDFS ontology of persons.

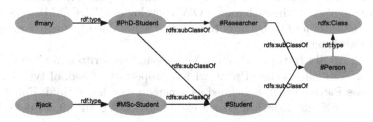

Fig. 2.2. RDFS ontology of persons

RDF(S) (referring to the combination of RDF and RDF Schema) is not very expressive compared with many other ontology languages, as it allows only the representation of concepts, concept taxonomies, binary relations, and simple domain and range restrictions on properties. The expressive limitations of RDF(S) were a major motivation for developing more expressive languages for the Semantic Web.

2.2.2 The Web Ontology Language OWL

The Web Ontology Language OWL [46] is an expressive ontology language that extends RDFS. OWL itself consists of three *species* of increasing expressiveness: Lite, DL, and Full. We are here mostly considered with OWL DL, which is based on the Description Logics knowledge representation paradigm [11].

Where statements in RDF(S) are triples, statements in OWL DL are either axioms or assertions. An axiom is either a class definition, a class axiom,

```
Class(Person partial
    restriction (hasChild allValuesFrom(Person)))

Class(Parent complete
    Person
    restriction (hasChild someValuesFrom(Person)))

ObjectProperty(hasChild)

Individual (John type(Person)
    value(hasChild Mary))
```

Listing 2.2. OWL example using abstract syntax

or a property axiom. Class definitions can be used to define subclass relationships, as well as certain property restrictions which hold for a particular class. With class and property axioms one can express more complex relationships between classes and between properties such as boolean combinations of class descriptions and transitive, inverse, and symmetric properties. Individual assertions can be used to express class membership, property values, and (in)equality of individuals.

OWL DL is defined in terms of an abstract syntax [115]. However, the normative syntax for the exchange of OWL ontologies is RDF/XML. The RDF representation of an OWL DL ontology can be obtained through a mapping from the abstract syntax.

Listing 2.2 illustrates OWL DL using an ontology written in abstract syntax form. We define a class Person with a property hasChild, of type Person, and a class Parent, which is defined as a person who has a child. Finally, we define an individual John, who has a child Mary. OWL DL allows us to infer that John is a Parent.

2.3 Web Service Technologies

The Web services paradigm is often depicted as the next step in software engineering and software architecture [4]. This facilitates developing distributed applications through combinations of services that are located in various places on the Web, as well as remotely accessing business services. Software architectures that are based on the Web services paradigms are called Service-Oriented Architectures (SOA).

In this section we first briefly review the principles of service-oriented architectures, after which we describe the three most prominent Web service technologies.

2.3.1 Principles of Service-Oriented Architectures

Web services are self-contained, atomic units of computation. In fact, a Web service can be seen as a function, which has an input (e.g., product and credit card information) and an output (e.g., purchase confirmation), but it might also have some side effects (e.g., credit card is charged with the price of the product). The W3C Web service Activity uses a technology-oriented definition of a Web service: "a software application identified by a URI, whose interfaces and bindings are capable of being defined, described, and discovered as XML artifacts. A Web service supports direct interactions with other software agents using XML-based messages exchanged via Internet-based protocols." [10]

From the definition we see that the use of standards, and especially XML and Internet-based protocols, is an important aspect of Web services. As we will see below when discussing the Web service technologies, the Web standards URI, HTTP, and XML play an important role.

Services do not maintain state across invocations; therefore, any two invocations are, to some extent, independent. However, if a service changes the state of the world two invocations might not be independent. For example, if the invocation of a media selling service results in the removal of the last copy of a book from the warehouse, rendering the item out of stock, a following invocation of the service requesting the sale of the same book will fail or result in a longer delivery time.

2.3.2 The Web service Technology Stack

SOAP

SOAP [69] is a protocol for the exchange of messages. It is used for both messages sent to (input) and messages received from (output) Web services.

SOAP defines both a format for messages, based on XML, and a processing model, which defines how a receiver should process a SOAP message. Furthermore, it defines a framework for protocol bindings, and (in [70]) a binding for the HTTP protocol, which defines how SOAP messages can be transferred using HTTP.

A SOAP message consists of a SOAP envelope, which in turn contains an optional header and a body. Listing 2.3 contains an example of a SOAP envelope.

The header of a soap message typically contains information regarding the processing of the message. In the example, it says that the message is concerned with a transaction with the number 5. The head also contains security-related information. Credit card information would typically not be sent as plain XML, like in example in Listing 2.3. Instead, the information would be encrypted, e.g., using WS-Security [111].

The body contains the actual information that is to be transferred to the application (i.e., the Web service input or output). In the example, chargeBasket is the name of the procedure (service) to be invoked. There are two inputs, namely the (shopping) basket, which has a specific code (IKGH6343GTW) and credit card information. SOAP provides a data model

```
<env:Envelope xmlns:env=" http://www.w3.org/2003/05/soap—envelope" >
 <env:Header>
   <t:transaction
       xmlns:t=" http://example.org/MSI/transaction"
       env:mustUnderstand=" true" >5</t:transaction>
 </env:Header>
 <env:Body>
  <m:chargeBasket
      env:encodingStyle=" http://www.w3.org/2003/05/soap—encoding"
        xmlns:m=" http://example.org/MSI" >
   <m:basket xmlns:m=" http://example.org/MSI" >
    <m:code>IKGH6343GTW</m:code>
   </m:basket>
   <o:creditCard xmlns:o=" http://example.org/MSI/financial" >
        ...
    <o:number>123456789000000</o:number>
    <o:expiration >2008—04</o:expiration>
   </o:creditCard>
  </m:chargeBasket>
 </env:Body>
</env:Envelope>)
```

Listing 2.3. SOAP envelope example

for the representation of application-defined data structures, such as the shop-ping basket and credit card in the example; this data model is close to XML and can be represented in XML. The value of the encodingStyle attribute (http://www.w3.org/2003/05/soap-encoding) in the example conveys the in-formation that the content is an XML encoding of this data model.

WSDL

The Web Services Description Language WSDL [40] is an XML language for describing Web services. It can be seen as an *interface definition language*, since it defines the interface of the service in terms of its inputs and outputs. However, a WSDL description is more intricate than most interface definition languages, since it also needs to describe how and where to access the service.

A WSDL description consists of an abstract and a concrete part. The abstract part of a WSDL description consists of

- types, which are the kinds of messages the surface will send or receive and
- interfaces, which describe the abstract functionality provided by the Web service.

The message types are defined using XML schema [132]. An interface de-fines the abstract interface of a Web service as a set of *operations*, where each operation represents an interaction between the client and the service. An operation typically has a name, a message exchange pattern, and inputs and outputs, which are specified in terms of types.

The concrete part consists of

- bindings, which describe how the service can be accessed and
- services, which describe where the service can be accessed.

A `binding` specifies the concrete message format and transmission protocol for an interface, and thus for every operation in the interface. WSDL provides specific support for bindings using SOAP and HTTP.

Finally, a `service` specifies a concrete service, which consists of a reference to an interface and the `endpoints` where the service can be accessed. Each `endpoint` must include a reference to a binding to indicate which protocol and which transmission format should be used when accessing the service, as well as the actual address of the service, which is typically (but not necessarily) a URI.

SAWSDL

SAWSDL [54] (Semantic Annotations for WSDL) extends WSDL with a number of attributes that can be used for the semantic annotation of services, e.g., through references to ontologies. Specifically, an interface, an operation, an XML schema type, or an XML schema element may be annotated with a `modelReference`, which is a list of URIs. These URIs are pointers to concepts in some semantic model (e.g., an ontology). Furthermore, XML schema types and elements may be annotated with *schema mappings*, which are references to mappings between an XML schema type or element and a concept in the semantic model; the mappings define how instances of the schema are translated to instances of the concept in the semantic model, and vice versa.

SAWSDL provides a means for referring to semantic annotations, but does not impose any restrictions on the shape of these annotations. For example, such annotations may be RDFS or OWL ontology classes or (parts of) WSML descriptions.

2.4 Web Service Usage Tasks

As we have seen in the previous section, a (WSDL) Web service description tells the client how to invoke the service, that is, the location of the service, the protocol to be used for invocation, and the format of the messages to be sent to the service.

Besides the obvious use for invoking Web services (*invoke*), there are a number of other uses for Web service descriptions. Specifically, before invoking a Web service,

1. it is necessary to find a service that provides the desired functionality (*discover*),
2. select the *best* service, according to user preferences, among those providing the required functionality and negotiate a Service Level Agreement (SLA) with the provider (*select/negotiate*), and
3. if multiple services need to be invoked, the order of invocation needs to be determined (*composition*).

Likewise, the service provider needs to advertise the description of the service so that potential users can find it (*publish*), negotiate SLAs with potential customers, and *execute* the service when invoked. This usage process is illustrated in Figure 2.3.

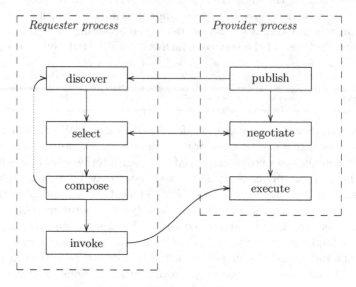

Fig. 2.3. Basic Web service usage process

We now describe each of the steps in the usage process in more detail.

2.4.1 Publication

The service provider needs to publish a description of the service such that it may be found by potential requesters. The description would be published at a Web service repository (e.g., UDDI [16]) that can be searched. It is crucial that the description of the service is written in such a form that potential requesters understand the functionality provided by the service and that potential customers that require this functionality will actually find it.

2.4.2 Discovery

Clients in search of a service that provides some desired functionality will query service repositories to find Web services that can provide it. In order to be able to find services, the query comprising the desired functionality has to be formulated in such a way as to allow matching the request with published service descriptions. In addition, if discovery is to be automated, both the service description and the user query need to be formulated using a language that can be processed by a machine (computer).

So, the functionality of the service and the client request both need to be formulated using a formal language, in order to allow automation of matching, and they need to use the same or related terminologies, to ensure that descriptions that are concerned with essentially the same thing can actually be matched.

2.4.3 Selection and Negotiation

The discovery step in the requester process may return a number of Web service descriptions, i.e., there may be several Web services providing the desired functionality. It is then necessary to select one particular Web service from the list and negotiate a Service Level Agreement (SLA) with the provider.

Selection of the service is done based upon matching user preferences with nonfunctional descriptions, e.g., quality of service (QoS), pricing, existing SLAs, etc. For example, a requester might look for a service that provides credit card payment processing services. The discovery step may return two Web services: the services A and B both provide payment processing services, but their quality of service differs: A guarantees processing each payment within 1 minute and charges €1, 00 per payment, whereas B guarantees processing within 1 day, but charges only €0, 10 per payment. Depending on whether the requester prefers a low price or quick processing, A or B will be selected.

In order to automate such matching and ranking of services with respect to user preferences the client needs to describe its preferences and the provider needs to include non-functional (QoS) descriptions of the service in the advertised service description. Furthermore, these descriptions need to use common vocabularies and need to be expressed using a formal language in order to enable automated selection and ranking.

Negotiating a Service Level Agreement typically requires complex interaction between the requester and the provider. Selection can be seen as a trivial form of negotiation.

2.4.4 Composition

The service may only provide part of the functionality desired by the user. For example, booking a trip may require both flight and hotel reservation, which are provided by 2 different services. In this case, the services need to be combined, or *composed*, to achieve all of the goals of the user.

Concretely, the task of Web service composition is: given a number of services that potentially provide part of the desired functionality, combine the services in such a way that they together provide the desired functionality, and specify how they should interact. In the example of flight and hotel reservation, the flight reservation service would have to be invoked first, because this will determine the actual travel days and times. Only after the invocation of the flight reservation service has been completed and the travel itinerary has been finalized, can the hotel reservation service be invoked.

During composition, new services need to be discovered and/or selected. This might require additional discovery and/or selection and negotiation activities during the composition process.

There are a number of challenges in Web service composition. First of all, the language that is used to represent the composition of services (e.g., BPEL4WS [6]) must be able to represent dependencies between the services, and it must be possible to verify that the composition of services indeed provides the desired functionality and that at any point in the process the conditions for invoking the next service (e.g., input data is available) are satisfied.

We distinguished two levels of Web service composition:

Functional composition: based on the functionality advertised by the Web services, they are composed in such a way that their combination provides the desired functionality. A particular challenge in this scenario is to determine the order of invocation of services, to ensure that the preconditions of the next service to be invoked are met.

Interface composition: at each stage in the process it must be possible to invoke the next service, so the information required for the input of service must be available at that stage; this information will typically depend on the outputs of other Web services in the composition.

2.4.5 Invocation and Execution

After the services has been discovered, selected, and composed, they need to be invoked. With service invocation we mean an interaction between the client and the service that involves messages being exchanged between the two. Web service description standards that are currently in place (i.e., WSDL) allow describing the location of services, as well as the protocol to be used for sending messages (e.g., HTTP) and the format of the messages (e.g., SOAP). Current standards, however, do not allow describing the *content* of messages. Therefore, it is not possible to automatically interpret such messages.

2.5 Challenges in Web Service description

We are concerned with a means of describing services that overcomes the difficulties mentioned in the previous section. We can conclude that we need three kinds of description for each individual service:

Functional description The tasks of publication, discovery, and composition all require a means for describing the functionality of a service. Furthermore, automation of these tasks requires a mechanism for matching functional descriptions.

Behavioral and interface description The task of invocation requires a description of messages to be sent to and received from a service. In general, a complex service (e.g., media selling service) requires a complex interaction between the requester and provider of the service, i.e., several messages are sent back and forth. This requires a description of the content of individual messages, as well as the interaction itself.

Nonfunctional description The task of selection requires nonfunctional properties, including Quality of Service (QoS) parameters such as price and availability, as well as such things as trust and security-related aspects; see [113].

Finally, in order to be able to find potential matches, a common terminology is required. Semantic Web technologies, as described in Section 2.2, provide languages for describing such terminologies (i.e., ontologies).

The Web Service Modeling Language WSML accounts for all these kinds of descriptions. Chapter 4 introduces WSML and illustrates how these kinds of descriptions are realized in WSML. Chapter 5 describes ontologies in WSML in more detail. Chapters 6 and 7 address functional and behavioral description using WSML. However, before introducing WSML, we describe the conceptual framework underlying the language, namely the Web Service Modeling Ontology WSMO, in the following chapter.

3

The Web Service Modeling Ontology

In the previous chapter we have identified several aspects of services that need to be described in order to effectively find and use these services. This includes the functional and nonfunctional description of the service, as well as a description of the behavior and the interface. We have also identified the need for common terminologies and suggested the use of ontologies for their description; using a common vocabulary across descriptions is a prerequisite to be able to match descriptions of Web services and user requirements.

The Web Service Modeling Ontology WSMO [57, 121] provides a conceptual model for the description of Web services. WSMO distinguishes between user *goals*, which are descriptions of the desires of the requester, and *Web service* descriptions, which are descriptions of the functionality and interface of the service offered by the provider. Thereby, WSMO acknowledges the separation between the requester and provider roles.

Another important principle of WSMO is the loose coupling of the descriptions of goals and Web services, allowing them to be described independently. *Mediators* (first identified in [138]) are used for overcoming possible discrepancies in the terminology and styles employed in the descriptions.

WSMO identifies four main top-level elements:

- *Ontologies* provide formal and explicit specifications of the vocabulary used by the other modeling elements in WSMO. The use of shared ontologies specified in formal languages increases interoperability and allows for automated processing of the descriptions. In the previous chapter we have mentioned two languages for describing ontologies, namely RDF Schema and OWL. As we shall see in the next chapter, WSML not only enables using RDF Schema and OWL ontologies, but also provides an ontology language of its own (Section 4.4.3; see also Chapter 5).
- A Web service is a piece of functionality accessible over the Web. A WSMO *Web service* is made up of three parts, namely
  - the *capability*, which describes the functionality offered by the service,

- the *interface*, which describes (a) how to interact with the service, through its *choreography* and (b) how the service makes use of other services in order to provide its functionality, through its *orchestration*, and
- the *non functional information*, comprising such things as costs of service invocation and Quality of Service (QoS) related parameters [113, 134].

- The way in which service requesters use Web services may be very different from what was envisaged by the provider of the service. Thus it is important that requirements of the requester are given the same importance as the description of services. Thus WSMO provides *goals* as a mechanism for describing the requirements a given service requester has when searching for services that meet these requirements. As is the case for the description of Web services, these requirements are broken down into
  - the requested capability, i.e., the functionality the requester expects the service to provide,
  - an optional requested interface, i.e., what the interaction pattern of the service should look like for interfacing with it and which services this service should make use of in order to achieve its functionality, and
  - non-functional information comprising and *user preferences* related to QoS parameters.

- The open and distributed nature of the Web requires resources to be decoupled. In other words, WSMO descriptions are created in (relative) isolation from one another and thus the potential for heterogeneity problems between resources is high. Such heterogeneity issues can exist between the formats of the data exchanged between service requesters and providers, the process is used for invoking them and the protocols used in communication. WSMO *mediators* are responsible for overcoming these heterogeneity problems; WSMO emphasizes the centrality of mediation by making mediators a first class component of the WSMO model. An example of a WSMO mediator for resolving data heterogeneity is a mediator that performs transformation of instant information from one ontology to another through the use of ontology mappings [106].

We focus here on the structure of Web service and goal descriptions and how they relate to each other. When clear from the context, we refer to WSMO Web service and goal descriptions simply as a (Web) *services* and *goals*, respectively. Recall that Web services define the information needed for a machine to interpret the usability of a Web service to fulfill a requester's requirements, which are encoded as a goal. Figure 3.1 presents the elements of a Web service description, namely non-functional properties, a capability, a choreography and an orchestration. The term interface is used to describe the combination of the choreography and orchestration of a service. Note that services may have zero or more interfaces; for reasons of understandability only one interface is depicted in the figure.

The structure of a goal is the same as that of a Web service and automating a given task in the process of using Web services is essentially the interaction of a given part of the goal description with a given part of one or more Web service descriptions. Therefore below we describe the elements that make up goals and Web services by describing how they interact with one another in the process of automatically finding and using Web services.

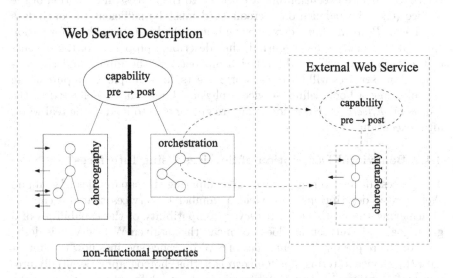

Fig. 3.1. Elements of a Web service description

3.1 Web Service and Goal Description

In this section we describe the individual elements that make up a Web service or goal description, namely the capability, the interfaces, and the non-functional properties.

3.1.1 Functional Description Using Capabilities

To perform Web service discovery, in other words to automatically find services that can fulfill the user's requirements, the capability of a goal is compared with the capabilities of known services. A capability is a description of the functionality provided by a service (or requested by a requester) and is described in terms of conditions on the state of the world that must exist for execution of the service to be possible and conditions on the state of the world that are guaranteed to hold after execution of the service. WSMO makes a distinction between the state of the information space, i.e., the inputs and outputs of the service, and the state of the world.

Based on these considerations a capability description comprises four main elements. *Preconditions* describe conditions on the state of the information space prior to execution. Therefore, preconditions specify requirements on the inputs the service, e.g., typing. There may exist additional conditions that must hold in the real world in order for the service to successfully execute. These conditions, called *Assumptions*, are not necessarily checked by the service before execution but are crucial to the successful execution of the service (e.g., the balance on a credit card must be sufficient to conclude a purchase). *Postconditions* describe conditions on the state of the information space after execution has occurred, thus describing properties of the outputs of the service, as well as the relationship between the inputs and the outputs. Many services will have real world effects, for example when purchasing a book using a book selling service a physical book will be delivered to the requester. *Effects* are conditions that are guaranteed to hold in the real world after execution.

3.1.2 Behavioral Description of Services Using Interfaces

The process of discovering services by comparing the capabilities of goal and Web service descriptions may yield a number of services that are capable of achieving the user's goals. However, compatibility of the capabilities of a given goal and Web service does not mean that a given Web service is desirable for the requester. The *interface* of a Web service specifies how to interact with the service in terms of a *choreography*, this choreography essentially provides information about the relationships between different operations on the Web service, for example the `login` operation of a book selling service must be invoked before the `buyBook` operation. A choreography can also be specified within the goal, essentially allowing the provider to specify the desired interaction pattern. The choreographies within the goal and discovered Web service descriptions can be compared in order to filter out those services whose interaction pattern is incompatible with that of the requester.

The interface of a Web service description also contains an *orchestration* description. An orchestration specifies which services this service relies upon to provide its functionality, for example the description of a book selling service may specify that a specific delivery service is relied upon for final delivery of books. The goal may also contain such an orchestration description specifying the desired external services the discovered service should rely upon. Discovered Web services that do not meet these requirements may be eliminated, e.g., services that do not use the requested delivery service are not desired by the requester and thus can be ignored.

3.1.3 Describing Nonfunctional Properties of Services

After discovering those services whose functionally meets the requester's requirements and filtering out those that do not match in terms of their interaction pattern or the services upon which they rely there may still be multiple

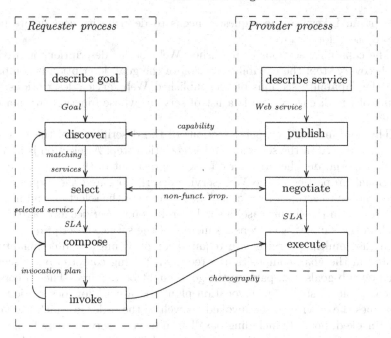

Fig. 3.2. Web service usage process in WSMO

services that can achieve the user's goal. In this case the most desirable a Web service must be selected from the list. To perform this selection the non-functional properties of the discovered Web services are compared against the requested non-functional properties within the goal. Non-functional properties, as their name suggests, are used to capture non-functional aspects of a given Web service. These non-functional properties typically provide a description of the Quality of Service of the service, e.g., reliability, scalability, and security. By comparing the requested non-functional properties of the goal to those of the discovered services we can eliminate those services that do not meet the minimum requirements laid out by the goal and rank the remaining services to find the service that best fits the requester's non-functional requirements. Having selected the right service for the requester, based on functional, interface and non-functional parameters, automatic invocation of the selected service is possible using the choreography description of the service.

3.2 Basic Usage Patterns of WSMO

Figure 3.2 shows the refinement of the Web service usage process (see Figure 2.3 on page 18) in the context of WSMO. Before publishing a service, the provider needs to describe the service, which results in a *Web service* description. Likewise, the requester needs to describe its *goal* before being able to use it for discovery.

The capability sections of published Web service descriptions is used for the discovery step; the capability section of the goal description is compared with the capability sections of the published Web service descriptions. The results of the discovery step is a list of services whose functionality matches the goal.

The nonfunctional property sections of the descriptions of the matching services are used in the selection and negotiation step. A selection is in fact a simple negotiation: the provider offers an agreement in the form of the nonfunctional properties in the Web service description, and the requester can either choose to accept or reject it. The outcome of the selection and negotiation step is (in the simple case) a single service plus a service level agreement, which in the simplest case consists merely of the service description.

In case multiple services are required for providing the functionality requested in the goal, composition is required. During composition, discovery based on sub-goals, i.e., parts of the goal, might be required. The outcome of the composition step is an invocation plan, i.e., a workflow description that prescribes the services to be invoked, as well as the order in which they need to be invoked, possibly including parallelism (several services may be invoked in parallel). Such an invocation plan may include goals, which would require dynamic discovery of services during execution. The orchestration description of a WSMO Web service can be seen as such an invocation plan. The simplest invocation plan is a single Web service.

Finally, the invocation plan is executed, which means that the Web services are invoked. The choreography of a Web service prescribes how the invocation takes place; it describes which messages need to be sent to the provider and in which order, as well as the messages which can be expected. In case a sub-goal is encountered in the invocation plan, dynamic discovery is required, i.e., a new service fulfilling this goal needs to be discovered. Furthermore, in case an exception occurs, e.g., the service cannot be reached or provides erroneous output information, the invocation plan may need to be updated, possibly requiring the discovery of additional services to fill the place of the erroneous service.

For more information about different uses of WSMO we refer the reader to [57]. For further information concerning Web service discovery we refer the reader to [114, 131, 94, 82]; the topic will also be discussed in more detail in Chapter 6. For further information concerning Web service composition we refer to the reader to [112, 129, 74, 19, 95].

In the remainder of this book we are concerned with a language for describing Semantic Web services based on WSMO, called the Web Service Modeling Language.

4

The Basic WSML Language

The Web Service Modeling Language WSML [68] is a concrete formal language based on the conceptual model of WSMO [57], which we described in the previous chapter. As such, it provides a language for describing ontologies, goals, Web services, mediators, and their interrelationships in the way envisioned by WSMO. Besides providing an ontology language for use with Web service description, WSML also allows using the Semantic Web ontology languages RDF schema [28] and OWL (DL) [46] (see also Section 2.2) for describing the terminologies used in goal and Web service descriptions.

The semantic foundation of any Web service description is the ontology language used for describing the terminology. WSML recognizes two important Knowledge Representation paradigms in this context, namely Description Logics [11] and logical rule-based languages [96]. The user may choose which paradigm to use: Description Logics, rules, a common subset, or a common superset. To this end, WSML defines a number of different *variants*: WSML-Core marks the common subset, WSML-DL marks the Description Logics paradigm, WSML-Rule marks the rules paradigm, and WSML-Full marks the common superset.

WSML defines an ontology language for WSML-Full. The other variants are obtained by suitably restricting the syntax of the language. The language variant also determines which Semantic Web ontology languages may be used. WSML-Core and Rule permit the use of a subset of OWL DL, inspired by [66]. The DL and Full variants permit the use of arbitrary OWL DL. Finally, a subset of RDF Schema may be used with WSML-Core and DL, and all of RDF Schema may be used with WSML-Rule and Full.

The WSML ontology language can be seen as a sub-language of WSML. The other sub-languages are the languages used for the functional, nonfunctional, and behavioral description, i.e., the languages used to realize WSMO capabilities, non-functional properties, and choreographies. These languages all allow using terminology defined in ontologies, and there is considerable overlap between the ontology languages, and specifically language of logical expressions, and the expressions used in these other sub-languages, as we shall see in this chapter.

Orthogonal to the 4 sub-languages are the three concrete syntaxes of WSML for the specification and exchange of WSML descriptions. The surface syntax is the primary syntax of WSML; its structure and keywords are based on the WSMO conceptual model, and it is primarily meant for the specification and viewing of WSML descriptions by human users. The XML and RDF representations are meant for the exchange of WSML descriptions over the Web, as well as RDF-based access of WSML descriptions.

This chapter is further structured as follows. In Section 4.1 we describe the role of the different components of Web service descriptions, namely ontology, functional, nonfunctional, and behavioral descriptions, in more detail. In Section 4.2 we describe the principles underlying the major choices underlying the design of the WSML language. Section 4.3 describes the WSML variants and their interrelationships in more detail. We introduce the WSML language through a description of its surface syntax in Section 4.4. Finally, we describe the XML and RDF syntaxes of WSML in Section 4.5.

We note here that the normative specification of the WSML syntax is in the form of an *abstract syntax* that may be found in [29]. The concrete surface syntax [68] and XML [133] and RDF [45] representations are based on this abstract syntax. We do not present the abstract syntax in detail in this book; instead we refer the interested reader to [29]. We do use parts of the abstract syntax in the following chapters where necessary to clarify specific aspects of the language.

4.1 Components of Web Service Descriptions

Figure 4.1 depicts the elements of a Web service description. The ontology is the basis for the description; it provides the terminology used in the other elements, and the ontology language provides the basic semantics used by the other descriptions. The other elements of the descriptions are the (i) nonfunctional properties (NFP), (ii) the functional description (i.e., capability), and (iii) the behavioral description (i.e., choreography).

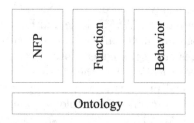

Fig. 4.1. Elements of a WSML Web service description

4.1.1 Ontologies

The basis of any Web service description is the ontology that defines the terminology used in the description. Such an ontology defines the concepts that are
relevant for the business, relationships between the concepts (i.e., attributes),
as well as additional background information (in the form of axioms). Examples of concepts are Product, Book, ShoppingBasket, and Customer. Examples
of attributes are hasPrice, hasAuthor, and hasLineItem, hasShoppingBasket. Examples of axioms are "each Product has a price", "a Customer has at most 1
Shoppingbasket", and "if a Customer has bought products with a total worth
of at least €1000 in the preceding year, he is a GoldCustomer".

Ontologies serve several purposes in Web service descriptions, namely:

- They form a common terminology for the description of Web services and
  goals that is shared between requesters and providers of services, thereby
  enabling interoperation.
- They contain background information about the domain, thereby enabling
  reasoning using this domain knowledge.
- They form the data model for the Web service inputs and outputs; the
  actual messages exchanged between the service requester and provider
  contain instances of concepts and relations in the ontology.

There are different languages that may be used for the description of such
ontologies. RDF Schema and OWL DL (described in Chapter 2) are two such
ontology languages. WSML also provides an ontology language, which is based
on the conceptual model of ontology description of WSMO.

In fact, WSML provides a range of increasingly expressive ontology languages through its language *variants*, which are described in more detail in
the next section. The chosen language variant determines the semantics of
the ontology description, which is used by the non-functional properties and
functional and behavioral description. Ontology descriptions, and specifically
the semantics of the WSML variants and combinations with RDF Schema and
OWL DL ontologies, are described in more detail in Chapter 5.

4.1.2 Functional Description

As prescribed by WSMO, a functional description is specified as the *capability*
of a goal or Web service. WSML defines two kinds of capabilities: set-based capabilities, which correspond to the concepts of a *task ontology* and state-based
capabilities, in which part of the WSML ontology language is used to describe
the assumptions, effects, pre-conditions, and post-conditions comprising the
capability; the terminology used in the description of the capability is defined
in (RDF Schema, OWL DL, or WSML) ontologies.

When considering set-based capabilities, a capability is viewed as a set
of pieces of functionality. When considering state-based capabilities, a Web
service is viewed as a *function*: the pre-conditions are conditions on the inputs

of this function (Web service), while the post-conditions are conditions on the outputs of the service.

The semantics of functional descriptions (see Chapter 6) uses (for the case of set-based capabilities) and extends (for the case of state-based capabilities) the semantics of ontology descriptions. The semantics of set-based capabilities is based on the semantics of ontologies. The semantics of state-based capabilities is based on a notion of *states*; the state before execution of the service is known as the pre-state, while the post-state is the state after execution of the service.

Both kinds of capability descriptions are primarily used for Web service discovery.

The requester would formulate the desired functionality using a goal description; the provider would formulate the provided functionality in a Web service description. A simple matching operator, match, takes two functional descriptions (i.e., capabilities) as its arguments and returns a degree of matching, as illustrated in Figure 4.2. The degrees

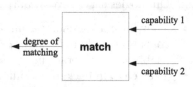

Fig. 4.2. The match operator

of match that can be returned are determined by the actual definition of the operator. A specific *discovery mechanism* implements the operator and defines the degrees of match that may be returned. Most discovery mechanisms would at least return a degree non-match in case the capabilities do not match at all, and a degree full match in case the two completely correspond.

4.1.3 Behavioral Description

With a description of the behavior of a Web service we mean a description of the input messages it expects, the output messages it sends, and their interdependencies: the kinds of output messages it sends, as well as the message it expects, might depend on the content of messages that have been received earlier in the interaction with the requester. Therefore, a behavioral description of a Web service may be a complex process description with such elements as sequencing (e.g., if a message of type A is received, a message of type B is sent) and conditional splits (e.g., if the method of delivery is "Postal Service", send only a confirmation; if the method of delivery is "Package service", send confirmation and a tracking number). This kind of information enables checking the compatibility of interfaces. Similar to matching capability descriptions, a compatibility checker determines whether two behavioral descriptions (i.e., choreographies) can communicate. In case communication is not possible, a list of conflicts may be returned by the checker. These conflicts may range from ontological mismatches to behavioral mismatches.

Like in functional descriptions, conditions in behavioral descriptions are written using the WSML ontology language and behavioral descriptions are based on terminology defined using ontologies. The behavior of a service is described in terms of state transition rules. Intuitively, if the condition of such a rule is satisfied, the rule is executed and the state of the conversation is changed accordingly. Such state changes may correspond to sending or receiving messages. Behavioral descriptions (choreographies) are illustrated later in this chapter and described in more detail in Chapter 7.

4.1.4 Non-Functional Properties

Like the functional and behavioral descriptions, non-functional properties also use terminology defined in ontologies, and their semantics is based on the semantics of the underlying WSML variant.

A nonfunctional property description consists of the name of the nonfunctional property and a condition that determines the value of the property. This value can be a simple data value (e.g., an integer or string) or identifier, but it might be a complex condition determining the actual value (e.g., the price of using the service might depend on the geographical location of the requester). From a semantic point of view, nonfunctional properties are queries over an ontology.

4.2 Design Principles of WSML

The leading principle of the design of WSML is the conceptual model of WSMO. All design choices regarding the structure of the language, constraints in the syntax, and the names of the keywords follow from the WSMO model. The design of WSML further follows three main principles.

A language based on two useful well-known formalisms

We conjecture that both Description Logics and Logic Programming are useful formal language paradigms for ontology description and knowledge representation on the Semantic Web [87], and, consequently, for Semantic Web services. In fact, the Web Ontology Language OWL is based on Description Logics and logical rule-based reasoning with RDF and rule-based extensions of RDF (e.g., [5, 79, 43]) are commonplace. The formal properties, as well as reasoning algorithms, for both paradigms have been thoroughly investigated in the respective research communities, and efficient reasoning implementations are available for both paradigms. WSML should leverage the research that has been done in both areas, and the implementations that are available, by catering for these language paradigms.

The difference in the expressiveness and underlying assumptions of both paradigms should be overcome by defining means for interaction between descriptions in both paradigms. On the one hand, it is desirable to use a common subset of both paradigms for such interaction (cf. [66]) so that it is not necessary to compromise on computational properties and so that existing implementations for both paradigms may be used. On the other hand, using a common subset requires compromising on expressiveness, which is not desirable in many situations; a common superset would include the expressiveness of both paradigms, but would require compromising on computational properties such as decidability (cf. [93]).

Web Language

WSML is meant to be a language for the Semantic Web. Therefore, WSML needs to take into account and adopt the relevant (Semantic) Web standards. We proceed with a description of the Web standards that are relevant to WSML.

The Web has a number of standards for object identification and the representation and manipulation of data that can be directly adopted by any Web language, including WSML. The Web architecture [80] prescribes the use of the standard URI [17], and its successor IRI [49], for the identification of objects on the Web. Therefore, such things as concepts, instances, relations, and axioms should be identified using URIs. XML Schema [20] describes a number of data types (e.g., string, integer, date) and XQuery [98] describes a number of datatype functions and operators for manipulating and comparing data conforming to these types. These data types and functions and operators can be adopted for the representation and manipulation of concrete data values.

There are, at the time of writing, three (Semantic) Web languages for the exchange of data and information that are relevant to WSML (see also Section 2.2). Recall that

- the most basic of the Semantic Web languages is XML [27], which provides a structured format for exchanging data over the Web. In fact, XML is part of the foundation for the Semantic Web; it is used, for example, for transmitting RDF data over the Web [14];
- RDF [90] is the standard language for exchanging (semi-)structured data over the Semantic Web. RDF Schema [28] provides a lightweight ontology language for RDF that allows representing classes, properties, and domain and range restrictions; and
- OWL [46] is the standard ontology language for the Semantic Web, extending RDF schema; the sub-language OWL DL provides a means for exchanging Description Logic-based ontologies over the Web.

One of the basic design principles for languages on the Semantic Web is to reuse existing (semantic) Web languages as much as possible. Therefore, WSML should use the mentioned languages as much as possible for the exchange of ontology (and Web service) descriptions.

At the time of writing, there is no standard rules language for the Semantic Web. However, such an effort is underway in the context of the Rule Interchange Format Working Group.[1] At the time of writing, there is a working

---

[1] http://www.w3.org/2005/rules/wg

draft comprising the specification of the basic logic dialect of RIF, which is a negation-free logical rules language [22], and there is a working draft specifying the interoperation between RIF and RDF/OWL [43].

RDF Schema and OWL provide ontology modeling capabilities. Since these are the standard languages for modeling ontologies on the Semantic Web, it may be expected that there will be many ontologies on the Web that are modeled using these languages. Therefore, it should be possible to use RDF Schema and OWL ontologies for defining terminologies used in WSML Web service descriptions.

We consider query languages such as SPARQL [117] beyond the scope of WSML. However, SPARQL may be used to query the RDF representation of WSML, as discussed in Section 4.5.

User-friendly surface syntax

It has been argued that tools hide language syntax from the user, and thus a user-friendly surface syntax is not necessary; however, as has been seen, for example, with the adoption of SQL, an expressive but understandable syntax is crucial for successful adoption of a language. Developers and early adopters of the language will have to deal with the concrete syntax of any new language. This trend is also visible on the Semantic Web, with the development of surface syntaxes for RDF (e.g., N-Triples [65, Chapter 3] and Turtle [15]) and OWL (e.g., [75]) which are easier to read and write for the human user than the standard exchange syntaxes based on RDF/XML [14, 46].

A drawback of using an expressive formal logical language is that statements in the language are often hard to understand and use by non-expert users. Therefore, WSML should provide a means for hiding complex logical formulas from non-expert users who are mainly interested in the conceptual modeling of ontologies and not in complex logical axioms.

The following sections describe how these design principles are realized in WSML. Section 4.3 describes the framework of WSML language variants, which correspond to the relevant well-known formalisms of the first design principle. Section 4.4 describes the different modeling constructs in WSML using the normative surface syntax, which is meant to be user-friendly, and in which URIs and XML datatypes play an important role. In Section 4.6 we describe how RDF and OWL ontologies can be leveraged in WSML descriptions. Finally, in Section 4.5 we describe how WSML descriptions can be exchanged using its XML and RDF representations, and we discuss how SPARQL can be used for querying WSML descriptions.

4.3 WSML Language Variants

Following the principle, detailed in the previous section, of using both the Description Logic (DL) and Logic Programming[2] (LP) paradigms, WSML incorporates a number of different language *variants*, corresponding to the DL and LP paradigms, and their possible (subset and superset) interaction. Figure 4.3 shows the WSML language variants and their interrelationships. The variants differ in logical expressiveness and underlying language paradigms; they allow users to make a trade-off between the expressiveness of a variant and the complexity of reasoning for ontology modeling on a per-application basis. Additionally, different variants are more suitable for different kinds of reasoning and representation.

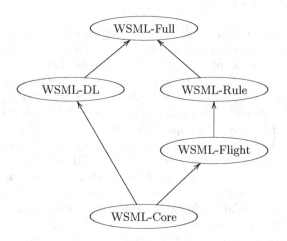

Fig. 4.3. The WSML variants

WSML-Core   is based on an intersection of the Description Logic $\mathcal{SHIQ}$ and Horn Logic, also known as Description Logic Programs [66]. It has the least expressive power of the WSML variants, and is a common subset of the DL-based and LP-based variants. That is, every WSML-Core description is also a WSML-DL and WSML-Flight/Rule description.

WSML Core ontologies, goals, and Web services may import OWL DLP (a subset of OWL DL) ontologies. See Section 4.6 for more details.

---

[2] With Logic Programming we mean a declarative logic-based rules language with negation under the Well-Founded [61] or the Stable Model [62] Semantics.

WSML-DL   is the Description Logic variant of WSML, and captures the Description Logic $\mathcal{SHIQ}(\mathbf{D})$, which corresponds to a large part of (the DL species of) OWL [46]. Furthermore, this variant is used for the interoperation with OWL DL ontologies. WSML-DL ontologies, goals, and Web services may import OWL DL ontologies.

WSML-Flight is the least expressive of the two LP-based variants of WSML. Compared with WSML-Core, it adds features such as meta-modeling, constraints, and nonmonotonic negation. WSML-Flight is based on a Logic Programming variant of F-Logic [88] and is semantically equivalent to Datalog with inequality and (locally) stratified negation [118].

Technical issues related to the layering between the (DL-based) WSML-Core and (F-Logic-based) WSML-Flight are discussed in detail in [34], and the specific layering issues in WSML are discussed in detail in [32].

Finally, the WSML-Flight variant can be used for combinations with RDF graphs and RDFS ontologies. WSML-Flight ontologies, goals, and Web services may import RDF graphs and RDFS ontologies.

WSML-Rule extends WSML-Flight with further features from Logic Programming, namely the use of function symbols, unsafe rules, and unstratified negation. There are two prominent semantics for logic programs with unstratified negation, namely the Stable Model Semantics [62] and the Well-Founded Semantics [61]; with respect to the task of query answering, the latter can be seen as an approximation of the former. Since the Stable Model Semantics is more general, WSML-Rule (in version 0.3 [29]) adopts the Stable Model Semantics, but implementations may use the Well-Founded Semantics as an approximation for the task of query answering. See Chapter 5 for more details.

WSML-Full   unifies WSML-DL and WSML-Rule. A definition of the semantics for WSML-Full, generalizing WSML-DL and WSML-Rule, is proposed in [32, 33]. However, as the combination of Description Logics and nonmonotonic logic programs is still an open research issue – some work has been done on the topic [51, 126, 30, 31, 107, 108, 36], but there is no consensus on which is the right semantics for the combination. Therefore, the current version of WSML does not define a semantics for WSML-Full, but instead outlines a number of properties such a semantics should have.

WSML has two alternative layerings, namely, WSML-Core $\Rightarrow$ WSML-DL $\Rightarrow$ WSML-Full and WSML-Core $\Rightarrow$ WSML-Flight $\Rightarrow$ WSML-Rule $\Rightarrow$ WSML-Full. For both layerings, WSML-Core and WSML-Full mark the least and most expressive layers. The two layerings are to a certain extent disjoint, namely the inter-operation between WSML-DL, on the one hand, and WSML-Flight and -Rule, on the other, is only possible through a common subset (WSML-Core) or through a very expressive superset (WSML-Full). The precise properties of language layering in WSML are shown Section 5.3 of this book.

4.4 WSML Language and Surface Syntax

In this section we introduce the WSML language through an introduction of its surface syntax. The other syntaxes of WSML (XML and RDF) are described in Section 4.5. Since different WSML language variants have different underlying language paradigms, there are differences in the language constructs which may be used in each of the variants, especially in the WSML ontology language.

Besides the mentioned mappings to XML and RDF, which allow exchanging descriptions over the Web, WSML addresses the "Web language" design principle through the use of IRIs [49] for the identification of objects and resources in WSML and the use of XML schema datatypes [20] for typing concrete data values, as described in Section 4.4.1. The reuse of XQuery comparators and functions is addressed through the use of corresponding built-in predicates, as described in [68, Appendix B.2].

The "user-friendly surface syntax" design principle is addressed through the definition of WSML in terms of a normative surface syntax with keywords based on WSMO. Furthermore, "inferring" and "checking" constraints on attributes (described below) are distinguished using the **impliesType** and **ofType** keywords.

Finally, WSML distinguishes between the modeling of the different conceptual elements on the one hand and the specification of complex logical definitions on the other. To this end, the WSML syntax is split into two parts: the *conceptual syntax* and *logical expression syntax*. The conceptual syntax is based on the structure of the WSMO conceptual model and is independent from the particular underlying language paradigm; it shields the user from the particularities of the formal language. The logical expression syntax provides access to the full expressive power of the language underlying the particular variant. The basic entry points for logical expressions in the conceptual syntax are the axioms in ontologies, the assumptions, preconditions, postconditions, and effects in capability descriptions, and the transition rules in choreography descriptions. We start with a description of identifiers in WSML, in Section 4.4.1. We proceed to describe the common elements of the conceptual syntax and WSML ontologies in the Sections 4.4.2 and 4.4.3. The logical expression syntax is described in Section 4.4.4. Finally, we describe Web services, goals, and mediators in Sections 4.4.5, 4.4.6, and 4.4.7.

4.4.1 Identifiers in WSML

WSML has three kinds of identifiers, namely, IRIs, compact IRIs, which are abbreviated IRIs, and data values. Compact IRIs are specific to the surface syntax, and do not appear in the XML and RDF serialization.

IRIs

An *IRI* (Internationalized Resource Identifier) [49] uniquely identifies a resource (e.g., concepts, relations, individual) in a Web-compliant way, following the W3C Web Architecture recommendation [80]. The IRI proposed standard is the successor of the popular URI standard and has already been adopted in various W3C activities such as SPARQL [117]. In the surface syntax IRIs are delimited using an underscore and double quote '_"', and a double quote '"', for example: _"http://www.wsmo.org/wsml/wsml-syntax#".

In order to enhance legibility in the surface syntax, an IRI can be abbreviated to a compact IRI, which is of the form *prefix#localname*. The prefix and separator '*prefix#*' may be omitted, in which case the name falls in the default namespace. Both the namespace prefixes and the default namespace are specified at the top of a WSML document (see Listing 4.1 for an example).

Our concept of a compact IRI corresponds with the use of QNames in RDF and is slightly different from QNames (Qualified Names) in XML, where a QName is not merely an abbreviation for an IRI, but a tuple <namespaceURI, localname>. Since WSML is a language for the Semantic Web, we follow the Semantic Web recommendation RDF in this respect.

We use the following prefixes throughout the book: wsml stands for the WSML namespace http://www.wsmo.org/wsml/wsml-syntax#; xsd stands for the XML schema namespace http://www.w3.org/2001/XMLSchema#; rdf stands for the RDF namespace http://www.w3.org/1999/02/22-rdf-syntax-ns#; rdfs stands for the RDFS namespace http://www.w3.org/2000/01/rdf-schema#; owl stands for the OWL namespace http://www.w3.org/2002/07/owl#. When not explicitly specified, the default namespace is assumed to be an example namespace, e.g., http://example.org/example#.

Data Values

Data values in WSML are either strings, integers, decimals, or structured data values (e.g., dates and XML content). Strings are Unicode character sequences delimited with double quotes (e.g., "John Smith"), where quotes are escaped using the backslash character '\'; integers are sequences of digits, optionally preceded with the minus symbol (e.g., -77 0 14 6789); decimals consist of two sequences of digits separated with a point, optionally preceded with the minus symbol (e.g., -56.93 -0.87 67.865 3458.7).

WSML defines constructor functions, called *datatype wrappers*, for creating structured data values using strings, integers, and decimals; the names of these wrappers correspond to the IRIs of the corresponding (XML schema) datatypes. For example, the date "March 15th, 2005" is represented as: xsd#date(2005,3,15).

Strings, integers, and decimals correspond to values of the respective XML schema datatypes [20] string, integer, and decimal. Furthermore, the datatypes recommended for use in WSML are the XML schema datatypes (see [68, Appendix B.1]), plus the RDF datatype rdf#XMLLiteral. Nonetheless, it is possible to use datatypes beyond this set.

4.4.2 Conceptual Syntax

The WSML conceptual syntax allows for the modeling of ontologies, Web services, goals and mediators. It is shared between all variants, with the exception of some restrictions that apply to the modeling of ontologies in WSML-Core and WSML-DL.

We first describe annotations and ontology imports, which are common to ontologies, Web services, goals and mediators. We then describe the conceptual syntax for modeling WSML ontologies, after which we describe the logical expression syntax and the conceptual syntaxes of WSML Web service, goal, and mediator descriptions.

Annotations

WSML descriptions may have annotations. Such annotations are used to describe metadata such as natural language names for WSML elements, data about the authors, and more elaborate natural language descriptions. An annotation consists of a property-value pair, and multiple annotations are grouped into annotation blocks which start with the keyword **annotations** and end with the keyword **endAnnotations**. Such annotation blocks always occur immediately after the definition of an element (e.g., Web service, ontology, concept, axiom) and the annotations in the block apply to the *identifier* of the element.

Consider the following description:

```
webService _"http://example.org/webservices/shopping/MediaShoppingService"
   annotations
      dc#creator hasValue "James Scicluna"
      dc#description hasValue "Describes a Web service that is capable of selling Multimedia
         items"
      wsml#version hasValue "1.2"
      dc#title hasValue "Multimedia Shopping Service"
   endAnnotations
```

It is the description of a Web service that is identified by the IRI http://example.org/webservices/shopping/MediaShoppingService. The description contains a number of annotations, namely a creator, a description, a version, and a title. This particular description reuses the creator, description, and title properties defined by Dublin Core [137], and the version property defined by WSML.

Ontology Imports

Ontologies may extend other ontologies by importing them. Goals, Web services, mediators, capabilities, interfaces, and choreographies may import ontologies for using the terminologies in the respective descriptions.

Ontology imports are declared using the **importsOntology** keyword, followed by a list of IRIs identifying the ontologies to be imported. The imported ontologies may be WSML, RDF Schema, or OWL DL ontologies. For more considerations about importing RDF and OWL in WSML see Section 4.6.

4.4.3 Ontologies

An ontology in WSML consists of the elements **concept, relation, instance, relationInstance** and **axiom**. Additionally, an ontology may have annotations and may import other ontologies. We start the description of WSML ontologies with an example which demonstrates the elements of an ontology, in Listing 4.1, and describe the individual elements in more detail below.

The top of the listing illustrates how the WSML variant is declared and how the default namespace and namespace prefixes are declared.

Concepts

The notion of concepts (sometimes also called 'classes') plays a central role in ontologies. Concepts form the basic terminology of the domain of discourse. A concept may have instances and may have a number of attributes associated with it. The annotations, as well as the attribute definitions, are grouped together in one syntactical construction, as can be seen from the example concept **book** in Listing 4.1.

Attribute definitions can take two forms, namely *constraining* (using **ofType**) and *inferring* (using **impliesType**) attribute definitions. Constraining attribute definitions define a typing constraint on the values for this attribute, similar to integrity constraints in Databases; inferring attribute definitions imply that the type of the values for the attribute is inferred from the attribute definition, similar to range restrictions on properties in RDFS and universal value restrictions in OWL.[3]

It is possible to declare several types for a single attribute; these are interpreted conjunctively, which means that every type applies. The list may be empty, if the type of the attribute is not known, as is the case for the property hasStageName of the concept Artist in Listing 4.1.

Each attribute definition may have a number of associated features, namely, transitivity, symmetry, reflexivity, and the inverse of an attribute, as well as minimal and maximal cardinality constraints.

---

[3] The distinction between inferring and constraining attribute definitions is explained in more detail in [37, Section 2].

```
wsmlVariant _"http://www.wsmo.org/wsml/wsml−syntax/wsml−flight"
namespace { _"http://example.org/ontologies/Media#",
    dc _"http://purl.org/dc/elements/1.1/",
    xsd _"http://www.w3.org/2001/XMLSchema#",
    foaf _"http://xmlns.com/foaf/0.1/",
    wsml _"http://www.wsmo.org/wsml/wsml−syntax#" }

ontology _"http://example.org/ontologies/Media"
  annotations
    dc#creator hasValue "Jos de Bruijn"
    dc#type hasValue {"Domain Ontology", wsml#Ontology}
    dc#description hasValue "Describes the media domain, where media are understood as books,
        CDs, and DVDs. Imports the FoaF ontology for description of persons."
    dc#subject hasValue "Media"
    wsml#version hasValue "Revision: 1.7 "
    dc#language hasValue "en−US"
    dc#title hasValue "Media Ontology"
    dc#date hasValue "2007−07−10"
  endAnnotations

  importsOntology
    { _"http://xmlns.com/foaf/0.1/" }


  concept MediaItem
    hasTitle ofType (1 *) xsd#string
    hasContributor ofType (1 *) Artist

  concept Artist subConceptOf foaf#Person
    hasStageName ofType { }
    contributorOf inverseOf(hasContributor) ofType MediaItem

  concept CD subConceptOf MediaItem

  concept Musician subConceptOf Artist

  instance prince memberOf Musician
    hasStageName hasValue "Prince"
    hasStageName hasValue "The Artist Formerly Known As Prince"
    hasStageName hasValue _"http://z.about.com/d/altreligion/1/0/i/S/2/tafkap.jpg"
    foaf#name hasValue "Prince Rogers Nelson"

  instance _"http://z.about.com/d/altreligion/1/0/i/S/2/tafkap.jpg"
    annotations
      dc#format hasValue "image/jpeg"
    endAnnotations
```

Listing 4.1. An example WSML ontology

Constraining attribute definitions, as well as cardinality constraints, require closed-world reasoning and are thus not allowed in WSML-Core and WSML-DL. As opposed to features of roles in Description Logics, attribute features such as transitivity, symmetry, reflexivity and inverse attributes are local to a concept in WSML. Thus, none of these features may be used in WSML-Core and WSML-DL.

Relations

Relations in WSML can have an arbitrary arity, may be organized in a hierarchy using **subRelationOf** and the parameters may be typed using parameter
type definitions of the form (**ofType** *type*) and (**impliesType** *type*), where *type* is
a concept identifier or a (possibly empty) list of concept identifiers. The usage
of **ofType** and **impliesType** correspond with the usage in attribute definitions.
Namely, parameter definitions with the **ofType** keyword are used to check the
type of parameter values, whereas parameter definitions with the **impliesType**
keyword are used to infer concept membership of parameter values.

The following is an example of a relation.

```
relation stageNameContributor(ofType {}, ofType xsd#string)
    annotations
        dc#description hasValue "Relation between (the stage names of) contributors to media items
            and the titles of these items."
    endAnnotations
```

WSML-Core and WSML-DL do not allow using relations; unary and binary relations in Description Logics correspond to concepts and attributes in WSML.

Instances

A concept may have a number of instances associated with it. Instances explicitly specified in an ontology are those that are shared as part of the ontology.
However, most instance data exists outside the ontology in private databases.
WSML does not prescribe how to connect such a database to an ontology, since
different organizations will use the same ontology to query different databases
and such corporate databases are typically not shared. In case the instance
data resides in an RDF document, the **importsOntology** construct can be used
for referring to (importing) the data.

An instance may be member of zero or more concepts and may have a
number of attribute values associated with it. Note that the specification
of concept membership is optional and the attributes used in the instance
specification do not necessarily have to occur in the associated concept definition. Consequently, WSML instances can be used to represent semi-structured
data, since without concept membership and constraints on the use of attributes, instances form a directed labeled graph. Because of this possibility to
capture semi-structured data, most RDF graphs can be represented as WSML
instance data, and vice versa.

Axioms

Axioms provide a means to add arbitrary logical expressions to an ontology.
Such logical expressions can be used to refine concept or relation definitions
in the ontology, but also to add arbitrary axiomatic domain knowledge or
express constraints. The following is an example of an axiom that that domain
knowledge to the ontology of Listing 4.1.

```
axiom stageNameContributorAxiom
  annotations
    dc#relation hasValue stageNameContributor
    dc#description hasValue "Defines the stageNameContributor relation as the  relation
        between stage names and titles  of media items they contributed to."
  endAnnotations
  definedBy
    stageNameContributor(?x,?y) :− ?z memberOf Artist and ?z[hasStageName hasValue ?x,
        contributorOf hasValue ?w] and ?w[hasTitle hasValue ?y].
```

Besides their use in ontologies, special kinds of axioms are used in goal and Web service capability descriptions; see Section 4.4.5. The syntax of logical expressions is explained in more detail below.

4.4.4 Logical Expression Syntax

The WSML logical expression syntax is used in axioms of ontologies and in Web service capabilities, as well as the transition rules of Web service choreographies and in non-functional properties. The use of logical expressions in axioms was described in the previous section. The use of logical expressions in capabilities and choreographies will be explained in the next section. We will first explain the general logical expression syntax, which encompasses all WSML variants, and then review the restrictions on this general syntax for each of the variants.

The general logical expression syntax for WSML has a first-order logic style, in the sense that it has constants, function symbols, variables, predicates and the usual logical connectives, namely negation, disjunction, conjunction, implication, and quantifiers. Furthermore, WSML has constructs for modeling concepts, attributes, attribute definitions, and subconcept and concept membership relationships, inspired by F-Logic [88]. Finally, WSML has a number of connectives specifically for the Logic Programming based variants, namely default negation (negation-as-failure), LP-implication and database-style integrity constraints.

Variables in WSML start with a question mark, followed by an arbitrary number of alphanumeric characters, e.g., ?x, ?name, ?123. Free variables in WSML (i.e., variables that are not explicitly quantified), are implicitly universally quantified outside of the formula (i.e., the logical expression in which the variable occurs is the scope of quantification), unless indicated otherwise, through the **sharedVariables** construct (see the next section) and unless the logical expression occurs in a non-functional property, in which case the variables are interpreted as parameters, that may be replaced with ground terms.

Terms are either identifiers (i.e., IRIs or data values), variables, or constructed terms of the form $f(t_1, \ldots, t_n)$. An atom is, as usual, a predicate symbol with a number of terms as arguments, e.g., $p(t_1, \ldots, t_n)$. Besides the usual atoms, WSML has a special kind of atoms, called *molecules*, which are used to capture information about concepts, instances, attributes and attribute values. WSML features two types of molecules:

- An *isa* molecule is a concept membership molecule of the form t_1 **memberOf** t_2 or a subconcept molecule of the form t_1 **subConceptOf** t_2, where t_1 and t_2 are terms.
- An *object* molecule is an attribute value expressions $t_1[t_2$ **hasValue** $t_3]$, a constraining attribute signature expression $t_1[t_2$ **ofType** $t_3]$, or an inferring attribute signature expression $t_1[t_2$ **ofType** $t_3]$, where t_1, t_2, and t_3 are terms.

WSML has the usual first-order connectives, written in ASCII style in the surface syntax: the unary negation operator **neg**, and the binary operators for conjunction **and**, disjunction **or**, right implication **implies**, left implication **impliedBy**, and dual implication **equivalent**. Variables may be universally quantified using **forall** or existentially quantified using **exists**. First-order formulae are obtained by combining atoms using the mentioned connectives in the usual way. The following are examples of first-order formulae in WSML:

```
//every person has a father
forall ?x (?x memberOf Person implies exists ?y (?x[father hasValue ?y])).
//john is member of a class which has some attribute called 'name'
exists ?x,?y (john memberOf ?x and ?x[name ofType ?y]).
```

Apart from first-order formulae, WSML allows using the negation-as-failure symbol **naf** in front of atomic formulas, the special logic programming implication symbol :-, and the integrity constraint symbol !-. A logic programming rule consists of a *head* and a *body*, separated by the :- symbol. An integrity constraint consists of the symbol !- followed by a rule body. Negation-as-failure **naf** is only allowed to occur in the body of a logic programming rule or an integrity constraint. The following logical connectives are allowed in the head of a logic programming rule: **and, implies, impliedBy,** and **equivalent**. The following connectives are allowed in the body of a rule (or constraint): **and, or,** and **naf**. The following are examples of LP rules and database constraints:

```
//every person has a father
?x[father hasValue f(?y)] :- ?x memberOf Person.
//Man and Woman are disjoint
!- ?x memberOf Man and ?x memberOf Woman.
//in case a person is not involved in a marriage, the person is a bachelor
?x memberOf Bachelor :- ?x memberOf Person and naf Marriage(?x,?y,?z).
```

Particularities of the WSML Variants

Each of the WSML variants defines a number of restrictions on the logical expression syntax. For example, LP rules and constraints are not allowed in WSML-Core and WSML-DL. Table 4.1 mentions a number of language features and indicates in which variant the feature may be used, to give an idea of the differences between the logical expressions of each variant.

- *WSML-Core* allows only first-order formulae that are equivalent to the DLP subset of $\mathcal{SHIQ}(\mathbf{D})$ [66]. This subset is very close to the 2-variable fragment of first-order logic, restricted to Horn logic. Although WSML-Core might appear in the Table 4.1 featureless, it captures most of the

Feature	Core	DL	Flight	Rule	Full
Classical Negation (**neg**)	-	X	-	-	X
Existential Quantification	-	X	-	-	X
(Head) Disjunction	-	X	-	-	X
n-ary relations	-	-	X	X	X
Meta Modeling	-	-	X	X	X
Default Negation (**naf**)	-	-	X	X	X
LP implication	-	-	X	X	X
Integrity Constraints	-	-	X	X	X
Function Symbols	-	-	-	X	X
Unsafe Rules	-	-	-	X	X

Table 4.1. Logical expression features in WSML variants

conceptual model of WSML, but has only limited expressiveness within the logical expressions.

- *WSML-DL* allows first-order formulae that can be translated to $\mathcal{SHIQ}(\mathbf{D})$. This subset is very close to the 2-variable fragment of first-order logic. Thus, WSML-DL allows classical negation and disjunction and existential quantification in the consequents of implications.

- *WSML-Flight* extends the set of formulae allowed in WSML-Core by allowing variables in place of instance, concept and attribute identifiers and by allowing relations of arbitrary arity. In fact, any such formula is allowed in the head of a WSML-Flight rule. The body of a WSML-Flight rule allows conjunction, disjunction and default negation.

  WSML-Flight additionally allows meta-modeling (e.g., classes-as-instances) and reasoning over the signature, because variables are allowed to occur in place of concept and attribute names.

- *WSML-Rule* extends WSML-Flight by allowing function symbols and unsafe rules, i.e., variables that occur in the head or in a negative body literal do not need to occur in a positive body literal.

- The logical syntax of *WSML-Full* is equivalent to the general logical expression syntax of WSML and allows the full expressiveness of all other WSML variants.

The separation between conceptual and logical modeling allows for easy adoption by non-experts, since the conceptual syntax does not require expert knowledge in logical modeling, whereas complex logical expressions require more familiarity and training with the language. Thus, WSML allows modeling of different aspects related to Web services on a conceptual level, while still offering the full expressive power of the logic underlying the chosen WSML variant through its logical expression syntax. Part of the conceptual syntax for ontologies has an equivalent in the logical syntax. The translation between the conceptual and logical syntax is illustrated in Table 4.2.

Conceptual syntax	Logical expression syntax

concept A
  annotations
    B hasValue C
  endAnnotations
	A[B hasValue C].

concept A subConcepOf B	A subConceptOf B.

concept A
  B ofType (0 1) C
	A[B ofType C].
	!− ?x memberOf A and
	  ?x[B hasValue ?y, B hasValue ?z] and ?y != ?z.

concept A B ofType C	A[B ofType C].
relation A/n subRelationOf B	$A(x_1,...,x_n)$ implies $B(x_1,...,x_n)$
instance A memberOf B C hasValue D	A memberOf B. A[C hasValue D].

Table 4.2. Translating conceptual to logical syntax

4.4.5 Web services

The functionality, behavior, and other aspects of Web services are described using WSML Web service descriptions. Such a description consists of a capability, which describes the functionality, one or more interfaces, which describe the possible ways of interacting with the service, and nonfunctional properties, which describe nonfunctional aspects of the service. Listing 4.2 shows the structure of a simple Web service for adding items to a shopping cart.

Capabilities

WSML allows using two kinds of capabilities: (1) capabilities as concepts of a task ontology and (2) detailed state-based description of the functionality. Since concepts represent sets of instances, capabilities of the former kind (1) are also referred to as *set-based capabilities*; capabilities of the latter kind (2) are referred to as *state-based capabilities*.

Set-based Capability Description

A set-based capability simply consists of the **capability** keyword followed by an IRI identifying a concept in a task ontology. Such a task ontology is typically imported in the Web service to which the capability belongs. The following is an example Web service with a capability concerned with buying media products.

```
webService _"http://example.org/webservices/shopping/SimpleMediaShoppingService"
  importsOntology {
    _"http://example.org/ontologies/tasks/MediaShoppingTasks"
}

  capability  _"http://example.org/ontologies/tasks/MediaShoppingTasks#BuyMedia"
```

```
wsmlVariant _"http://www.wsmo.org/wsml/wsml−syntax/wsml−flight"

namespace { _"http://example.org/ontologies/commerce/Commerce#",
     dc _"http://purl.org/dc/elements/1.1/",
     wsml _"http://www.wsmo.org/wsml/wsml−syntax#",
     xsd _"http://www.w3.org/2001/XMLSchema#",
     product _"http://example.org/ontologies/products/Products#",
     prop _"http://example.org/ontologies/WebServiceProperties#" }

webService _"http://example.org/webservices/shopping/AddItemsToCart"
  annotations
     dc#creator hasValue "Jos de Bruijn"
     dc#description hasValue "A Web service for adding items to a shopping cart"
     wsml#version hasValue "Revision : 1.53"
     dc#title hasValue "Add items to cart  service"
     dc#language hasValue "en−US"
     dc#date hasValue "2008−01−30"
  endAnnotations

  importsOntology {
     _"http://example.org/ontologies/commerce/Commerce",
     _"http://example.org/ontologies/products/Products"
  }

  capability
     ...

  interface
     ...

  nonFunctionalProperty
     ...
```

Listing 4.2. An example Web service description

State-Based Capability Description

Preconditions and assumptions describe the state before the execution of a Web service. While preconditions describe conditions over the information space – that is, conditions over the input, e.g., correct typing of inputs – assumptions describe conditions over the state of world that cannot be verified by the requester of the service, but which might explain failure of the service, e.g., there must exist a cart with the given (input) identifier, and this cart must be unique. Postconditions describe the relation between the input and the output, e.g., a search returns all products related to the given search criteria. In this sense, they describe the information state after execution of the service. Effects describe changes caused by the service beyond the inputs and outputs, e.g., the item is added to the shopping cart.

Listing 4.3 describes the capability of the simple Web service for adding items to a shopping cart: given a shopping cart identifier and a number of items, the items are added to the shopping cart with this identifier. The **sharedVariables** construct is used to identify variables that are shared between the pre- and postconditions and the assumptions and effects. Shared variables

```
capability
    sharedVariables {?cartId, ?item, ?number}
    precondition
        annotations
            dc#description hasValue "The cart ID must be a string and the item must be a book."
        endAnnotations
        definedBy
            ?cartId memberOf xsd#string and ?item memberOf product#Product.
    assumption
        annotations
            dc#description hasValue "There must exist a cart with the given ID
                and there must not exist another cart with the same ID.
                Furthermore, if there exists a line item with the input item, the variable
                    ?number reflects the quantity currently in the shopping cart; otherwise it
                    is 0."
        endAnnotations
        definedBy
            exists ?cart (?cart memberOf Cart and ?cart[hasId hasValue ?cartId] and
            (
                exists ?li (?cart [hasItems hasValue ?li] and ?li [hasProduct hasValue ?item] and
                    ?li [hasQuantity hasValue ?number]) or
                ?number = 0
            ) and
            neg exists ?x (?x memberOf Cart and
                ?x[hasId hasValue ?cartId] and ?x != ?cart))
    effect
        annotations
            dc#description hasValue "The item is added to the cart; if the product was already
                in the cart, the quantity is increased with 1."
        endAnnotations
        definedBy
            forall ?cart (?cart [hasId hasValue ?cartId] memberOf Cart implies
                exists ?li (?li memberOf LineItem and
                ?li [hasProduct hasValue ?Item] and ?li [hasQuantity hasValue ?number+1])).
```

Listing 4.3. An example capability: adding items to a shopping cart

can be used to refer to the input (?cartId and ?item) or share variables between the pre- and post-condition or assumption and effect (e.g., ?number).

More details about the modeling of capabilities can be found in Chapter 6.

Interfaces and Choreographies

Interfaces describe how to interact with a service from the requester point-of-view (**choreography**) and how the service interacts with other services and goals it needs to fulfill its capability (**orchestration**). Orchestration descriptions are external to WSML; WSML allows referring to any orchestration description identified by an IRI.

WSML provides a language for describing choreographies, called the *WSML choreography language*. It is also possible to refer to any choreography that has an IRI. However, WSML does not say anything about how such a choreography should be interpreted. We will now give a brief overview of the WSML choreography language.

A choreography description is a model for possible conversations – that is, sequences of message exchanges – between the service requester and provider. Patterns of message exchanges are governed by transition rules; given the current state, the transition rules determine the next step in the conversation. The messages themselves consist of ontology instance information, and the background knowledge contained in ontologies is taken into account when evaluating transition rules.

A central notion in WSML choreographies is the *state* of a conversation. Technically, a state consists of instance data of some ontology. State transitions correspond to update, insertion, or deletion of instance data. Communication between the requester and provider is modeled by marking certain ontology concepts as **in** or **out** concepts; an incoming message (from the requester to the provider) results in the insertion of an instance of an **in** concept; inserting an instance of an **out** concept results in a message being sent from the provider to the requester.

A single conversation corresponds to a choreography run, which consists of a start state, a sequence of intermediate states, and an end state. State transitions are governed by the transition rules; firing of a rule corresponds to a state transition. Such a state transition may or may not correspond to a message exchange between the requester and provider.

Listing 4.4 shows an example of an interface description with a choreography. A choreography is defined by a *state signature* and a set of *rules*. The state signature defines the state ontology over which the rules are evaluated and updates performed. In addition, the state signature assigns *modes* to ontology concepts and relations. These modes determine the role that a particular concept/relation plays in the choreography, as well as the relationship between instances of such a concept/relation and message formats, defined using, for example, WSDL.

Following the state signature block are the *transition rules*, which express conditions that are evaluated with respect to the state and the background ontologies. If the condition of a transition rule holds in the state, the rule is *fired*. If a transition rule fires, the enclosed *update rules* update to the state by adding, deleting, or updating facts in the state.

The WSML choreography language is very general, and can be used in a number of different ways. For example, there is no explicit control flow between the transition rules – that is, the order of rule firing is not determined by the order the rules are written, but rather by the conditions at the time of execution. It is certainly possible to add control flow to the transition rules, for example by defining a controlled concept that mimics an explicit state using an integer.

More details about the interface and choreography descriptions can be found in Chapter 7.

```
interface mediaSearchInterface
  annotations
    dc#title hasValue "Media Search Choreography"
    dc#description hasValue "An example of a choreography for searching for media items"
  endAnnotations

choreography mediaSearchChoreography

  stateSignature mediaSearchSignature

    importsOntology _"http://example.org/bookOntology"

    in
      shoptasks#SearchCatalog withGrounding
      _"http://example.org/webservices/shopping/mediashoppingservice#wsdl.
          interfaceMessageReference(MediaShoppingServicePortType/SearchCatalog/In)",

    out
      mediaproduct#MediaProduct withGrounding
      _"http://example.org/webservices/shopping/mediashoppingservice#wsdl.
          interfaceMessageReference(MediaShoppingServicePortType/SearchCatalog/Out)",


  transitionRules mediaSearchTransitions

    forall ?search
    with
      (?search [
        hasTitle hasValue ?title ,
        hasArtist hasValue ?artist ,
        hasMinPrice hasValue ?minPrice,
        hasMaxPrice hasValue ?maxPrice,
        hasMinRating hasValue ?minRating,
        hasMaxRating hasValue ?maxRating
      ] memberOf shoptasks#SearchCatalog
      and ?artist memberOf media#Artist
      and exists{?item}(
          ?item memberOf mediaproduct#MediaProduct and(
            ?item[hasContributor hasValue ?artist ] or
            ?item[hasTitle hasValue ?title ] or
            (
              ?item[hasPrice hasValue ?price] and
              ?price >= ?minPrice and
              ?price <= ?maxPrice
            ) or
            (
              ?item[hasRating hasValue ?rating] and
              ?rating >= ?minRating and
              ?rating <= ?maxRating
            )
          )
        )
      )
    do
      add(?item[
        hasContributor hasValue ?artist ,
        hasTitle hasValue ?title ,
        hasPrice hasValue ?price ,
        hasRating hasValue ?rating
      ] memberOf mediaproduct#MediaProduct
      )
      delete(?search memberOf shoptasks#SearchCatalog)
    endForall
```

Listing 4.4. An example interface declaration

```
nonFunctionalProperty
  prop#provider hasValue prop#mediaseller
  annotations
    dc#description hasValue "The agent providing the service ."
  endAnnotations

nonFunctionalProperty
  prop#security hasValue prop#highGradeEncryption
  annotations
    dc#description hasValue "There is a high grade of encryption, only if the requester is
       unique and is known."
  endAnnotations
  definedBy
    exists ?x(?x memberOf prop#ServiceRequester and naf exists ?y(?y memberOf
       prop#ServiceRequester and ?y != ?x) and prop#knownCustomer(?x)) .

nonFunctionalProperty
  prop#price hasValue ?price
  annotations
    dc#description hasValue "The price for service invocation is determined by the relation
       servicePrice , which is defined in the service properties ontology."
  endAnnotations
  definedBy
    exists ?x(?x memberOf prop#ServiceRequester and servicePrice(?x, ?price)) .
```

Listing 4.5. Example nonfunctional properties

Non-Functional Properties

The non-functional properties of a service are concerned with aspects of the service not directly related to its functionality, but that are nonetheless of interest to the requester. Examples of non-functional properties are: provider of the service, cost of service invocation, availability, and security.

Non-functional properties should not be confused with annotations: where annotations are concerned with the *description* of the service – e.g., creator of the description, natural language description – non-functional properties are concerned with the service itself.

As the name indicates, nonfunctional properties are *properties*, and are thus essentially name-value pairs. However, in contrast to annotations, it is possible to say a bit more about nonfunctional properties using logical expressions. Consequently, there are three kinds of non-functional properties: (i) simple name-value pairs, (ii) conditional name-value pairs, which should only be considered if the given logical expression is true (i.e., follows from the ontology), and (iii) open name-value pairs, where a given logical expression determines the value(s) of the property. Listing 4.5 shows examples of all three kinds of nonfunctional properties, all related to the service description in Listing 4.2.

4.4.6 Goals

Goal descriptions are symmetric to Web service descriptions in the sense that goals describe desired functionality and Web services describe offered functionality. Therefore, goal descriptions comprise the same modeling elements as Web service descriptions, namely, a capability, one or more interfaces, and non-functional properties.

There are, however, two (potential) differences between goals and Web services: (i) goals and Web services may be described using different terminologies (ontologies) and (ii) whereas services are described from the provider point of view, goals are described from the requester point of view.

Different Terminologies

In an ideal world, requesters and providers would use the same domain ontologies for the description of their goals and Web services, respectively. However, this cannot be assumed in general. The requester might find it more convenient to use his own terminology rather than the terminology of providers; different providers may use different terminologies to describe the same functionality; in general, it cannot be assumed that the requester is aware of the terminologies used by the providers.

In case there is a mismatch between the terminologies used in a goal and a Web service, mapping or mediation is required during discovery, selection, as well as usage of the service. To mediate between the requester and provider ontologies during discovery, it is necessary to be aware of the mappings between the ontologies. Certain kinds of simple mappings (e.g., subclass axioms) can be expressed using RDFS or OWL, as well as WSML-Core ontologies; more expressive mappings can be expressed using the Flight, Rule, or Full variants of WSML. Besides ontology languages, there are also dedicated mapping languages that might be used (e.g., [127, 116]).

WSML does not prescribe how a discovery engine should specify or use ontology mappings. There are, however, a number of ways in which such mappings can be made explicit in WSML. A **wgMediator** specifies a link between a goal and a Web service. Such a mediator can import an ontology that contains mappings between the ontologies used in the goal and Web service descriptions. WSML does not prescribe how such a mediator should be used, or how the mappings in the imported ontology should be processed.

In case a requester or provider knows about ontologies that are used in potentially matching Web services or goals, the mappings can be imported in the goal or Web service directly using the **importsOntology** directive. Mappings that are imported in this way are virtually added to the ontologies that are used for the goal or Web service specification.

Provider versus Requester Point of View

Even if the requester and provider use the same ontologies, or their ontologies have been mapped onto one another, there will be other differences in the ways the goal and Web service are described. For example, on the one hand, a requester will describe the information he can provide, but this information may be incomplete because the requester is not willing to disclose everything he knows due to privacy considerations. The provider, on the other hand, will describe all information that is required to execute the service.

We now proceed to outline the differences in the points of view of capability and interface descriptions.

Capability

On the level of a set-based capability description, there is not much difference between the requester and provider point of view. In a state-based capability description, however, the requester and provider will have different objectives in their descriptions of the preconditions, postconditions, assumptions, and effects.

Preconditions The service provider will want to make sure that all information required to execute the service is present when the service is executed. Therefore, he has an interest in describing the preconditions of the service in detail. The requester, on the other hand, may want to disclose some of his (personal) information, but most likely not all of it. Furthermore, if requesters were to include all their information in the preconditions of every goal, the task of writing the goal would become unmanageable, and even more so the processing of the goal. Therefore, we may assume that the requester might include some of his information in the pre-condition, but it will in no way be complete. This has implications for possible discovery mechanisms: even if a Web service provides exactly the requested functionality, it cannot be assumed in general that the preconditions of a goal will exactly match the preconditions of the service.

Assumptions With respect to assumptions, neither the requester nor the provider will want to be really complete. There are many things that must hold in the real world to ensure that the service can be executed successfully, e.g., a delivery address must exist, the company providing the service must not go bankrupt, and war must not break out. While a provider may want to model the assumption that the provided delivery address must exist in the real world in order to deliver a product, he will not be poised to model aspects related to bankruptcy and war. Considerations for the requester are similar: the requester can guarantee a number of things to hold, but an exhaustive list (e.g., including guarantees that his house does not have a leaky roof and his car will have enough gas to drive to the supermarket) would become too long for any practical use. In general, it may be expected that the provider will include some assumptions that are directly related to the provided service (e.g., for payment, the limit of the credit card must not have been reached) that might help a potential requester to determine whether the service is suitable and to explain possible failures in execution of the service, but the description will not be exhaustive.

From the above description it may seem that the prospect of using state-based capabilities for automated matching is rather bleak when looking at our expectations concerning the description of preconditions and assumptions, especially from the side of the requester; if the formal descriptions are not detailed enough, or even missing, automated matching is not possible. Fortunately, the situation looks a bit better when considering postconditions and effects. There are two reasons for this: postconditions and effects are only concerned with the desired and actual outputs and real-world effects of the service; therefore, requesters have an interest in including detailed descriptions of the postconditions and effects in their goals.

Postconditions and Effects The requester has a big interest in what the service actually "does" for him. If he is interested in specific information (e.g., product availability) that should be an output of the service, he will describe the postconditions concerning this information. If he is interested in certain real-world effects (e.g., product delivery), he will describe the corresponding effects. The provider may find it more important to ensure that all preconditions and assumptions are met before executing the service, rather than describing the output and effects in detail; however, if the provider wants the service to be found, he will have to describe the postconditions and effects in sufficient detail.

More details about the modeling of capabilities can be found in Chapter 6.

Interfaces and Choreographies

Considerations for interfaces are similar to those for preconditions. There is typically a fixed way (or number of ways) in which a service can interact with a requester. The service provider has an interest in accurately describing this interface so that potential requesters know how to invoke it. The requester, on the other hand, may have a large repository of information that could be sent over the wire; however, it is not practical to describe this all in a goal. We conjecture that there will be many situations in which a Web service description contains an accurate interface description, but a matching goal description does not. That said, if the requester is an automated agent, there may be a limited number of ways it can interact with services. In that case, the goal would contain descriptions of the ways the requester can interact with services. Note that it is, in the general case, unlikely that such interface descriptions and goals would easily match with interface descriptions in Web services, even if ontology mapping is applied; it might be necessary to use a *mediator* (see the next section).

More details about the interface and choreography descriptions can be found in Chapter 7.

4.4.7 Mediators

Mediators connect different goals, Web services and ontologies, and enable inter-operation by reconciling differences in representation formats, encoding styles, business protocols, etc. Connections between mediators and other WSML elements can be established in two different ways:

1. Each WSML element allows for the specification of a number of used mediators through the **usesMediator** keyword.
2. Each mediator has (depending on the type of mediator) one or more **source**s and one **target**. Both source and target are optional in order to allow for generic mediators.

A mediator achieves its mediation functionality either through a Web service, which provides the mediation service, or a goal, which can be used to dynamically discover the appropriate (mediation) Web service.

4.5 XML and RDF Exchange Syntaxes

In the previous section we have introduced the WSML language through its surface syntax. The surface syntax is a plain text format that uses keywords resembling natural language. Therefore, this syntax is especially suitable for consumption by human readers and for writing WSML descriptions by hand. However, it might not be suitable for exchange over the Web, because it does not allow reusing existing tools and techniques for such things as parsing, storing, and retrieving descriptions.

For the purposes of exchange and interoperation with existing Web languages, WSML comes with an XML syntax [133] and an RDF syntax [45], called WSML/XML and WSML/RDF, respectively.

WSML/XML documents conform to an XML schema, which has been specified following the structure of the WSML abstract syntax [29], leveraging built-in XML mechanisms such as character encoding and namespaces.

WSML/RDF consists of an RDF Schema that captures the structure of WSML descriptions. Individual WSML descriptions are written as RDF graphs using vocabulary defined in the schema.

4.5.1 WSML XML Syntax

The WSML XML syntax is essentially an XML version of the surface syntax, and is thus very similar, both in keywords and in structure. In fact, there is a one-to-one correspondence between the structure of the WSML abstract syntax defined in [29] and the structure of WSML/XML.

WSML/XML is defined using an XML schema document.[4] XML schema [53] is a schema language for XML; it defines thee allowed structure of XML

---

[4] http://www.wsmo.org/TR/d36/v0.1/xml-syntax/wsml_xml_syntax.xsd

```
<wsml xmlns="http://www.wsmo.org/wsml/wsml-syntax#" variant="http://www.wsmo.org/wsml/
    wsml-syntax/wsml-flight">
  <WebService name="http://example.org/webservices/shopping/AddItemsToCart">
    <Annotations>
      <AttributeValue name="http://purl.org/dc/elements/1.1#title">
        <Value type="http://www.w3.org/2001/XMLSchema#string">
          Add items to cart  service
        </Value>
      </AttributeValue>
      ...
    </Annotations>
    <importsOntology>http://example.org/ontologies/commerce/Commerce</importsOntology>
    <importsOntology>http://example.org/ontologies/products/Products</importsOntology>
    <Capability>
      <SharedVariables>
        <Variable name="?cartId"/>
        <Variable name="?item"/>
        <Variable name="?number"/>
      </SharedVariables>
      ...
    </Capability>
    <Interface> ... </Interface>
    <NonFunctionalProperty> ... </NonFunctionalProperty>
  </WebService>
</wsml>
```

Listing 4.6. Example Web service written in WSML/XML

instance documents. Every WSML/XML description (e.g., goal, Web service) is an instance document that must conform to the schema.

Listing 4.6 shows the WSML/XML rendering of the Web service description in Listing 4.2 on page 48. As can be seen from the listing, the structure of the XML rendering is very close to that of the surface syntax. The root element of any WSML/XML document is wsml; the variant is indicated using the variant attribute on the root element. Certain syntactic shortcuts in the surface syntax, such as the list of imported ontologies in Listing 4.2, are not used in WSML/XML. For example, every imported ontology requires a separate importsOntology tag.

Notice that all WSML elements fall in the WSML namespace http://www.wsmo.org/wsml/wsml-syntax#.

The WSML/XML schema can be found at the following location: http://www.wsmo.org/TR/d36/v0.1/xml-syntax/wsml_xml_syntax.xsd. For a detailed description of WSML/XML we refer the reader to [133].

4.5.2 WSML RDF Syntax

WSML/RDF [45] is an RDF Schema [28] vocabulary for writing WSML descriptions. WSML/RDF descriptions are RDF graphs that use this vocabulary. We refer to the RDF Schema that defines WSML/RDF as the WSML/RDF schema.

WSML descriptions group all data related to a particular ontology, Web service, goal or mediator. In the WSML surface syntax this is achieved by grouping all descriptions under the **ontology**, **webService**, **goal**, **ggMediator**, **wgMediator**, **wwMediator**, and **ooMediator** keywords. The same holds for lower-level entities: concepts in an ontology, for example, group a number of attribute definitions and state-based Web service capabilities group pre-conditions, postconditions, assumptions and effects. Conceptually, a WSML description can be seen as a part-whole hierarchy. An ontology has as parts the concept, relation, axiom, and instance definitions; in turn, these definitions are part of the ontology. Similar for Web services, goals and mediators.

To represent the part-whole hierarchy of WSML descriptions we use a part-whole[5] ontology inspired by the work of the Semantic Web Best Practices Working Group [119]. Each ontology, Web service, goal, and mediator is a node in the RDF graph that is connected to all its parts using the relationship hasPart_directly. Figure 4.4 shows part of the part-whole hierarchy.

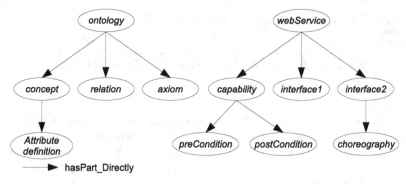

Fig. 4.4. WSML descriptions as part-whole hierarchies

In some cases it is necessary to disambiguate between different parts of a whole; is not possible to use the hasPart property for all parts of a whole. This is for example the case for the preconditions, postconditions, assumptions and effects of a capability: one axiom may be a pre-condition of one capability and a post-condition of another capability. For this reason, we define sub-properties of hasPart_directly, namely hasPrecondition, hasPostcondition, hasAssumption, and hasEffect.

RDF is not suitable for representing complex statements such as WSML logical expressions. Therefore, such expressions are either represented as XML literals using the WSML/XML format or represented as plain literals, using the WSML surface syntax described in Section 4.4.4.

Listing 4.7 contains part of the Web service description of Listing 4.2 in WSML/RDF format. The listing uses the Turtle syntax [15] for representing RDF.

---

[5] http://www.wsmo.org/TR/d32/v0.2/part.owl

```
@prefix  :  <http://www.wsmo.org/wsml/wsml−syntax#> .
@prefix  part−whole: <http://www.wsmo.org/TR/d32/v0.2/part.owl#> .
@prefix  xsd:  <http://www.w3.org/2001/XMLSchema#> .
@prefix  rdf:  <http://www.w3.org/1999/02/22−rdf−syntax−ns#> .
@prefix  dc:  <http://purl.org/dc/elements/1.1/> .
@prefix  ex:  <http://example.org/webservices/shopping/"> .

ex:AddItemsToCart rdf:type  :WebService .
ex:AddItemsToCart :variant  <http://www.wsmo.org/wsml/wsml−syntax/wsml−flight> .

ex:AddItemsToCart dc:title  "Add items to cart  service" .

ex:AddItemsToCart :importsOntology <http://example.org/ontologies/commerce/Commerce> .
ex:AddItemsToCart :importsOntology <http://example.org/ontologies/products/Products> .

ex:AddItemsToCart part−whole:hasPart_directly _:c .
_:c  rdf:type  :Capability .
_:c  :sharedVariable  "?cartId" .
_:c  :sharedVariable  "?item" .
_:c  :sharedVariable  "?number" .

ex:AddItemsToCart part−whole:hasPart_directly _:i .
_:i  rdf:type  :Interface .

_:i  part−whole:hasPart_directly _:ch .
_:ch  rdf:type  :Choreography .

ex:AddItemsToCart part−whole:hasPart_directly _:n .
_:n  rdf:type  :NonFunctionalProperty.

...
```

Listing 4.7. Example Web service description written in WSML/RDF

Since an RDF graph does not have a root element, the variant is an attribute of the actual description (in this case a Web service description). As can be seen from the example, annotations are written simply as RDF triples. Three parts of the example Web service are shown in the listing, through the use of part-whole:hasPart_directly: the capability, an interface, and a nonfunctional property. These elements did not have names in Listing 4.2; therefore, blank nodes are used to represent them. The interface (_:i) has a further part, which is an unnamed choreography.

The WSML/RDF schema can be found at the following location: http://www.wsmo.org/TR/d32/v0.2/wsml.rdf. For more details about WSML/RDF we refer the reader to [45].

4.6 Leveraging RDF and OWL Ontologies in WSML Web Services

In the previous section we described WSML/RDF, which enables the use of RDF for the exchange, storage, and retrieval of WSML descriptions using RDF-based tools. In particular, it enables the use of SPARQL [117], a query language for RDF, for retrieving and querying WSML descriptions. In addition, WSML repositories may be implemented as SPARQL endpoints [41], which may consequently be seen as Web-based interfaces to the repositories.

Another use of RDF in the context of WSML, and Semantic Web services in general, is the use of RDF Schema [28, 73] ontologies to define the terminology of goal and Web service descriptions. Such RDF Schema ontologies can be used in addition to, or instead of, WSML ontologies.

Besides RDF Schema ontologies, it is also possible to use OWL DL [46, 77] ontologies in combination with WSML. There are, however, certain restrictions on the use of RDFS and OWL DL in the various WSML variants. Namely, RDFS ontologies cannot be used with the Core and DL variants of WSML, and only a subset of OWL DL can be used with the Core, Flight, and Rule variants of WSML. This is not necessarily a big problem. For example, when importing an RDFS ontology in a WSML-Core Web service description, the variant under consideration will automatically become WSML-Flight, and there are known effective procedures for processing WSML-Flight descriptions. However, when importing an OWL DL ontology in a WSML-Flight description (or, likewise, when importing an RDFS ontology in a WSML-DL description) the variant under consideration will become WSML-Full, and there are no known procedures for processing WSML-Full descriptions. For more details about the exact relationship between RDFS and OWL DL and the various WSML variants, see the next chapter.

References to RDFS and OWL DL ontologies are written using the **importsOntology** directive, which is the same directive used for importing WSML ontologies. It is up to the implementation to determine whether the referenced ontology is a WSML, RDFS, or OWL DL ontology. One could imagine that the IRI is dereferenced, the application initiates an HTTP request, and the result will be either a WSML, RDFS, or OWL DL ontology. Now, a WSML ontology can be written using one of three syntaxes: surface syntax, WSML/XML, or WSML/RDF. Distinguishing the surface syntax and WSML/XML from RDFS and OWL DL is straightforward. Distinguishing WSML/RDF from RDFS is not completely straightforward. A possible guideline is be the following: in case there is a triple of the form o rdf:type wsml:Ontology in the graph, the ontology is most likely a WSML ontology (every WSML/RDF ontology contains such a triple); otherwise, it is an RDFS ontology.

It is more tricky to distinguish RDFS and OWL DL ontologies, because the syntax of both kinds of ontologies is based on RDF graphs. In fact, every RDF graph that is an OWL DL ontology is an RDFS ontology (but not necessarily the other way around). Therefore, an RDF graph that is an OWL DL ontology can be interpreted either way. A guideline that could be used to decide how to interpret the graph is to check whether any OWL vocabulary is used in the graph. If this is the case (every OWL DL ontology contains OWL vocabulary), and the RDF graph is an OWL DL ontology, then it should be interpreted as such; otherwise it should be interpreted as an RDFS ontology.

Note that, if this guideline is strictly followed, OWL Full ontologies that are not OWL DL ontologies are interpreted as RDFS ontologies.

Consider, for example, the FOAF ontology,[6] which is an RDF graph. This ontology does not contains a triple of the form o rdf:type wsml:Ontology, and is thus not a WSML ontology. The ontology does contain OWL vocabulary, and could thus be considered an OWL ontology. It turns out, however, that the ontology is not an OWL DL ontology,[7] but an OWL Full ontology (and thus also an RDFS ontology). The application should consequently interpret the RDF graph as an RDFS ontology.

In this chapter we have introduced various aspects of the Web Service Modeling Language. In the following three chapters we will describe the three core parts of WSML – ontology, functional, and behavioral description – in more detail.

---

[6] The IRI identifying this ontology is http://xmlns.com/foaf/0.1/; the ontology can be found at http://xmlns.com/foaf/spec/index.rdf.

[7] This can be verified, for example, using the WonderWeb OWL Ontology Validator: http://www.mygrid.org.uk/OWL/Validator.

Part II

The WSML Description Components

5

Description of Ontologies

As we discussed in Chapter 4, ontologies form the basic vocabularies for goal and Web service descriptions. More specifically, they define the terminologies used in the functional and behavioral descriptions, as well as the nonfunctional properties. This chapter is concerned with ontologies; the following two chapters are concerned functional and behavioral Web service descriptions, respectively.

WSML includes the *WSML ontology language*. In this chapter we define this language and the interaction between this language and the RDF schema [28] and OWL DL [46] ontology languages. We define the basic semantic notions that are used for representing and reasoning with ontologies, but also for representing and reasoning with functional and behavioral descriptions. To that end, Chapters 6 and 7 extend the notions defined in this chapter to suit the needs of the respective types of descriptions.

Recall from Section 4.3 the WSML language variants. They are based on different knowledge representation paradigms. WSML-Rule is based on the paradigm of logical rules with negation, specifically the Stable Model Semantics [62], which is a popular semantics for declarative logic programs with negation – another popular semantics for logic programs with negation is the Well-Founded Semantics [61], which may be used as an approximation of the Stable Model Semantics for the task of query answering. WSML-DL, in contrast, is based on the paradigm of Description Logics [11], which are, for our purposes, subsets of classical first-order logic [25]. Consequently, it is hard to define a single semantics for all WSML variants – a straightforward combination of positive function-free rules with a simple Description Logic already leads to undecidability of reasoning [93]. We note that there are approaches to combining Description Logics with logical rules (e.g., [93, 48, 123, 125, 124, 126, 109, 108, 76, 51, 51, 50, 31]); these approaches, however, are not as well investigated as the individual paradigms of Description Logics and Logic Programming, and they are generally computationally harder to deal with. Therefore, the semantics of WSML-DL is defined in a way that is close to the first-order version of the Description Logics [25] and base the semantics of WSML-Core, Flight, and Rule is based on the Stable Model Semantics for logic programs [62].

We note that one of the approaches to combining rules and ontologies (de Bruijn et al. [31]) was adapted to WSML, to provide a semantic framework for all variants, including WSML-Full, by De Bruijn and Heymans [32, 33]. However, as the combination of rules and ontologies is still very much an open research issue, this semantics for WSML-Full is not included in the language recommendation.

The semantics of WSML ontologies, and their combination with RDFS and OWL DL, is defined on the logical expression syntax. The semantics of the conceptual syntax is defined through a mapping from the logical expression syntax, which is described in Section 5.1. This mapping also shows the overlap between conceptual and logical expression syntax, and how expressions in the conceptual syntax can be accessed from the logical expression syntax.

WSML defines a model theory, which is shared between the variants; individual variants impose additional restrictions to achieve correspondence with the respective knowledge representation paradigms: Description Logics, in the case of WSML-DL, and the Stable Model Semantics for logic programs, in the case of WSML-Rule. The model theory is defined in Section 5.2. Section 5.3 describes the relationship between the variants. Specifically, it turns out that all WSML- Core derivations are WSML-DL derivations.

Finally, the combination of WSML ontologies with RDFS and OWL DL is defined in Section 5.4. The combinations are achieved by connecting the model theories of RDFS, OWL DL, and WSML ontologies. Notions of satisfiability and entailment for the different variants in combinations with RDFS and OWL DL are defined. Combinations of WSML and RDFS/OWL ontologies not only result from importing RDFS/OWL ontologies in WSML ontologies, but also from importing RDFS/OWL ontologies in WSML Web service and goal descriptions

Sections 5.2 and 5.4 are quite technical and require a basic understanding of model theory in logics. Therefore, the reader may want to skip the sections on first reading.

5.1 Relationship between the Conceptual and Logical Expression Syntaxes

The WSML conceptual and logical expression syntaxes (see the Sections 4.4.2 and 4.4.4, respectively) have a certain overlap in their expressiveness. It was mentioned in Section 4.4.4 that certain expressions in the conceptual syntax have a counterpart in the logical expression syntax (see Table 4.2 on page 47). Indeed, it is possible to write statements about classes, attributes, relations, instances, and relation instances in the logical expression syntax. It is in fact the case that most statements in the conceptual syntax of WSML ontologies can be expressed using the logical expression syntax. Exceptions are ontology import and mediator usage statements and declarations of WSML elements. For example, the ontology declaration ontology_"http://example.org/ontologies/Media" cannot be expressed in the logical expression syntax. In fact, such declarations are not reflected in the WSML semantics.

If an ontology has associated annotations, these are reflected in the semantics and can be expressed in the logical expression syntax. Consider the following description:

```
ontology _"http://example.org/ontologies/Media"
  annotations
    dc#title  hasValue "Media Ontology"
    wsml#version hasValue "Revision: 1.25"
  endAnnotations
  importsOntology { _"http://xmlns.com/foaf/0.1/" }
```

The ontology declaration and the import statement are not reflected in the semantics and do not have an equivalent in the logical expression syntax; the annotations are and do. In fact, ontology import statements play an important role in the definition of the ontology semantics: all imported ontologies are taken into account.

The following formulas are the logical expression-equivalent of the annotations in the example. The annotations are in fact attribute values of the ontology:

```
_"http://example.org/ontologies/Media" [dc#title hasValue "Media Ontology"] .
_"http://example.org/ontologies/Media" [wsml#version hasValue "Revision: 1.25"] .
```

This is not to say that ontology declarations and import statements should not be used or are not important. The identifier of the ontology can be used for other purposes, such as importing this ontology into other ontologies. The ontology import statements themselves are not directly reflected in the semantics of WSML, but they do play a role in the definition of entailment. Namely, to decide whether a formula is entailed by an ontology, all imported ontologies are taken into account in making this decision. This aspect is discussed in more detail in the next section. In fact, the union of the ontology and all (recursively) imported WSML ontologies is considered when checking entailment (or satisfiability, for that matter).

In the example above, the imported ontology (the FOAF ontology) is an RDFS ontology. Since an RDFS ontology is not a WSML ontology, additional considerations need to be taken into account when defining the semantics of imports of RDFS ontologies. See Section 5.4 for an in-depth discussion.

The correspondence between the conceptual syntax and the logical expression syntax, outlined in Table 4.2, on page 47, and formally defined in [29, Section 3.1.4], is used to define the semantics of WSML ontologies. This semantics is directly defined for logical expressions; the semantics for the conceptual syntax is obtained through its mapping to the logical expression syntax.

Abstract Syntax	Surface Syntax
$tr(p(t_1,\ldots,t_n))$	$p(t_1,\ldots,t_n)$
$tr(\top)$	**true**
$tr(\bot)$	**false**
$tr(t_1 = t_2)$	$t_1 = t_2$
$tr(t_1 : t_2)$	t_1 **memberOf** t_2
$tr(t_1 :: t_2)$	t_1 **subConceptOf** t_2
$tr(t_1[t_2 \text{ hv } t_3])$	$t_1[t_2$ **hasValue** $t_3]$
$tr(t_1[t_2 \text{ ot } t_3])$	$t_1[t_2$ **ofType** $t_3]$
$tr(t_1[t_2 \text{ it } t_3])$	$t_1[t_2$ **impliesType** $t_3]$
$tr(\neg\phi)$	**neg** $tr(\phi)$
$tr(not\ \phi)$	**naf** $tr(\phi)$
$tr_{rule}((\forall)b_1 \wedge \ldots \wedge b_l \wedge$ $not\ c_1 \wedge \ldots \wedge not\ c_m \supset \bot),$ with $l+m \geq 1$	**!-** $tr(b_1)$ **and** $\ldots$ **and** $tr(b_l)$ **and naf** $tr(c_1)$ **and** $\ldots$ **and naf** $tr(c_m)$
$tr_{rule}((\forall)b_1 \wedge \ldots \wedge b_l \wedge$ $not\ c_1 \wedge \ldots \wedge not\ c_m \supset h),$ with $h \neq \bot$	$tr(h)$ **:-** $tr(b_1)$ **and** $\ldots$ **and** $tr(b_l)$ **and naf** $tr(c_1)$ **and** $\ldots$ **and naf** $tr(c_m)$
$tr(\phi \wedge \psi)$	$tr(\phi)$ **and** $tr(\psi)$
$tr(\phi \vee \psi)$	$tr(\phi)$ **or** $tr(\psi)$
$tr(\phi \supset \psi)$	$tr(\phi)$ **implies** $tr(\psi)$
$tr(\phi \equiv \psi)$	$tr(\phi)$ **equivalent** $tr(\psi)$
$tr(\forall x(\phi))$	**forall** ?x$(tr(\phi))$
$tr(\exists x(\phi))$	**exists** ?x$(tr(\phi))$

Table 5.1. Mapping between abstract and surface syntax of logical expressions

In the remainder of this chapter we are primarily concerned with the logical expression syntax. We will use the abstract syntax for logical expressions as defined in [29, Section 1.22]. Table 5.1 shows the correspondence between the abstract syntax and the surface syntax for logical expressions, through a mapping tr that translates logical expressions from the abstract to the surface syntax. The mapping tr_{rule} is used in the rule-based variants of WSML, namely WSML-Flight and WSML-Rule.

The semantics of WSML ontologies is defined relative to sets of WSML formulas in abstract syntax form, called *theories*. Given a WSML ontology O, the *corresponding* theory Φ is the set of WSML formulas in abstract syntax form obtained by mapping the conceptual syntax to the logical expression syntax.

5.2 Semantics of WSML Ontologies

In this section we give an outline of the semantics of WSML ontologies. For detailed definitions we refer the reader to [29, Section 3.1]. Instead, we focus on the differences between the variants.

The semantics of WSML ontologies is based on a model theory, similar to the standard model theory used for classical first-order predicate logic (see, e.g., [59]), extended with certain features inspired by the model theory of F-Logic [88]. This model theory defines a notion of interpretation, and defines the conditions under which an interpretation $\mathcal{I}$ *satisfies* a formula or a set of formulas (also called a *theory*), which are WSML logical expressions written in abstract syntax form (cf. Table 5.1; [29]). An interpretation that satisfies a formula or theory is called a *model*. Finally, the most important notion for reasoning (deduction) is that of *entailment*, which corresponds to derivation (or logical deduction). A set of formulas Φ *entails* a formula ϕ if every model of Φ is a model of ϕ.

Recall that different WSML variants are based on different knowledge representation paradigms. It turns out that, because of the differences between the paradigms, it is not known how to use the same model theory for all variants. However, there is a basic notion of a WSML interpretation and there is a basic notion of a model. Different variants extend these definitions in different ways. WSML-DL imposes certain additional restrictions on interpretations, such as a separation of the interpretation of concept, instance, and attribute identifiers, but uses the basic notion of a model. WSML-Core, Flight, and Rule use the basic notion of WSML interpretation, but impose certain additional restrictions on conditions under which an interpretation is a model; models need to be minimal or *stable*. The latter is necessary for the nonmonotonic interpretation of the default negation symbol *not* .

The model theory of WSML-DL has been constructed in such a way that it is close to the usual model theory of the first-order variant [25] of the Description Logic $\mathcal{SHIQ}(\mathbf{D})$ [78]. See, e.g., [44, Section 8.2] for a first-order style definition of the $\mathcal{SHIQ}(\mathbf{D})$ semantics.

WSML-Core, Flight, and Rule share the same model theory, which has been constructed in such a way that there is a correspondence with the Stable Model Semantics of normal logic programs [62], i.e., logic programs with no disjunction in the head and with negation in the body of the rules. Note that WSML-Flight theories are locally stratified, and that for locally stratified logic programs the Stable Model Semantics corresponds with the other prominent semantics for logic programs with negation, such as the Well-Founded Semantics [61] and the perfect model semantics [118]. Finally, WSML-Core theories do not contain negation; for negation-free logic programs the Stable Model Semantics corresponds with the minimal Herbrand model semantics [96].

For more details of the correspondence between WSML-DL and $\mathcal{SHIQ}(\mathbf{D})$ and between WSML-Core, Flight, and Rule and the Stable Model Semantics for normal logic programs, and how these formalisms can be used for reasoning with WSML, see Chapter 8.

In the remainder of this section we first describe the basic WSML model theory. We proceed with a description of the extension to the WSML-DL model theory and the notion of entailment in WSML-DL. We then describe the notions of minimal Herbrand model and stable model for WSML-Core,

Flight, and Rule, and define the notion of entailment for these variants. We conclude this section with a discussion of the differences between the variants and language layering in WSML, most notably the layering between the Core and DL variants.

5.2.1 The Basic WSML Model Theory

The basic WSML model theory defines a notion of interpretation and a notion of satisfaction, which are conditions under which a WSML interpretation is a model of a formula, or a set of formulas.

As usual, an interpretation has an *abstract domain of interpretation*, which is an abstract set of objects used for the interpretation of IRIs. Additionally, an interpretation has a *concrete domain*, which is used for the interpretation of data values. Different interpretations may have different abstract domains and different mappings of IRIs to this abstract domain. The concrete domains of all interpretations under consideration must be the same, as must be the mapping of data values to elements of this domain. This means that any data value is mapped to the same element (value) in the concrete domain, in every interpretation under consideration. For example, an IRI ex#abc may be mapped to some abstract object a in one interpretation and to b in some other interpretation, but the integer 1 must be mapped to the number 1 in every interpretation.

The concrete domain to be considered is given by a *concrete domain scheme*, which defines a concrete domain, a mapping of data values to elements of this domain, and a number of built-in functions and predicates (e.g., numeric addition, string concatenation, and numeric comparison). Since the list of datatypes that may be used with WSML is not fixed, there is not a single concrete domain scheme for WSML. However, WSML does impose certain requirements on so-called *WSML-compliant* domain schemes, namely, the scheme must include the XML schema datatypes *string*, *integer*, and *decimal* [20], the RDF datatype *XMLLiteral*, and a number of built-in predicates defined for WSML (see [68, Appendix B.2]).

We now proceed to define the notions of interpretation, satisfaction, and concrete domain scheme.

WSML Interpretations

An interpretation is a tuple $\mathcal{I} = \langle U, \prec_U, \in_U, U^D, \mathcal{I}_F, \mathcal{I}_P, \mathcal{I}_{\mathsf{hv}}, \mathcal{I}_{\mathsf{it}}, \mathcal{I}_{\mathsf{ot}} \rangle$, where

- U is a nonempty countable set, called the *abstract* domain,
- U^D is a non-empty set that is disjoint from U, called the *concrete* domain,
- $\prec_U$ is an irreflexive partial order over $U \cup U^D$, representing the strict sub-concept relation,
- $\in_U$ is a binary relation over $U \cup U^D$, representing the concept membership relation,

- $\mathcal{I}_F$ is a mapping from constant and function identifiers to elements of U and functions over $(U \cup U^D)$,
- $\mathcal{I}_P$ is a mapping from relation identifiers to relations over $(U \cup U^D)$, and
- $\mathcal{I}_{hv}$, $\mathcal{I}_{it}$, and $\mathcal{I}_{ot}$ are mappings from $U \cup U^D$ to binary relations over $U \cup U^D$, representing the attribute value (**hasValue**) and the two kinds of attributes typing relations (**impliesType** and **ofType**): $\mathcal{I}_{hv}, \mathcal{I}_{it}, \mathcal{I}_{ot} : U \cup U^D \rightarrow 2^{(U \cup U^D) \times (U \cup U^D)}$.

Additionally, the following two conditions ((5.1) and (5.2)) must hold on every WSML interpretation. These conditions that WSML interpretations obey the semantics of the sub-concept and **impliesType** relations. The first condition requires that if the sub-concept relation holds between two elements, the set of instances of the sub-concept is a subset of the set of instances of the super-concept.

We write $a \preceq_U b$ when $a \prec_U b$ or $a = b$, for any two $a, b \in U \cup U^D$. For every interpretation must hold that

$$\text{if } a \in_U b \text{ and } b \preceq_U c \text{ then } a \in_U c \qquad (5.1)$$

The second condition requires that if the **impliesType** typing relation holds between an attribute p and a concept d, for a concept c, then it must be the case that for every instance a of c, whenever the attribute p has a value b, then b must be an instance of d:

if $\langle c, d \rangle \in \mathcal{I}_{it}(p)$, then for every $a \in_U c$ holds that

$$\text{for every } b \in U \cup U^D \text{ such that } \langle a, b \rangle \in \mathcal{I}_{hv}(p), b \in_U d \quad (5.2)$$

From condition 5.1 follows that, if $b \preceq_U c$, then the set of instances of b is a subset of the set of instances of c, i.e., $\{k \mid k \in_U b, k \in U \cup U^D\} \subseteq \{k \mid k \in_U c, k \in U \cup U^D\}$. We call the set $\{k \mid k \in_U b, k \in U \cup U^D\}$ the *class extension* of b, and denote the class extension of an element b with b_{cext}. Thus,

$$\text{if } b \preceq_U c, \text{ then } b_{cext} \text{ is a subset of } c_{cext} \qquad (5.3)$$

However, the converse of (5.3) is not always true: if b_{cext} is a subset of c_{cext}, then it is not necessarily the case that $b \preceq_U c$.

Note that a consequence is that it is not possible to derive a subconcept statement $c :: d$ from a formula $\forall x (x : c \supset x : d)$. Note that this kind of derivation is common in Description Logics; in fact, in DLs there is no distinction between subconcept statements and formulas of the mentioned form; both are written as $c \sqsubseteq d$. Consequently, WSML-DL requires an additional conditions that ensures the converse of 5.3 is be true in every interpretation; see the following subsection.

Before proceeding with the definitions of the interpretation of identifiers, we must make a note about anonymous identifiers. In the following we assume that

- each unnumbered anonymous identifier _# is replaced with a globally unique new IRI and
- for every formula ϕ and every numbered anonymous identifier _#n occurring in ϕ, each occurrence of _#n is replaced with the same new globally unique IRI.

We now proceed with the definition of the interpretation functions for identifiers, namely $\mathcal{I}_F$ and $\mathcal{I}_P$. Note that all identifiers (after replacement of anonymous identifiers) are IRIs, with the exception of elementary data values.

An instance identifier is interpreted as an element of the abstract domain U: $\mathcal{I}_F(f) = u \in U$. A function identifier is interpreted as a function over the domain U, for every arity $i \geq 1$: $\mathcal{I}_F(f)^i : U^i \rightarrow U$. An n-ary datatype wrapper or elementary data value (elementary data values have arity 0) f is interpreted as a function over the domain U^D: $\mathcal{I}_F(f) : (U^D)^n \rightarrow U^D$. A relation identifier p is interpreted as a relation over the domain $U \cup U^D$ for every arity $i \geq 0$: $\mathcal{I}_P(p)^i \subseteq (U \cup U^D)^i$. An n-ary built-in predicate identifier p is interpreted as a relation over the domain U^D: $\mathcal{I}_P(p) \subseteq (U^D)^n$.

After defining the interpretation of constant, predicate, and function symbols, we can now define the interpretation of terms. To do that, we first need to define the notion of variable assignment. We need to distinguish between *abstract* and *concrete* assignments.

A variable assignment B assigns each variable x to an individual $x^B \in U \cup U^D$. A variable assignment B' is an abstract (resp., concrete) x-variant of B if $x^{B'} \in U \cup U^D$ (resp., $x^{B'} \in U^D$) and $y^{B'} = y^B$ for every $y \neq x$.

We are now ready to define interpretation of terms.

The interpretation of a term t in some interpretation $\mathcal{I}$ with respect to some variable assignment B, written $t^{\mathcal{I},B}$, is defined as: $t^{\mathcal{I},B} = t^B$ if $t \in \mathcal{V}$, and $t^{\mathcal{I},B} = \mathcal{I}_F(f)(t_1^{\mathcal{I},B}, \ldots, t_n^{\mathcal{I},B})$ if t is of the form $f(t_1, \ldots, t_n)$, with $n \geq 0$.

Satisfaction

Satisfaction is a relation between interpretations and formulas. Whenever a pair of an interpretation $\mathcal{I}$ and a formula ϕ are in the satisfaction relation, the interpretation $\mathcal{I}$ *satisfies* the formula ϕ, denoted $\mathcal{I} \models \phi$. If $\mathcal{I} \models \phi$ we say that $\mathcal{I}$ is a *model* of ϕ; in other words, ϕ is *true* in $\mathcal{I}$. If $\mathcal{I}$ and ϕ are not in the satisfaction relation, i.e., $\mathcal{I}$ is not a model of ϕ, we write $\mathcal{I} \not\models \phi$.

To define satisfaction of formulas with free variables, we formally define the satisfaction relation relative to a given variable assignment B. We first define satisfaction of atomic formulas and molecules and subsequently extend it to arbitrary formulas.

Satisfaction of atomic formulas and molecules ϕ in an interpretation $\mathcal{I}$, given a variable assignment B, denoted $(\mathcal{I}, B) \models \phi$, is defined as:

- $(\mathcal{I}, B) \models \top$,
- $(\mathcal{I}, B) \not\models \bot$,

- $(\mathcal{I}, B) \models p(t_1, \ldots, t_n)$ iff $(t_1^{\mathcal{I},B}, \ldots, t_n^{\mathcal{I},B}) \in \mathcal{I}_P(p)$,
- $(\mathcal{I}, B) \models t_1 : t_2$ iff $t_1^{\mathcal{I},B} \in_U t_2^{\mathcal{I},B}$,
- $(\mathcal{I}, B) \models t_1 :: t_2$ iff $t_1^{\mathcal{I},B} \preceq_U t_2^{\mathcal{I},B}$,
- $(\mathcal{I}, B) \models t_1[t_2 \, \mathsf{hv} \, t_3]$ iff $\langle t_1^{\mathcal{I},B}, t_3^{\mathcal{I},B} \rangle \in \mathcal{I}_{\mathsf{hv}}(t_2^{\mathcal{I},B})$,
- $(\mathcal{I}, B) \models t_1[t_2 \, \mathsf{it} \, t_3]$ iff $\langle t_1^{\mathcal{I},B}, t_3^{\mathcal{I},B} \rangle \in \mathcal{I}_{\mathsf{it}}(t_2^{\mathcal{I},B})$,
- $(\mathcal{I}, B) \models t_1[t_2 \, \mathsf{ot} \, t_3]$ iff $\langle t_1^{\mathcal{I},B}, t_3^{\mathcal{I},B} \rangle \in \mathcal{I}_{\mathsf{ot}}(t_2^{\mathcal{I},B})$, and
- $(\mathcal{I}, B) \models t_1 = t_2$ iff $t_1^{\mathcal{I},B} = t_2^{\mathcal{I},B}$.

This extends to arbitrary formulas as follows:

- $(\mathcal{I}, B) \models \phi_1 \wedge \phi_2$ iff $(\mathcal{I}, B) \models \phi_1$ and $(\mathcal{I}, B) \models \phi_2$,
- $(\mathcal{I}, B) \models \phi_1 \vee \phi_2$ iff $(\mathcal{I}, B) \models \phi_1$ or $(\mathcal{I}, B) \models \phi_2$,
- $(\mathcal{I}, B) \models \phi_1 \supset \phi_2$ iff $(\mathcal{I}, B) \not\models \phi_1$ or $(\mathcal{I}, B) \models \phi_2$,
- $(\mathcal{I}, B) \models \phi_1 \equiv \phi_2$ iff $(\mathcal{I}, B) \models \phi_1 \supset \phi_2$ and $(\mathcal{I}, B) \models \phi_2 \supset \phi_1$,
- $(\mathcal{I}, B) \models \neg \phi_1$ iff $(\mathcal{I}, B) \not\models \phi_1$,
- $(\mathcal{I}, B) \models not \, \phi_1$ iff $(\mathcal{I}, B) \not\models \phi_1$,
- $(\mathcal{I}, B) \models \forall_a x(\phi_1)$ iff for every B'_a, which is an abstract x-variant of B, $(\mathcal{I}, B'_a) \models \phi_1$,
- $(\mathcal{I}, B) \models \exists_a x(\phi_1)$ iff for some B'_a, which is an abstract x-variant of B, $(\mathcal{I}, B'_a) \models \phi_1$,
- $(\mathcal{I}, B) \models \forall_c x(\phi_1)$ iff for every B'_c, which is a concrete x-variant of B, $(\mathcal{I}, B'_c) \models \phi_1$,
- $(\mathcal{I}, B) \models \exists_c x \, (\phi_1)$ iff for some B'_c, which is a concrete x-variant of B, $(\mathcal{I}, B'_c) \models \phi_1$.

If a variable x is quantified using a concrete quantifier ($\forall_c, \exists_c$), we call x a *concrete variable*; otherwise, we call x an *abstract variable*.

An interpretation $\mathcal{I}$ satisfies a formula ϕ, written $\mathcal{I} \models \phi$ if $(\mathcal{I}, B) \models \phi$ for every variable assignment B.

Notice that we did not say anything about the concrete domain or the interpretation of the concrete domain functions and predicates. We now proceed to define the notion of concrete domain schemes and the notion of models relative to concrete domain schemes.

Concrete Domain Schemes

A concrete domain scheme consists of a concrete domain, which is a set of values (e.g., integers and strings), a set of concrete predicate symbols (e.g., numeric comparison such as greater-than), a set of data values identifiers (e.g., strings and integers), a set of datatype identifiers, a set of concrete function symbols, and an interpretation function that maps concrete function symbols to functions and concrete predicate symbols to relations.

We note that, generally, WSML uses concrete predicate symbols for built-in functions. For example, numeric addition $x + y = z$ correspond to an atomic formula with a concrete predicate symbol wsml#numericAdd(z, x, y). Concrete function symbols are used as constructors of data values (they are *datatype wrappers*).

Formally, a *concrete domain scheme* $\mathfrak{S}$ is a tuple $\mathfrak{S} = \langle U^{\mathfrak{S}}, \mathcal{F}^{\mathfrak{S}}, \mathcal{D}^{\mathfrak{S}}, \mathcal{P}^{\mathfrak{S}}, \cdot^{\mathfrak{S}} \rangle$, where

- $U^{\mathfrak{S}}$ is a non-empty set of concrete values,
- $\mathcal{F}^{\mathfrak{S}}$ and $\mathcal{P}^{\mathfrak{S}}$ are disjoint sets of concrete function and predicate symbols, which are IRIs, each with an associated nonnegative arity n,
- $\mathcal{D}^{\mathfrak{S}} \subseteq \mathcal{F}^{\mathfrak{S}}$ is a set of datatype IRIs, and
- $\cdot^{\mathfrak{S}}$ is an interpretation function which assigns a function $f^{\mathfrak{S}} : (U^{\mathfrak{S}})^n \to U^{\mathfrak{S}}$ to every $f \in \mathcal{F}^{\mathfrak{S}}$, and a relation $p^{\mathfrak{S}} \subseteq (U^{\mathfrak{S}})^n$ to every $p \in \mathcal{P}^{\mathfrak{S}}$.

As an abuse of notation, for every datatype IRI $d \in \mathcal{D}^{\mathfrak{S}}$, with $d^{\mathfrak{S}}$ we denote both the function assigned to d by $\cdot^{\mathfrak{S}}$ and the range of this function. In the latter case, we also speak about $d^{\mathfrak{S}}$ as the *domain* of the datatype identified by d. In other words, we use the same identifier d to denote both the datatype and the datatype wrapper.

Intuitively, a datatype function $d^{\mathfrak{S}}$ defines a datatype as a set of values that are *constructed* from other values. For example, a date 2008-02-13 is constructed from the integers 2008, 2, and 13 using the function xsd#date: xsd#date(2008, 2, 13). In addition, xsd#date denote the range of the constructor function xsd#date, which is the set of all dates, i.e., the value space of the datatype xsd#date.

We illustrate the concept of concrete domain schemes through the definition of a scheme for integers and strings.

Example 5.1. We define $\mathfrak{S} = \langle U^{\mathfrak{S}}, \mathcal{F}^{\mathfrak{S}}, \mathcal{D}^{\mathfrak{S}}, \mathcal{P}^{\mathfrak{S}}, \cdot^{\mathfrak{S}} \rangle$ as follows: $U^{\mathfrak{S}}$ is the union of the sets of integer numbers and finite-length sequences of Unicode characters. $\mathcal{F}^{\mathfrak{S}}$ is the union of the set of finite-length sequences of decimal digits, optionally with a leading minus (-), and the set of finite-length sequences of Unicode characters, delimited with " (for simplicity, we assume that the character '"' does not occur in such strings), all with arity 0. $\mathcal{P}^{\mathfrak{S}}$ consists of unary predicate symbols xsd#integer and xsd#string, and the binary predicate symbol wsml#numeric-equals. The interpretation function $\cdot^{\mathfrak{S}}$ interprets (signed) sequences of decimal digits and "-delimited sequences of characters as integers and strings, respectively, in the natural way; $\cdot^{\mathfrak{S}}$ interprets the unary predicate symbols xsd#integer and xsd#string as the sets of integers and strings, respectively; finally, $\cdot^{\mathfrak{S}}$ interprets wsml#numeric-equals as identity over the set of integers.

WSML Compliance

It is not allowed to use just any kind of concrete domain scheme with WSML. The scheme must at least include the datatypes and built-in predicates required by WSML. Additionally, if any XML schema datatype is used, the scheme must conform to the definition of the datatype in the XML schema datatypes specification [20].

Formally, a concrete domain scheme $\mathfrak{S} = \langle U^{\mathfrak{S}}, \mathcal{F}^{\mathfrak{S}}, \mathcal{D}^{\mathfrak{S}}, \mathcal{P}^{\mathfrak{S}}, \cdot^{\mathfrak{S}} \rangle$ is *WSML-compliant* if the following conditions are met. We first define the condition which make sure all XML schema datatypes in $\mathfrak{S}$ conform with the specification. The IRI of an XML schema datatype is obtained by concatenating XML schema namespace and the name of the datatype. For example, the IRI of the datatype *string* is http://www.w3.org/2001/XMLSchema#string.

- if $d \in \mathcal{D}^{\mathfrak{S}}$ is the IRI of an XML schema datatype dt, then the range of $d^{\mathfrak{S}}$ corresponds to the value space of dt and the domain of $d^{\mathfrak{S}}$ corresponds to the definition in [68, Table B.1], if it exists; otherwise it is the set of strings comprising the lexical space of dt, and the mapping $d^{\mathfrak{S}}$ corresponds to the lexical-to-value mapping for dt defined in [20].

The following conditions ensure that the required data types, namely the XML schema datatypes *string*, *integer*, and *decimal* and the RDF datatype *XMLLiteral*, are included in the scheme.

- the IRIs xsd#string, xsd#integer, and xsd#decimal are included in $\mathcal{D}^{\mathfrak{S}}$, and for any string, integer, or decimal v in $\mathcal{F}^{\mathfrak{S}}$, $v^{\mathfrak{S}}$ is the value obtained by applying the corresponding lexical to value mapping, as defined in [20], to v,
- the IRI rdf#XMLLiteral is included in $\mathcal{D}^{\mathfrak{S}}$, every string x representing valid XML content [90, Section 1] is included in $\mathcal{F}^{\mathfrak{S}}$ with arity 0, and for any string x representing valid XML content, rdf#XMLLiteral$^{\mathfrak{S}}(x)$ is the XML value of x according to [90, Section 5.1], and
- the built-ins defined for WSML in Appendix C.2 of [68] are included in $\mathcal{P}^{\mathfrak{S}}$ and are interpreted to the definition in Appendix C.2 of [68].

In the remainder, we require that every domain scheme under consideration is WSML-compliant.

Conformance of Interpretations

The intention of concrete values and concrete predicate and function symbols is that they are interpreted in the same way in all interpretations under consideration. The way this is achieved in WSML is by associating a single concrete domain scheme with all considered interpretations. A concrete domain scheme is associated with an interpretation if the interpretation *conforms* with the scheme, is defined below.

An interpretation $\mathcal{I} = \langle U, \prec_U, \in_U, U^D, \mathcal{I}_F, \mathcal{I}_P, \mathcal{I}_{\mathsf{hv}}, \mathcal{I}_{\mathsf{it}}, \mathcal{I}_{\mathsf{ot}} \rangle$ *conforms to* a concrete domain scheme $\mathfrak{S}$ if the following conditions are satisfied.

- $U^D = U^{\mathfrak{S}}$,
- $\mathcal{I}_F(f) = f^{\mathfrak{S}}$ for every concrete n-ary function symbol $f \in \mathcal{F}^{\mathfrak{S}}$, and
- $\mathcal{I}_P(p) = p^{\mathfrak{S}}$ for every concrete n-ary predicate symbol $p \in \mathcal{P}^{\mathfrak{S}}$.

We note here that a datatype identifier is also a concept identifier, and the set of instances of this concept is the set of values of the datatype. This is guaranteed by the following condition.

- for every datatype identifier $d \in \mathcal{D}^{\mathfrak{S}}$ holds that $u \in d^{\mathfrak{S}}$ iff $u \in_U \mathcal{I}_F(d)$, for every $u \in U^D$.

Models

Using the above notion of conformance we can now define the notion of a model relative to a concrete domain scheme.

Given a concrete domain scheme $\mathfrak{S}$, an interpretation $\mathcal{I}$ is a $\mathfrak{S}$-*model* of a formula ϕ if $\mathcal{I}$ conforms to $\mathfrak{S}$ and $\mathcal{I} \models \phi$. A formula ϕ is $\mathfrak{S}$-*satisfiable* if it has a $\mathfrak{S}$-model; ϕ is $\mathfrak{S}$-*valid* if every interpretation that conforms to $\mathfrak{S}$ is a $\mathfrak{S}$-model of ϕ.

Likewise, an interpretation $\mathcal{I}$ is a $\mathfrak{S}$-model of a theory $\varPhi$ if $\mathcal{I}$ is a $\mathfrak{S}$-model of every formula $\phi \in \varPhi$ and $\varPhi$ is $\mathfrak{S}$-satisfiable if it has a $\mathfrak{S}$-model.

We have defined the basic notion of models in WSML. The subsequent sections extend this notion in two different ways, for the DL and Core, Flight, and Rules variants, respectively. These extended notions will be used to define the semantic notions for the respective variants.

5.2.2 WSML-DL Extensions

WSML-DL makes a syntactic separation between concepts, attributes, and instance identifiers, and the places they may occur (e.g., a concept identifier may only occur in a concept positions). Additionally, the places where abstract and concrete terms and variables may occur are distinct. In order to enable DL-based reasoning it is necessary to reflect these distinctions in the semantics as well. Specifically, WSML-DL imposes additional conditions on interpretations.

We first need to define the notions of concept, attribute, and instance position. We say that a term occurs in a *concept position* if occurs as the third term in a it or ot molecule, as the second term in a :-molecule, or the term occurs in a ::-molecule; it occurs in an *attribute position* if it occurs as the second term in a hv, it or ot molecule; otherwise, the term occurs in an *instance position*. That is, in the molecules and atoms $a : c$, $c :: c$, $a[p \, \text{hv} \, a]$, $a[p \, \text{it} \, c]$, $a[p \, \text{ot} \, c]$, $q(a, \dots, a)$, and $a = a$ the term c occurs in concept, p occurs in relation, and a occurs in instance positions.

WSML-DL Semantic conditions

Observe that the syntax of WSML-DL makes a distinction between identifiers used in concept, attribute and instance positions. In fact, the sets of instances, concept, attribute, and annotation property identifiers are mutually disjoint. WSML interpretations, defined in the previous subsection, do not distinguish between the interpretations of these different identifiers; they are all interpreted in the same domain. This separation is reflected in the conditions on WSML-DL interpretations, as well as conditions on WSML-DL variable assignments.

An interpretation $\mathcal{I} = \langle U, \prec_U, \in_U, U^D, \mathcal{I}_F, \mathcal{I}_P, \mathcal{I}_{hv}, \mathcal{I}_{it}, \mathcal{I}_{ot} \rangle$ is a *WSML-DL interpretation* if the following conditions hold. Firstly, we require a separation between the interpretations of instance, concepts, and attributes identifiers.

- U is partitioned into three sub-domains U^i, U^a, and U^c, such that U^i is not empty,
- $\mathcal{I}_F$ maps instance identifiers to elements in U^i,
- $\mathcal{I}_F$ maps concept identifiers to elements in U^c, and
- $\mathcal{I}_F$ maps attribute and annotation property identifiers to elements in U^a.

Then, we need to ensure that the elements of the interpretation that are used for the interpretation of subclass, class instance, and attribute statements are defined only on the appropriate sub-domains.

- the partial order $\prec_U$ is only defined on elements in U^c,
- $\in_U$ is a relation between U^i and U^c, and
- $\mathcal{I}_{hv}(u) = \mathcal{I}_{it}(u) = \mathcal{I}_{ot}(u) = \emptyset$ for any $u \in U^c \cup U^i$.

Finally, WSML-DL requires an *extensional* interpretation of the subclass and implies-type constructs, i.e., the converse of the conditions (5.1) and (5.2) must hold:

for any two elements $a, b \in U^c$ holds that
$$\text{whenever } a_{cext} \subseteq b_{cext}, \ a \preceq_U b \quad (5.4)$$

for any three elements $c, p, d \in U$ it is the case that
whenever for every $a, b \in U$ such that $a \in_U c$ and $\langle a, b \rangle \in \mathcal{I}_{hv}(p)$
$$\text{it holds that } b \in_U d, \ \langle c, d \rangle \in \mathcal{I}_{it}(p) \quad (5.5)$$

WSML-DL Satisfaction

The conditions on WSML-DL interpretations are not yet enough to define satisfaction for WSML-DL. Namely, it is necessary to ensure that variables are only mapped to the subdomain U^i and the concrete domain U^D, and abstract variables must only be mapped to U^i.

Formally, given a variable assignment B, a variable assignment B' is an abstract DL-x-variant of B if B' is an abstract x-variant of B and $x^{B'} \in U^i$.

DL satisfaction, denoted by the symbol $\models_{DL}$, is obtained from satisfaction as described in the previous section by modifying the definition of satisfaction of abstractly quantified formulas in the following way:

- $(\mathcal{I}, B) \models_{DL} \forall_a x(\phi_1)$ iff for every variable assignment B'_a, which is an abstract DL-x-variant of B whose range is U^i, $(\mathcal{I}, B'_a) \models_{DL} \phi_1$ and
- $(\mathcal{I}, B) \models_{DL} \exists_a x(\phi_1)$ iff for some variable assignment B'_a, which is an abstract DL-x-variant of B whose range is U^i, $(\mathcal{I}, B'_a) \models \phi_1$.

As can be seen from the definition, the difference with the definition of satisfaction given earlier is the following: abstractly quantified variables are only assigned to the individual domain U^i, and not to the concrete domain U^D, the concept domain U^c, or the attribute domain U^a. The notions of a model, satisfiability, and validity in WSML-DL are defined analogously to the corresponding notions in WSML.

Given a concrete domain scheme $\mathfrak{S}$, an interpretation $\mathcal{I}$ is a *WSML-DL* $\mathfrak{S}$-*model* of a WSML-DL formula ϕ if $\mathcal{I}$ is a WSML-DL interpretation, $\mathcal{I}$ conforms to $\mathfrak{S}$, and $\mathcal{I} \models_{DL} \phi$. A formula ϕ is WSML-DL $\mathfrak{S}$-*satisfiable* if it has a WSML-DL $\mathfrak{S}$-model; ϕ is WSML-DL $\mathfrak{S}$-*valid* if every WSML-DL interpretation which conforms to $\mathfrak{S}$ is a model of ϕ.

Likewise, an interpretation $\mathcal{I}$ is a $\mathfrak{S}$-model of a theory Φ if $\mathcal{I}$ is a $\mathfrak{S}$-model of every formula $\phi \in \Phi$ and Φ is $\mathfrak{S}$-satisfiable if it has a $\mathfrak{S}$-model.

Semantics of WSML-DL Ontologies

We are now ready to define the semantics of WSML-DL ontologies. The main notions we are interested in are (1) satisfiability of a concept relative to an ontology, (2) satisfiability of an ontology, and (3) entailment between ontologies.

The definitions of these notions follow straightforwardly from the above definitions with the complication that we need to take imported ontologies into account. We first define the notion of a model of a WSML-DL ontology. Given a concrete domain scheme $\mathfrak{S}$, an interpretation $\mathcal{I}$ is a *WSML-DL* $\mathfrak{S}$-*model* of a WSML-DL ontology O if

1. $\mathcal{I}$ is a WSML-DL $\mathfrak{S}$-model of a theory Φ which corresponds to O and
2. $\mathcal{I}$ is a WSML-DL $\mathfrak{S}$-model of every ontology imported by O.

Notice that we require every model of an ontology to be also a model of every imported ontology. Consequently, the interpretation must also be a model of every ontology imported by any imported ontology, etc. So, if an ontology O_1 imports an ontology O_2 and O_2 imports an ontology O_3, then every model of O_1 must be a model of O_2, by condition 2 above. But, every model of O_2 must also be a model of O_3, again by condition 2 above. Consequently, every model of O_1 must be a model of O_3.

We now proceed with definitions of the WSML-DL semantic notions, which are in line with the semantic notions typically used in Description Logic reasoning [11].

Concept Satisfiability Given a concrete domain scheme $\mathfrak{S}$, let c be a concept identifier. We say that c is *WSML-DL $\mathfrak{S}$-satisfiable* with respect to a WSML-DL ontology O if there is a WSML-DL $\mathfrak{S}$-model $\mathcal{I}$ of O such that $\mathcal{I}_F(c)_{cext} \neq \emptyset$, i.e., the concept extension of c is not empty.

Ontology Satisfiability Given a concrete domain scheme $\mathfrak{S}$, a WSML-DL ontology O is *WSML-DL $\mathfrak{S}$-satisfiable* if O has a WSML-DL $\mathfrak{S}$-model.

Formula Entailment Given a concrete domain scheme $\mathfrak{S}$, a WSML-DL ontology O *WSML-DL $\mathfrak{S}$-entails* a formula ϕ if every WSML-DL $\mathfrak{S}$-model of O is a WSML-DL $\mathfrak{S}$-model of ϕ.

Ontology Entailment Given a concrete domain scheme $\mathfrak{S}$, a WSML-DL ontology O_1 *WSML-DL $\mathfrak{S}$-entails* a WSML-DL ontology O_2 if every WSML-DL $\mathfrak{S}$-model of O_1 is a WSML-DL $\mathfrak{S}$-model of O_2.

See Chapter 8 for a description of how Description Logic reasoning techniques can be used for processing WSML-DL descriptions.

5.2.3 Stable Models for Core, Flight, and Rule

WSML-Flight and Rule allow the use of *default negation* (*not* in the abstract syntax; **naf** in the surface syntax) in rule bodies: by default a literal *not a* is assumed to be true. Furthermore, the **ofType** attribute typing construct requires that the types of attribute values are *known*; by default it is assumed that the type of an attribute value does not conform with the constraint.

Since in both cases there is a notion of defaults that may be overwritten, the language is *nonmonotonic*, i.e., adding rules or facts to the ontology may invalidate entailments. Notice that classical negation ($\neg$; **neg**) may not be used in WSML-Core, Flight, and Rule.

We illustrate this nonmonotonicity with an example.

Example 5.2. Consider the following small ontology:

$$GoldCustomer :: Customer$$
$$x : GoldCustomer \supset x[hasDiscount\,\mathsf{hv}\,15]$$
$$x : Customer \wedge not\ x : GoldCustomer \supset x[hasDiscount\,\mathsf{hv}\,5]$$
$$john : Customer$$

which says that every gold customer is a customer, gold customers get a discount of 15 (percent), customers that are not gold customers get a discount of 5 (percent), and John is a customer. Now, because John is a customer and it is not known that he is a gold customer, he has a discount of 5. If we add the fact *john*: *GoldCustomer* to the ontology, John will no longer get a discount of 5%, because the corresponding (third) rule does not become active, but he will get a discount of 5%, because the second rule becomes active. Notice that if we were to remove the condition *not x*: *GoldCustomer* from the third rule, then John would have two discounts: 5% and 15%.

We now add the following axioms to the ontology:

$$Customer[hasPurchased \text{ ot } Product]$$
$$john[hasPurchased \text{ hv } myBook]$$

which say that every purchase of every customer must be known to be a product, and John has purchased the book *myBook*. Since it is not known that *myBook* is a product, the ontology is inconsistent. If we add the fact *myBook*: *Product* to the ontology, it will no longer be inconsistent.

The model theory described in Section 5.2.1 is not adequate to capture such nonmonotonic behavior, because adding formulas to an ontology will only decrease the number of models, and hence increase the number of entailments. Therefore, we need to go beyond this model theory to define an adequate semantics for default negation.

A solution to this problem is to consider only one or a few *preferred* models. The question is then: which models should we select as the preferred models, so that negation indeed behaves as default negation?

There is a nonmonotonic logic, called *default logic* [120], that defines a notion of defaults in a logical setting. This logic is, however, too broad for our purposes, and does not define a notion of preferred models, but rather a notion of extensions, which are sets of formulas. In contrast, the Stable Model Semantics for normal logic programs with negation [62] defines a notion of preferred (*stable*) model that essentially corresponds to the notion of extension in default logic [99]. So, since the Stable Model Semantics defines a notion of preferred model that exactly captures the notion of default negation, we have chosen to use it as the underlying semantics for WSML-Flight and Rule. We also use it as the underlying semantics for WSML-Core, but since WSML-Core does not allow the use of negation, the semantics corresponds to the usual minimal Herbrand model semantics for logic programs [96].

In addition, since all WSML-Flight rules must be *locally stratified*, the semantics corresponds with the perfect model semantics [118] and the Well-Founded Semantics [61] for WSML-Flight ontologies. Finally, it is the case that every consequence under the Well-Founded Semantics is a consequence under the Stable Model Semantics [61]; we explicitly allow implementations to use the Well-Founded Semantics as an approximation to the Stable Model Semantics of WSML-Rule for the task of query answering.

We first define the notion of a Herbrand model, in which each ground term is interpreted as itself, and the notion of a *minimal* Herbrand model. We then define the notion of a stable model, which is based on the *reduct* (i.e., removal of negation) of the grounding of a set of WSML rules. Based on the notion of stable models we define satisfiability and entailment for WSML-Core, Flight, and Rule ontologies.

Herbrand Models

We first define a specific kind of WSML interpretations and models, namely Herbrand interpretations and models. In these interpretations, the domain of interpretation consists of all ground terms and every ground term is interpreted as itself.

We define Herbrand interpretations relative to a concrete domain scheme $\mathfrak{S} = \langle U^{\mathfrak{S}}, \mathcal{F}^{\mathfrak{S}}, \mathcal{D}^{\mathfrak{S}}, \mathcal{P}^{\mathfrak{S}}, \cdot^{\mathfrak{S}} \rangle$. With $\mathcal{D}$ we denote the set of all data values in $\mathfrak{S}$: $\mathcal{D} = \bigcup \{ d^{\mathfrak{S}} \mid d \in D^{\mathfrak{S}} \}$.

When defining the Herbrand universe we consider symbols from the language for defining abstract terms, but concrete data values are represented by themselves. This is necessary because a concrete data value may have several syntactical representations (e.g., 1.0=1).

The *Herbrand $\mathfrak{S}$-universe* of a theory Φ is the union of the set of all ground terms that can be formed from the constant and function symbols in Φ that are not data values and the set of all values $t^{\mathfrak{S}}$ in $\mathcal{D}$ whose lexical representation t occurs in Φ.

A Herbrand $\mathfrak{S}$-interpretation $\mathcal{I} = \langle U, \prec_U, \in_U, U^D, \mathcal{I}_F, \mathcal{I}_P, \mathcal{I}_{\mathsf{hv}}, \mathcal{I}_{\mathsf{it}}, \mathcal{I}_{\mathsf{ot}} \rangle$ is a $\mathfrak{S}$-interpretation such that

- U is the Herbrand $\mathfrak{S}$-universe of Φ and
- for every ground term t that is not a data value, $t^{\mathcal{I}} = t'$, where t' is obtained from t by replacing every data value d in t with $d^{\mathfrak{S}}$.

We can view a Herbrand $\mathfrak{S}$-interpretation $\mathcal{I}$ as a set of ground atomic formulas, namely that set of ground atomic formulas that is satisfied by $\mathcal{I}$: $\{ \alpha \mid \mathcal{I} \models \alpha \}$. In the following, we will use the symbol $\mathcal{I}$ to denote both the interpretation and the corresponding set of ground atomic formulas.

We can now define the notion of a *minimal Herbrand $\mathfrak{S}$-model*. Given a concrete domain scheme $\mathfrak{S}$, a Herbrand $\mathfrak{S}$-interpretation $\mathcal{I}$ is a *minimal Herbrand $\mathfrak{S}$-model* of a theory Φ if $\mathcal{I} \models \Phi$ and for every Herbrand $\mathfrak{S}$-interpretation $\mathcal{I}'$ holds that if $\mathcal{I}' \models \Phi$, then $\mathcal{I} \subseteq \mathcal{I}'$.

Stable Models

It turns out that a WSML-Core or Flight theory has at most one Herbrand model, which can be computed using a fixpoint operator in the usual way [96]. However, there is no known computational procedure for finding minimal Herbrand models in case there are multiple models due to the presence of negation in rules. The Stable Model Semantics provides a procedure for finding minimal models, but not every minimal model is a stable model. However, as we have mentioned before, stable models correspond to extensions in default logic, and therefore adequately capture our desired notion of default negation.

The computation of a stable model roughly works as follows:

1. Guess a $\mathfrak{S}$-model $\mathcal{I}$ of Φ,
2. create the *reduct* of the grounding of Φ, which "evaluates" the negation in Φ according to $\mathcal{I}$, and
3. if $\mathcal{I}$ is the minimal Herbrand $\mathfrak{S}$-model of Φ, then it is a stable model.

The *grounding* of a set of WSML formulas Φ, denoted $gr(\Phi)$, is the union of all possible ground instantiations of Φ, obtained by

- replacing each abstract (resp., concrete) variable in a formula $\phi \in \Phi$ with a ground (resp., ground concrete) term in the Herbrand $\mathfrak{S}$-universe and
- replacing each data value d in ϕ with the corresponding concrete data value $d^{\mathfrak{S}}$,

for each formula $\phi \in \Phi$.

Following [63], the *reduct* of Φ with respect to a $\mathfrak{S}$-interpretation $\mathcal{I}$, denoted $\Phi^{\mathcal{I}}$, is obtained from $gr(\Phi)$ by

- deleting each formula r with a *not* c in the antecedent such that $c \in \mathcal{I}$ and
- deleting *not* c from the antecedent of every remaining formula r.

We are now ready to define the notion of stable $\mathfrak{S}$-model.

Given a concrete domain scheme $\mathfrak{S}$, a Herbrand $\mathfrak{S}$-interpretation $\mathcal{I}$ is a *stable $\mathfrak{S}$-model* of a WSML-Core, Flight, or Rule theory Φ if $\mathcal{I}$ is a minimal Herbrand $\mathfrak{S}$-model of $\Phi^{\mathcal{I}}$.

Example 5.3. Consider the following ground WSML-Rule theory:

$$not \; p(1.0) \;\supset\; p(2.0)$$
$$not \; p(2) \;\supset\; p(1)$$
$$p(1.00) \;\supset\; p(3.0)$$
$$p(2.00) \;\supset\; p(3)$$

Given any WSML-compliant domain scheme $\mathfrak{S}$, the theory has two stable $\mathfrak{S}$-models:

$$\mathcal{I}_1 = \{p(1), p(3)\}$$
$$\mathcal{I}_2 = \{p(2), p(3)\}$$

Observe that the decimals and integer $1.0, 1.00, 1$ are all syntactical representations of the integer value 1. Likewise for $2.0, 2.00, 2$ and $3.0, 3$. The stable models only contain the values corresponding to be syntactical representations.

We leave it as an exercise to the reader to verify that $\mathcal{I}_1$ and $\mathcal{I}_2$ are indeed the stable models of the theory.

Semantics of WSML-Core, Flight, and Rule Ontologies

We are now ready to define the semantics of WSML-Core, Flight, and Rule ontologies. We are interested in (1) satisfiability of an ontology and (2) entailment of ground formulas.

To deal with imported ontologies we generally followed the same scheme as with WSML-DL.

Note that we have not addressed the semantics of ot-molecules (**ofType**) so far. We address the semantics of such molecules in the definition of stable models of ontologies. Specifically, stable models may not satisfy the following formula:

$$\exists c, p, d, a, b(c[p \, \mathsf{ot} \, d] \wedge a : c \wedge a[p \, \mathsf{hv} \, b] \wedge not \; b : d) \tag{5.6}$$

which is true in a model if there is a concept c with an attribute p, which is **ofType** d, there is an instance a of c that has a value b for the attribute p and it is not known that b is an instance of d. In other words, if (5.6) is satisfied, some **ofType** constraint is violated.

Every WSML ontology O that imports a set of ontologies $\{O_1, \ldots, O_n\}$ has an *imports-closed* corresponding theory $\Phi^\cup$, which is defined as follows: $\Phi^\cup = \Phi \cup \Phi_1 \cup \cdots \cup \Phi_n$, where Φ is the theory that corresponds to O and $\Phi_1, \ldots, \Phi_n$ are the imports-closed theories of the ontologies $O_1, \ldots, O_n$, respectively.

Given a concrete domain scheme $\mathfrak{S}$, an interpretation $\mathcal{I}$ is a *stable $\mathfrak{S}$-model* of a WSML-Core, Flight, or Rule ontology O if

1. $\mathcal{I}$ is a stable $\mathfrak{S}$-model of the imports-closed theory Φ corresponding to O and
2. $\mathcal{I}$ does not satisfy (5.6).

Satisfiability   Given a concrete domain scheme $\mathfrak{S}$, a WSML-Core, Flight, or Rule ontology O is *$\mathfrak{S}$-satisfiable* if O has a stable $\mathfrak{S}$-model.

Entailment   Given a concrete domain scheme $\mathfrak{S}$, a satisfiable WSML-Core, Flight, or Rule ontology O *$\mathfrak{S}$-entails* a ground atomic formula α if for every stable $\mathfrak{S}$-model $\mathcal{I}$ of O holds that $\mathcal{I} \models \alpha$.

Example 5.4. Consider the theory in Example 5.3. Since the theory as a stable model, it is satisfiable. Additionally, the theory entails $p(3)$, $p(3.0)$, $p(3.00)$, $p(3.000)$, etc.; recall that $3, 3.0, 3.00, 3.000, \ldots$ are all syntactical representations of the integer 3. The theory does not entail $p(1)$ or $p(2)$, since these are both not satisfied in every stable model of the theory.

See Chapter 8 for a description of how reasoning techniques for logic programs can be used for processing WSML-Core, Flight, and Rule descriptions.

5.3 Layering of WSML Variants

Recall Figure 4.3 on page 36, which depicts WSML language layering. When introducing language layering in Section 4.3 we did not explain exactly what

the arrows in the figure mean. We have also seen in the definitions of the
semantics of WSML ontologies above that the semantics of variants differs.
Most notably, Figure 4.3 suggests that WSML-DL should be layered on top
of Core. However, the definition of the notions of models and entailment of
the respective variants is different. Since we did not discuss the semantics of
WSML-Full, we are not concerned with the layering between the DL and Full,
respectively the Rule and Full variants.

Since the semantics of the Core, Flight, and Rule variants is the same, and
since Flight syntactically extends Core and Rule syntactically extends Flight,
layering between these variants is trivial. Therefore, we primarily focus our
discussion on the layering between WSML-Core and DL.

The differences between the semantics of WSML-Core and DL can be sum-
marized as follows:

1. WSML-DL interpretations partition the domain, thereby distinguishing
   between concepts, attributes, and instances,
2. WSML-DL interpretations impose additional conditions on subclass ($::$)
   and implies-type (it) constructs, thereby strengthening their interpretation (see below for an example),
3. the semantics of WSML-Core is defined with respect to a single minimal
   model, whereas WSML-DL theories may have multiple models, and
4. entailment in WSML-Core is only defined for ground atomic formulas
   and molecules, whereas entailment in WSML-DL is defined for arbitrary
   formulas and ontologies.

It turns out that the first difference (partitioning of the domain in WSML-DL
interpretations) does not have practical implications due to the fact that the
equality symbol is not used in WSML-Core (this is discussed in more detail
below). The fourth difference indicates that it is only meaningful to discuss
layering in the context of entailment of ground atomic formulas and molecules;
it turns out that in that context, the third difference (single versus multiple
models) does not have practical implications (this is also discussed in more
detail below). The second difference – different interpretation of the subclass
and implies-type constructs – does have practical implications, as illustrated
in the following example.

Example 5.5. Consider the WSML-Core theory Φ:

$$Person[hasChild \text{ it } Person]$$
$$Astronaut :: Person$$
$$\forall_a x (x : Person \supset x : Animal)$$

which says that, for every instance of the class *Person*, each value of the
attribute *hasChild* is an instance of *Person*, *Astronaut* is a subclass of *Person*,
and every instance of *Person* is also an instance of *Animal*. Now consider
the formulas $\phi_1 = Astronaut[hasChild \text{ it } Person]$ and $\phi_2 = Person :: Animal$;

ϕ_1 and ϕ_2 are both WSML-DL entailments of Φ, but neither is a WSML-Core entailment of Φ, due to the conditions (5.4) and (5.5) on WSML-DL interpretations, respectively.

It is the case, as we will see later, that the set of WSML-Core entailments of a given Core theory Φ is a subset of the set of WSML-DL entailments of the same theory Φ. However, in certain situations it would be more desirable if the entailments under both semantics would be the same, e.g., when using a WSML-DL reasoner for processing WSML-Core theories. It turns out, also discussed below, that for a subset of the WSML-Core theories the sets of (ground) WSML-Core and WSML-DL entailments are the same.

5.3.1 Definition of Language layering

The above considerations lead us to defining two approaches to language layering in WSML. When considering *loose* layering, a variant L_2 is layered on a variant L_1 if, considering an arbitrary theory of L_1, every L_1-formula that is a consequence under L_1 semantics, is also a consequence under L_2 semantics. When considering *strict* layering, additionally every L_1-formula that is a consequence under L_2 semantics must be a consequence under L_1 semantics. Note that loose layering implies strict layering.

Considering these notions of language layering in the context of OWL, we observe that OWL Lite and OWL DL are strictly layered, and that OWL Full is not strictly, but only loosely layered on OWL DL; furthermore, OWL Full is loosely layered on RDFS (see [77]).

It turns out that if we want to guarantee strict language layering in WSML, we must pose certain restrictions on the entailments that are considered; namely, subclass and implies-type statements may not be considered. Additionally, we need to pose restrictions on the antecedents of WSML-Flight and Rule formulas; namely, subclass and implies-type statements may not appear in the antecedents, because they could be used to "simulate" entailment of such statements.

With WSML-Flight$^-$ (resp., Rule$^-$) we mean the WSML variant obtained from WSML-Flight (resp., Rule) by disallowing ::- and it-molecules in the antecedents of formulas (rule bodies). WSML-Core$^-$ is the same as WSML-Core.

Admissible entailments are subsets of all formulas of a given WSML variant. The admissible entailments of the WSML variants are defined as follows:

- Core$^-$/Flight$^-$/Rule$^-$: every it- and ::-free WSML-(Core/Flight/Rule) ground atomic formula is an admissible entailment;
- Core/Flight/Rule: every WSML-(Core/Flight/Rule) ground atomic formula is an admissible entailment;
- DL: every WSML-DL sentence is an admissible entailment.

Using this notion of admissible entailment, we can now formally define language layering.

Definition 5.6. *Let L_1, L_2 be two WSML variants. Then, L_2 is loosely layered on top of L_1, denoted $L_1 \Rightarrow_l L_2$, if for every L_1 theory Φ and admissible entailment of L_1, α is an L_2 entailment of Φ whenever α is an L_1 entailment of Φ.*

If, in addition, α is an L_1 entailment of Φ whenever α is an L_2 entailment of Φ, L_2 is strictly layered on top of L_1, denoted $L_1 \Rightarrow_s L_2$.

5.3.2 WSML Language Layering

With the necessary definitions of language layering in place, we are now nearly ready to state the properties of language layering in WSML. However, we first need the following result for overcoming the differences related to the partitioning of the domain in WSML-DL interpretations and the difference in the definition of the semantics of models of WSML-Core and DL (minimal versus multiple models).

Lemma 5.7. *Given a concrete domain scheme $\mathfrak{S}$. Let Φ be a WSML-Core theory and let α be a ground atomic formula.*

- *Φ has a single minimal Herbrand $\mathfrak{S}$-model iff Φ has a $\mathfrak{S}$-model and*
- *α is satisfied in every minimal Herbrand $\mathfrak{S}$-model of Φ iff α is satisfied in every $\mathfrak{S}$-model of Φ.*

Proof (Sketch). Φ can straightforwardly be transformed to an equi-satisfiable first-order theory Φ' by (1) replacing every data value d with its interpretation $d^{\mathfrak{S}}$, (2) replacing molecules with binary and ternary predicates (e.g., replace $a::b$ with $\_subclass(a,b)$), and (3) add axioms that captures the semantic conditions of the subclass and implies-type molecules; these axioms axiomatize the conditions (5.1) and (5.2). Φ' is obviously a Horn logic theory. The lemma follows immediately from the classical results by Herbrand (e.g., [59]). $\square$

Theorem 5.8 (WSML Language Layering).

1. *WSML-Core $\Rightarrow_l$ WSML-Flight $\Rightarrow_l$ WSML-Rule.*
2. *WSML-Core $\Rightarrow_l$ WSML-DL.*
3. *WSML-Core$^-$ $\Rightarrow_s$ WSML-Flight$^-$ $\Rightarrow_s$ WSML-Rule$^-$.*
4. *WSML-Core$^-$ $\Rightarrow_s$ WSML-DL.*

Proof. 1. and *3.* follow immediately from the definition of the semantics of WSML-Core, WSML-Flight, and WSML-Rule.

Recall the four differences between WSML-Core and WSML-DL from the introduction to the section. Discrepancy 4. (ground versus arbitrary entailment) is overcome by the definition of admissible entailments: we only consider ground formulas. Discrepancies 1. (partitioning of the domain) and 3. (single versus multiple models) are overcome by Lemma 5.7: we need to consider only a single minimal model for checking satisfiability and ground entailment, even if a theory as multiple models and the domain of the minimal model is partitioned.

The minimal Herbrand model $\mathcal{I}$ of a WSML-Core theory Φ can be straightforwardly transformed into an interpretation $\mathcal{I}'$ that satisfies the conditions (5.4) and (5.5). Since $\mathcal{I}'$ is a Herbrand model and since there is a distinction in the WSML-Core syntax between instance, concept, and attribute identifiers, it is easy to find a partitioning of the domain into instance, attribute, and concept domains. Additionally, by the fact that $\mathcal{I}$ is a minimal model and by the syntactical restrictions on WSML-Core theories, $\prec_U$ is only defined on U^c, $\in_U$ is a relation between U^i and U^c, and $\mathcal{I}_{\mathsf{hv}}(u) = \mathcal{I}_{\mathsf{it}}(u) = \mathcal{I}_{\mathsf{ot}}(u) = \emptyset$ for any $u \in U^c \cup U^i$. Therefore, $\mathcal{I}'$ is a WSML-DL interpretation.

By the syntactical restrictions on WSML-Core theories it is easy to verify that $\mathcal{I}'$ WSML-DL satisfies Φ and that $\mathcal{I}'$ is in fact a minimal WSML-DL model of Φ, establishing loose layering (2.).

Given an it- and ::-free ground atomic formula α, clearly $\mathcal{I} \models \alpha$ iff $\mathcal{I}' \models_{DL} \alpha$. This establishes strict layering between WSML-Core$^-$ and WSML-DL (4.).

□

Consider example 5.5. Observe that ϕ_1 and ϕ_2 are not admissible WSML-Core$^-$ consequences. In fact, the sets of WSML-Core and WSML-DL entailment of Φ coincide when considering only admissible WSML-Core$^-$ entailment, as was demonstrated with Theorem 5.8.

Comparing strict and loose language layering, we observe that if strict language layering is considered, the definitions of the language variants we consider, specifically WSML-(Core$^-$/Flight$^-$/Rule$^-$), are more restrictive, and there are certain (some may argue, unintuitive) restrictions on the kinds of admissible entailments. In fact, the Core$^-$, Flight$^-$, and Rule$^-$ variants are less expressive than the usual Core, Flight, and Rule variants, which we consider under loose layering, because inferences of it- and ::-statements may not be considered for strict layering.

The use of loose layering seems more attractive than strict layering. Indeed, we have chosen to use loose layering for the standard language variants. In addition, the use of loose language layering is common in Semantic Web standards; for example, RDFS is loosely layered on top of RDF, OWL Full is loosely layered on top of RDFS, and OWL Full is loosely layered on top of OWL DL. However, one could imagine scenarios in which strict language layering is more attractive. For example, when directly using a WSML-DL reasoner for reasoning with WSML-Core theories, one needs to be sure that the semantics correspond; otherwise, certain inferences might be incorrect with respect to the WSML-Core semantics. In this case, one needs to restrict oneself to WSML-Core$^-$.

	Core	DL	Flight	Rule
RDFS	no	no	yes	yes
OWL DL	DLP subset	yes	DLP subset	DLP subset

Table 5.2. Use of RDFS/OWL in WSML variants

5.4 Combination with RDFS and OWL DL

Recall that a WSML ontology may import RDFS and/or OWL DL ontologies. Furthermore, Web service descriptions may directly import RDFS and OWL DL ontologies, besides WSML ontologies. In this section we address the semantics of such combinations of WSML ontologies with RDFS and/or OWL DL. Specifically, we extend the notions of satisfiability and entailment defined in Section 5.2 to such combinations.

Recall that there are certain restrictions on the use of RDFS and OWL ontologies with specific WSML variants. See Table 5.2 for a summary of the restrictions.

Recall also that when an ontology imports an ontology with a higher variant, the ontology automatically adopts the higher variant. For example, if a WSML-Core ontology imports an RDFS ontology, the variant automatically becomes WSML-Flight and if a WSML-Core ontology imports an OWL DL ontology that is not in the DLP subset, the variant automatically becomes WSML-DL. If, however, a WSML-DL ontology imports an RDFS ontology or a WSML-Rule ontology imports an OWL DL ontology that is not in the DLP subset, the variant becomes WSML-Full.

The remainder of this section is structured as follows. We first extend the notion of $\mathfrak{S}$-model with RDFS ontologies, based on the RDFS model theory [73]. We then extend the notions of WSML-DL $\mathfrak{S}$-model and $\mathfrak{S}$-model with OWL DL ontologies (resp, the DLP subset), based on the OWL DL model theory [115, Section 3]. Finally, we define the notions of satisfiability and entailment for combinations of WSML-DL with OWL DL and combinations of WSML-Rule with RDFS and (the DLP subset of) OWL DL, respectively.

5.4.1 Combination with RDFS

The RDF semantics specification [73] defines the semantics of RDFS with data types using the notions of D-interpretation and D-entailment for RDFS with datatypes. We define the semantics of combinations of WSML and RDFS ontologies by combining WSML interpretations with D-interpretations.

To this end, we first establish a correspondence between concrete domain schemes and datatype maps, after which we define the notion of combined WSML-RDF interpretations. Note that concrete domain schemes are more general than datatype maps, because they include built-in functions and predicates.

Data Types, Datatype Maps, and Concrete Domain Schemes

The symbol D in D-interpretation and D-entailment denotes a *datatype map*, which provides the datatypes that are to be considered in a particular entailment question. So, their purpose is similar to that of concrete domain schemes.

We proceed with the formal definitions of datatypes and datatype maps, following [73, Section 5], and define the notion of compatibility between concrete domain schemes and datatype maps.

Datatypes define sets of concrete data values (e.g., strings and integers), along with their lexical representations. Formally, a *datatype d* consists of

- a *lexical space* L^d, which is a set of Unicode character strings (e.g., "0", "1", "01", ..., in the case of the xsd#integer datatype), which are the lexical representations of the data values,
- a *value space* V^d, which is a set of values (e.g., the numbers 0, 1, 2, ..., in the case of the xsd#integer datatype), and
- a *lexical-to-value mapping* $L2V^d$, which is a mapping from the lexical space to the value space (e.g., { "0" $\mapsto$ 0, "1" $\mapsto$ 1, "01" $\mapsto$ 1, ...}, for the xsd#integer datatype).

A *datatype map D* is a partial mapping from IRIs to datatypes. With $dom(D)$ we denote the domain of D and with $ran(D)$ we denote the range of D. So, $dom(D)$ is the set of datatype identifiers and $ran(D)$ is the set of datatypes.

We assume that if any two datatype maps D_1 and D_2 are both defined on a datatype identifier d, i.e., they both interpret the same datatype identifier, then they map d to the same datatype: if $d \in dom(D_1)$ and $d \in dom(D_2)$, then $D_1(d) = D_2(d)$. This assumption is reasonable, because IRIs are global identifiers; therefore, a single IRI may not identify two different datatypes.

Compatibility between Concrete Domain Schemes and Datatype Maps

Intuitively, a concrete domain scheme is compatible with a datatype map if the sets of datatype identifiers are the same, these datatype identifiers can be used to identify the same sets of values, and there is a correspondence between the mappings from the syntax to the semantics.

Formally, we say that a concrete domain scheme $\mathfrak{S} = \langle U^{\mathfrak{S}}, \mathcal{F}^{\mathfrak{S}}, \mathcal{D}^{\mathfrak{S}}, \mathcal{P}^{\mathfrak{S}}, \cdot^{\mathfrak{S}} \rangle$ is *compatible* with a datatype map D if

- $dom(D) = \mathcal{D}^{\mathfrak{S}}$,
- for each n-ary $d \in \mathcal{D}^{\mathfrak{S}}$ holds that
  - the range of $d^{\mathfrak{S}}$ is the same as $V^{D(d)}$, and
  - there is a 1-to-1 correspondence between n-tuples $\langle t_1, \ldots, t_n \rangle$, where $t_1, \ldots, t_n$ are elementary data values, in the domain of $d^{\mathfrak{S}}$ and character sequences $s \in L^{D(d)}$ such that $d^{\mathfrak{S}}(\langle t_1, \ldots, t_n \rangle) = L2V^{D(d)}(s)$.

Since we assume that there is no difference in the mapping of datatype identifier D between any two datatype maps, each concrete domain scheme $\mathfrak{S}$ has a unique minimal (wrt. $dom(D)$) compatible datatype map D, which we denote with $D_\mathfrak{S}$.

Consider, for example, a concrete domain scheme $\mathfrak{S}$ that includes the xsd#date datatype (i.e., xsd#date $\in \mathcal{D}^\mathfrak{S}$). The domain of $D_\mathfrak{S}$ includes xsd#date and the lexical-to-value mapping is compatible with xsd#date$^\mathfrak{S}$; for example, xsd#date$(2007, 7, 6)$ is the same as $L2V^D$(xsd#date)("2007-07-06"), namely it is the date "July 6, 2007".

Combined WSML-RDF Interpretations

We first review the notion of D-interpretation, after which we define the notion of a combined WSML-RDF $\mathfrak{S}$-interpretation, which is used to interpret both WSML ontologies and RDF graphs.

A D-interpretation [73] is a tuple $I = \langle U, U_P, LV, I_\mathcal{F}, IL, I_{ext} \rangle$, where U is a non-empty set, called the domain, $U_P \subseteq U$ is a countable set of properties, $LV \subseteq U$ is a set of literal values that includes all Unicode character sequences, $I_\mathcal{F}$ is a mapping from IRIs to elements of U, IL is a mapping from typed literals (i.e., pairs of Unicode character sequences and datatype IRIs) to elements of U, and I_{ext} is an extension function that maps elements in U to sets of pairs of elements in U: $I_{ext} : U_P \to 2^{(U \times U)}$. Additionally, every D-interpretation must satisfy a number of conditions, as specified in [73]; these conditions govern the behavior of the RDFS ontology modeling vocabulary and the connection between interpretations and datatype maps.

Given a concrete domain scheme $\mathfrak{S}$. Let $D_\mathfrak{S}$ be the minimal compatible datatype map. A combined WSML-RDF $\mathfrak{S}$-interpretation is a pair $\langle \mathcal{I}, I \rangle$, where $\mathcal{I} = \langle U, \prec_U, \in_U, U^D, \mathcal{I}_F, \mathcal{I}_P, \mathcal{I}_{hv}, \mathcal{I}_{it}, \mathcal{I}_{ot} \rangle$ is a WSML $\mathfrak{S}$-interpretation and $I = \langle U', U_P, LV, I_\mathcal{F}, IL, I_{ext} \rangle$ is a $D_\mathfrak{S}$-interpretation, such that the following conditions hold:

1. $U' = U \cup U^D$,
2. $LV = U^D$,
3. $U_P \supseteq \{p \mid \exists s, o.\langle s, o \rangle \in \mathbf{I}_\twoheadrightarrow(p)\}$,
4. $I_\mathcal{F}(t) = \mathbf{I}_F(t)$ for every IRI t,
5. $I_{ext} = \mathbf{I}_{hv}$,
6. $I_{ext}(I_\mathcal{F}(rdf{:}type)) = \in_U$, and
7. $I_{ext}(I_\mathcal{F}(rdfs{:}subClassOf)) = \{\langle a, b \rangle \mid a, b \in U \ \& \ a \preceq b \ \& \ a \in_U I_\mathcal{F}(rdfs{:}Class) \ \& \ b \in_U I_\mathcal{F}(rdfs{:}Class)\}$.

Note that the interpretation of (well-)typed literals in I corresponds with the interpretation of data values in $\mathcal{I}$ due to the compatibility of $\mathfrak{S}$ and $D_\mathfrak{S}$. Likewise, the interpretation of plain literals without language tags corresponds with the interpretation of strings, due to the way plain literals are interpreted in RDF [73]. Note also that there is no representation in WSML of ill-typed literals (e.g., "a"^^$xsd{:}integer$).

Conditions 1 and 2 ensures that the domains under consideration are the same. Condition 3 ensures that the set of properties in the RDF interpretation includes at least those elements that are used as properties in the WSML interpretation. Condition 4 ensures that all IRIs are interpreted in the same way.

Due to condition 5, there is a correspondence between RDF triples of the form $\langle s, p, o \rangle$ and WSML molecules of the form $s[p\,\mathsf{hv}\,o]$. Likewise, there is a correspondence between RDF triples of the form $\langle a, rdf\text{:}type, c \rangle$ and WSML molecules of the form $a\!:\!c$ and a correspondence between RDF triples of the form $\langle c, rdfs\text{:}subClassOf, d \rangle$ and WSML molecules of the form $c\!::\!d$, by the conditions 6 and 7. Namely, whenever $\langle c, rdfs\text{:}subClassOf, d \rangle$, then $c\!::\!d$. Note that it is not necessarily the case that if $c\!::\!d$, then $\langle c, rdfs\text{:}subClassOf, d \rangle$, because $c\!::\!d$ holds whenever $c = d$, whereas $\langle c, rdfs\text{:}subClassOf, d \rangle$ may not hold even if $c = d$; in RDFS, the subclass relation may only hold between elements which have the type $rdfs\text{:}Class$.

Before defining models, and entailment we first define interpretations of combinations with OWL DL. We then define satisfiability and entailment of combinations of the three kinds of ontologies.

5.4.2 Combination with OWL DL

We now extend the notion of combined WSML-RDF interpretations to include OWL DL interpretations, leading to the notion of WSML-RDF-OWL interpretation. The OWL DL interpretations are used for interpreting OWL ontologies, and correspondence between the WSML and OWL interpretations is defined through a number of conditions, analogous to the correspondence between RDF and WSML interpretations.

We note that the notion of OWL DL interpretation we use here corresponds to the notion of *abstract OWL interpretation* [115, Section 3.1].

Given a datatype map D, an abstract OWL interpretation with respect to D is a tuple $\mathfrak{I} = \langle R, EC, ER, L, S, LV \rangle$, where

- R is a nonempty set,
- $LV \subseteq R$ is the set of literal values,
- EC maps class and datatype identifiers to sets,
- ER maps properties to binary relations,
- L maps typed literals to literal values, and
- S maps IRIs to elements of R.

Additionally, every abstract OWL interpretation has to satisfy a number of conditions, as specified in [115, Section 3].

Given a concrete domain scheme $\mathfrak{S}$ and the minimal compatible datatype map $D_{\mathfrak{S}}$, a *combined WSML-RDF-OWL $\mathfrak{S}$-interpretation* is a tuple $\langle \mathcal{I}, I, \mathfrak{I} \rangle$, where $\mathcal{I} = \langle U, \prec_U, \in_U, U^D, \mathcal{I}_F, \mathcal{I}_P, \mathcal{I}_{\mathsf{hv}}, \mathcal{I}_{\mathsf{it}}, \mathcal{I}_{\mathsf{ot}} \rangle$ is a WSML interpretation that conforms with $\mathfrak{S}$, $I = \langle U, U_P, I_{\mathcal{F}}, I_{ext} \rangle$ is a $D_{\mathfrak{S}}$-interpretation, and

$\mathfrak{I} = \langle R, EC, ER, L, S, LV \rangle$ is an OWL DL interpretation with respect to $D_{\mathfrak{S}}$, such that $\langle \mathcal{I}, I \rangle$ is a combined WSML-RDF $\mathfrak{S}$-interpretation and the following conditions hold:

1. $R = U \cup U^D$,
2. $LV = U^D$,
3. for every concept or datatype identifier c, $EC(c) = \{k \mid k \in U \cup U^D \ \& \ k \in_U \mathcal{I}_F(c)\}$,
4. for every property identifier p, $ER(p) = \{\langle a, b \rangle \mid a, b \in U \cup U^D \ \& \ \langle a, b \rangle \in \mathcal{I}_{\rightarrow}(\mathcal{I}_F(p))\}$, and
5. $S(t) = \mathcal{I}_F(t)$ for every IRI t.

Conditions 1 and 2 ensure that all ontologies talk about the same domain. Conditions 3 and 4 ensure that classes of properties are interpreted the same way. Finally, condition 5 ensures that IRIs are interpreted in the same way.

5.4.3 Satisfiability and Entailment of Combinations

We are now ready to define the semantics of WSML ontologies that import RDFS and/or OWL DL ontologies and of combinations of WSML, RDFS, and OWL DL ontologies. Such combinations may arise, for example, if several different ontologies are imported in a Web service description.

As before we distinguish between the semantics of the WSML-DL variant, on the one hand, and the WSML-Core, Flight, and Rule variants, on the other. The notions of model, satisfiability, and entailment are extensions of the corresponding notions for WSML ontologies defined in Section 5.2.

WSML-DL Semantics of Combinations

Recall that, when considering the WSML-DL variant, combinations with RDFS ontologies are not allowed. Therefore, we only consider WSML-DL and OWL DL ontologies in the combination.

In the definition of the semantics of WSML-DL ontologies, in Section 5.2.2, we defined the notions of models, satisfiability, and entailment for WSML-DL ontologies that import other WSML-DL ontologies. We now consider both WSML-DL and OWL DL ontologies that possibly import both WSML-DL and OWL DL ontologies.

Given a concrete domain scheme $\mathfrak{S}$, a combined WSML-RDF-OWL interpretation $\langle \mathcal{I}, I, \mathfrak{I} \rangle$ is a *DL $\mathfrak{S}$-model* of a WSML-DL or OWL DL ontology O if

1. $\mathcal{I}$ is WSML-DL interpretation,
2. in case O is a WSML-DL ontology, $\mathcal{I}$ is a WSML-DL $\mathfrak{S}$-model of a theory Φ that corresponds to O,
3. in case O is an OWL DL ontology, $\mathfrak{I}$ satisfies O with respect to $D_{\mathfrak{S}}$ according to [115, Section 3.4], and

4. $\langle \mathcal{I}, I, \mathfrak{J} \rangle$ is a DL $\mathfrak{S}$-model of every ontology imported by O.

We are now ready to define the semantic notions of WSML-DL, analogous to the notions defined in Section 5.2.2.

Concept Satisfiability Given a concrete domain scheme $\mathfrak{S}$, let c be a concept identifier. We say that c is *DL $\mathfrak{S}$-satisfiable* with respect to a set of WSML-DL and OWL DL ontologies **O** if there is a combined WSML-RDF-OWL interpretation $\langle \mathcal{I}, I, \mathfrak{J} \rangle$ that is a model of every $O \in$ **O** such that $\mathcal{I}_F(c)_{cext} \neq \emptyset$, i.e., the concept extension of c is not empty.

Ontology Satisfiability Given a concrete domain scheme $\mathfrak{S}$, a set of WSML-DL and OWL DL ontologies **O** is *DL $\mathfrak{S}$-satisfiable* if there is a combined WSML-RDF-OWL interpretation $\langle \mathcal{I}, I, \mathfrak{J} \rangle$ that is a model of every $O \in$ **O**.

Formula Entailment Given a concrete domain scheme $\mathfrak{S}$, a set of WSML-DL and OWL DL ontologies **O** *DL $\mathfrak{S}$-entails* a formula ϕ if for every combined WSML-RDF-OWL interpretation $\langle \mathcal{I}, I, \mathfrak{J} \rangle$ that is a model of every $O \in$ **O** holds that $\mathcal{I}$ is a WSML-DL $\mathfrak{S}$-model of ϕ.

Ontology Entailment Given a concrete domain scheme $\mathfrak{S}$, a set of WSML-DL and OWL DL ontologies **O** *DL $\mathfrak{S}$-entails* a WSML-DL or OWL DL ontology O if for every combined WSML-RDF-OWL interpretation $\langle \mathcal{I}, I, \mathfrak{J} \rangle$ that is a model of every $O' \in$ **O** holds that $\langle \mathcal{I}, I, \mathfrak{J} \rangle$ is a DL $\mathfrak{S}$-model of O'.

WSML-Core, Flight and Rule Semantics of Combinations

As we did for WSML ontologies, we define the semantics of WSML-Core, Flight, and Rule combinations using a notion of stable models. The domains of these stable models are somewhat extended, compared with the stable models of WSML ontologies, in order to account for the blank nodes in RDF graphs. So, we essentially *Skolemize* the blank nodes by replacing them with constant symbols.

We note that the semantics of these three variants is only defined for OWL DL ontologies that fall within the DLP fragment, i.e., those ontologies that are equivalent to sets of equality-free Horn formulas, and are hence essentially negation-free rules.

We first extend the notion of Herbrand models to combinations. We then define the notion of a stable model of a combination.

Herbrand Models of Combinations

Recall that we define Herbrand interpretations relative to a concrete domain scheme $\mathfrak{S} = \langle U^\mathfrak{S}, \mathcal{F}^\mathfrak{S}, \mathcal{D}^\mathfrak{S}, \mathcal{P}^\mathfrak{S}, \cdot^\mathfrak{S} \rangle$. Recall also that $\mathcal{D}$ denotes the set of all data values in $\mathfrak{S}$: $\mathcal{D} = \bigcup \{d^\mathfrak{S} \mid d \in D^\mathfrak{S}\}$.

In the remainder of this section, the symbol **O** denotes a set of WSML, RDFS, and OWL DL ontologies. The *set of constant symbols* of **O** is the set of IRIs, blank nodes, literals, and data values in every ontology in **O** (we assume anonymous identifiers have been replaced with IRIs, as described in Section 5.2.3). The set of function symbols of **O** is the set of all symbols occurring in a function position in any WSML ontology in **O**. The *set of ground terms* of **O** is the set of all ground terms that can be formed from the constant and function symbols of **O**.

The *Herbrand $\mathfrak{S}$-universe* of **O** is the union of set of ground terms of **O** that are not data values and the set of values $t^\mathfrak{S}$ in $\mathcal{D}$ whose lexical representation t occurs in any of the ontologies in **O**.

A Herbrand WSML-RDF-OWL $\mathfrak{S}$-interpretation $\langle \mathcal{I}, I, \mathfrak{I} \rangle$ of **O** is a WSML-RDF-OWL $\mathfrak{S}$-interpretation where

- the domain of $\mathcal{I}$, U, is the Herbrand $\mathfrak{S}$-universe of **O** and
- for every ground term t of **O**, $t^\mathcal{I} = t'$, where t' is obtained from t by replacing every data value d in t with $d^\mathfrak{S}$.

Recall the conditions on combined WSML-RDF-OWL interpretations in Sections 5.4.1 and 5.4.2. These conditions ensure that the parts of the domains of RDF and OWL interpretations that are not literal values correspond to the domain of the WSML interpretation $\mathcal{I}$. Therefore, these domains correspond to the Herbrand $\mathfrak{S}$-universe as well. Additionally, due to the fact that IRIs are interpreted the same in all three interpretations, all ground terms are interpreted in the same way in all three interpretations.

We are now ready to define the notions of model and minimal model. As before, a model of an ontology is required to be a model of every imported ontology.

A set of WSML, RDFS, and OWL DL ontologies **O** is *imports-closed* if for every ontology O imported by any ontology O' in **O** holds that $O \in$ **O**.

Now, a Herbrand WSML-RDF-OWL $\mathfrak{S}$-interpretation $\langle \mathcal{I}, I, \mathfrak{I} \rangle$ is a $\mathfrak{S}$-*model* of an imports-closed set of ontologies **O** if

- for every WSML ontology $O \in$ **O**, $\mathcal{I}$ is a $\mathfrak{S}$-model of the theory Φ corresponding to O,
- for every RDFS ontology $O \in$ **O**, I satisfies O, and
- for every OWL DL ontology $O \in$ **O**, $\mathfrak{I}$ satisfies O.

We can now define the notion of a *minimal Herbrand $\mathfrak{S}$-model*. A Herbrand WSML-RDF-OWL $\mathfrak{S}$-interpretation $\langle \mathcal{I}, I, \mathfrak{I} \rangle$ is a *minimal Herbrand $\mathfrak{S}$-model* of an imports-closed set of ontologies **O** if

- $\langle \mathcal{I}, I, \mathfrak{I} \rangle$ is a $\mathfrak{S}$-model of $\mathbf{O}$ and
- whenever a Herbrand $\mathfrak{S}$-interpretation $\langle \mathcal{I}', I', \mathfrak{I}' \rangle$ is an $\mathfrak{S}$-model of $\mathbf{O}$ and $\mathcal{I}' \subseteq \mathcal{I}$, then $\mathcal{I}' = \mathcal{I}$.

Stable Models of Combinations

The definition of stable models of combinations is similar to the definition of stable models for WSML ontologies. Likewise, we guess a model, "evaluate" the grounding of a combination by computing the reduct, and check whether the model we guessed is the minimal Herbrand model of the reduct.

It turns out that in a set of WSML, RDFS, and OWL DL ontologies we only need to ground the WSML ontologies, because the RDFS and OWL DL ontologies do not contain negation (recall that the OWL DL ontologies are required to be in the DLP fragment, which is negation-free).

The *grounding* of $\mathbf{O}$, denoted $gr(\mathbf{O})$, is obtained from $\mathbf{O}$ by replacing every WSML ontology $O \in \mathbf{O}$ by $gr(O)$, which is the union of all possible ground instantiations of the corresponding WSML theory Φ, obtained by

- replacing each abstract (resp., concrete) variable in a formula $\phi \in \Phi$ with a ground (resp., ground concrete) term in the Herbrand $\mathfrak{S}$-universe of $\mathbf{O}$ and
- replacing each data value d in ϕ with the corresponding concrete data value $d^{\mathfrak{S}}$,

for each formula $\phi \in \Phi$.

The *reduct* of $\mathbf{O}$ with respect to a combined Herbrand $\mathfrak{S}$-interpretation $\langle \mathcal{I}, I, \mathfrak{I} \rangle$, denoted $\mathbf{O}^{\langle \mathcal{I}, I, \mathfrak{I} \rangle}$, is obtained from $gr(\mathbf{O})$ by, for each WSML ontology $O \in gr(\mathbf{O})$,

- deleting each formula r with a *not* c in the antecedent such that $c \in \mathcal{I}$ and
- deleting *not* c from the antecedent of every remaining formula r.

Given a concrete domain scheme $\mathfrak{S}$, a Herbrand WSML-RDF-OWL $\mathfrak{S}$-interpretation $\langle \mathcal{I}, I, \mathfrak{I} \rangle$ is a *stable* $\mathfrak{S}$-*model* of an imports-closed set of ontologies $\mathbf{O}$ if $\langle \mathcal{I}, I, \mathfrak{I} \rangle$ is a minimal Herbrand $\mathfrak{S}$-model of $\mathbf{O}^{\langle \mathcal{I}, I, \mathfrak{I} \rangle}$.

Using the notion of stable $\mathfrak{S}$-model we define the semantic notions for WSML-Core, Flight, and Rule combinations.

Satisfiability Given a concrete domain scheme $\mathfrak{S}$, an imports-closed set of ontologies $\mathbf{O}$ is $\mathfrak{S}$-*satisfiable* if $\mathbf{O}$ has a stable $\mathfrak{S}$-model.

Entailment Given a concrete domain scheme $\mathfrak{S}$, an imports-closed set of ontologies $\mathbf{O}$ $\mathfrak{S}$-*entails* a ground atomic formula α if for every stable $\mathfrak{S}$-model $\langle \mathcal{I}, I, \mathfrak{I} \rangle$ of $\mathbf{O}$ holds that $\mathcal{I} \models \alpha$.

In this chapter we have defined WSML ontologies, and the semantics of their combination with RDFS and OWL DL ontologies. We have defined two notions of satisfiability and entailment, one for WSML-DL and one for WSML-Core/Flight/Rule. We have subsequently extended these notions to combinations with RDFS and OWL DL ontologies.

The notions defined in this chapter can be used directly for reasoning with WSML ontologies, as well as their combination with RDFS and OWL DL ontologies, bearing in mind the restrictions outlined in Table 5.2 on page 88. As such, these notions also provide the basis for using ontologies in the functional and behavioral Web service descriptions. In fact, the semantics of functional and behavioral descriptions, described in the following two chapters, are parameterized with respect to the satisfiability and entailment relations. Therefore, these descriptions can be used with any of the WSML variants.

6

Functional Description of Services

Where the previous chapter defined the semantics of WSML ontologies (the static knowledge component of Web service descriptions), this chapter describes how WSML can be used to capture the functionality of Web services. We consider both set-based and state-based capabilities, describing the models underlying these kinds of description, as well as the formal relations that can be defined between goals and Web services based on these models.

In general it is important to understand the conceptual model and the particular assumptions underlying each specific approach to service description. Different approaches vary greatly in the level of detail that can be expressed. In terms of functional descriptions we are interested in modelling what a service does as opposed to how a certain functionality is achieved. If we consider for example a Web service capable of processing credit card payments, we are interested in the details of this functionality, i.e., which credit cards are accepted (Visa, Master Card, JCB, ...), which currencies and what kind of fraud checking is provided. In this chapter we are not concerned with non-functional aspects such as the supported transport layer security or the guarantees in terms of service availability.

Describing the functionality of a service explicitly has many advantages. Most notably it allows potential users to easily find a certain Web service. In terms of discovery the Web service life cycle starts once it has been created and published by a provider (cf. the Web service usage process in Figure 3.2 on page 3.2). Web service technology allows to the invoking of services over the internet, however without knowing about a service a potential user will not be able to use it. So if someone is in the need of a certain functionality he needs to perform some kind of search in order to find a list of services that is able to provide the functionality desired. In order to decide whether a service does actually provide a certain functionality or not a matchmaking procedure based on some kind of description has to be performed. Semantic annotations can reduce the amount of manual labor involved in this process by providing accurate descriptions of client requests and the services offered.

Consider, in contrast, a discovery service that only allows to query services by keyword will require a human to manually asses a potentially large list of matches to determine which are actually providing the functionality desired. When both the request and the response are semantically described a matching engine can guarantee that all results indeed fulfill the desire expressed in the request. For example a request for a payment service to handle Visa cards can be matched against a service offering all *major* credit cards by using the appropriate background knowledge (in an ontology). However, performing a keyword query for "visa creditcard" will not necessarily return only payment services. In fact using an existing search engine for Web services[1] one quarter of the results of this query have been validation services.

In the remainder of the chapter we will first give an overview of the most prominent approaches to the functional description of Web services, in Section 6.1. We then proceed with a description of the models underlying capability descriptions, as well as notions of consistency and capability matching, both for set-based and state-based capability descriptions, in the Sections 6.2 and 6.3, respectively.

6.1 Approaches to Functional Description

When describing functionality we can do this in various ways. The simplest possible way is to base it on natural language text, i.e., to use a set of keywords to capture the functionality. For the payment service this could be "payment", "credit card", etc. Obviously this type of description has the advantage of not requiring complex logical expressions and trained knowledge engineers, however the descriptions are not very precise and tend to be ambiguous. Imagine you want to express that a service that accepts all major credit cards, but only does business with merchants based in North America. With keywords alone one cannot capture these facts in a way that they can be easily understood and processed by a machine.

With an ontology language we can express this specific information. We can model the concept of a payment service that has numerous properties. An example of such a property would be "accepted credit cards", whose values are the accepted credit cards. We refer to this kind of functional description as "set-based". The functionality is described by an ontological concept that describes the service (i.e., what it delivers).

Although a set-based description using an expressive ontology language can be used to describe many aspects of a service it has limitations: we can not explicitly refer to constraints that must hold in order for the service to be able to execute, nor can we describe the concrete dependencies between the pre and post-states. For example this is required in order to describe that before some service is executed some service the available credit of the card

---

[1] http://seekda.com

holder must be at least as high as the payment amount. We will refer to this type of description as "state-based".

Still finer grained levels of description are sometimes required. Suppose we want to describe a service conducting bank transfers; besides single bank transfers the service offers processing of multiple transfers at once, in a batch processing fashion. Assuming that a batch can contain credits as well as withdrawals the lowest intermediate balance will depend on the order of how the transfers are internally executed. In case all withdrawals are performed first and only then all credits, the account will have a lower intermediate balance then if the order would be reversed. Although in general the functional description is not concerned about how a particular functionality is achieved we still might be interested in modeling execution invariants, i.e., some conditions that must hold in all states that exist between invoking the Web Service and after that invocation has completed. This might be for example that the account balance must be always greater then zero. However, in this chapter we are not concerned with this level of detail. Such constraints are part of the behavioral description of the service (see Chapter 7).

Every of these levels implies a different description of Web services, ranging from detailed characterizations of pre- and post-states to less detailed descriptions using (complex) concepts in an ontology and simple unstructured keywords. Consequently, the achievable accuracy of a result in the discovery process varies significantly, as more or less structure is reflected in the descriptions. On the other hand, the ease of providing the descriptions varies drastically between these levels as well. Whereas simple keywords are easy to provide, using ontological concepts already requires the publisher to either familiarize himself with the applicable domain ontologies or create their own ones. The provision of detailed state-based descriptions requires most effort. The more fine-grained the information, that the descriptions reveal, the more complex the algorithms must be that to deal with these descriptions. Therefore, there is a trade-off between the accuracy and complexity of descriptions. In turn, lower accuracy of a Web service descriptions leads to a lower precision of the discovery process and higher complexity of descriptions leads to increased effort and skills required for service description, as well as decreased efficiency of the discovery process. This trade off is illustrated in Figure 6.1.

In principle the different models (state- versus set-based) are not tied to particular representation formalisms. WSML, however allows writing service descriptions at all of theses different levels of granularity. Moreover we can use different WSML variants to describe Web services at each of those levels. For example the set-based approach can be realized using WSML-DL. WSML leaves the choice of the concrete variant to the user, so that he can choose the expressivity suitable for his particular task.

Since a keyword based description (and the appropriate matchmaking) do not require a semantic language such as WSML we omit further discussion here. The interested reader can find additional information on how keyword

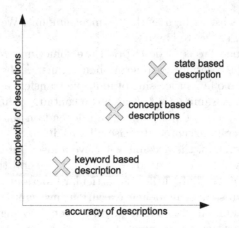

Fig. 6.1. Trade-off between accuracy and complexity for service descriptions

based technologies have been applied to the domain of Web service discovery in [47, 92].

6.2 Set-Based Web Service Description

In this section we present a formal modeling approach for Web services and goals that is based on set theory and exploits ontologies as formal, machine-processable representation of domain knowledge. We discuss Web service discovery based on this approach for simple semantic descriptions and describe how the set-based model in WSML is implemented.

The set-theoretic notions discussed in this section give rise to a set-based *discovery mechanism*.

6.2.1 The Model

One main characteristic of object oriented approaches is that the problem domain is understood as a collection of objects and objects with similar properties can be grouped together into sets or classes. Each class captures common (syntactic and semantic) features of their elements. Features can be inherited from one class to another by defining class hierarchies. In this way, the domain of discourse can be structured as a collection of classes and each class is a set of things. We apply this model to describe the functionality of a Web service as a set.

A Web service provides some value to the entity that invokes it. The invocation itself is based on Web service technologies like SOAP and WSDL, however these technical details of invocation are not necessarily relevant for discovery based on functional specifications. Only if one considers discovery together with the adaptation/invocation of the service does one need to cater for the particularities of the invocation mechanism. To judge wether the functionality offered by a Web service matches the one requested it is not necessary to check compatibility on the interface level, since it might be possible to bypass mismatches by mediators. The execution of the Web service with particular input values generates certain piece of information as an output and achieves certain changes in the state of the world. An output as well as an effect can be considered as objects which can be embedded in some ontology.

Goals on the other hand specify the desire of a client that he wants to have resolved after invoking a Web service, that means they describe the information the client wants to receive as output of the Web service execution as well as the effects on the state of the world. This desire can be represented as sets of elements that are relevant to the client as the outputs and the effects of a service execution. Goals therefore refer to the desired state of the world.

Both Web services and goals are represented by sets of objects. These sets of objects are described in ontologies that capture general knowledge about the domain under consideration. Matching a Web service to a Goal requires that there exists some mutual relationship between the objects used in their descriptions. This relationship can be established with reference to the ontology (or ontologies) used to describe these objects. We define domain-independent notions of matching in Section 6.2.2.

An important observation is that the description of a set of objects for representing a goal or a Web service actually can be interpreted in different ways and thus the description by means of a set is not semantically unique: A modeler might want to express that either all of the elements that are contained in the set are requested or can be delivered ($\forall$), or that only some of these elements are requested or can be delivered ($\exists$). Consider for example someone who wants to find pricing information of some multimedia product ($\exists$), versus someone who wants to know about the prices of all available products in a certain product category ($\forall$).

Clearly, a modeler has some intuition in mind when specifying such a set of relevant objects for a goal or Web service description and this intention essentially determines whether we consider two descriptions to match or not. Thus, this intuition should be stated explicitly in the descriptions of service requests or service advertisements.

Given our previous considerations we can model goals and Web services as follows: A goal G and a Web service W are represented by sets of objects from some common universe U (i.e., $G, W \subseteq U$). These sets represent relevant objects for the description. In addition, both G and W have an associated *intention* $I \in \{\forall, \exists\}$.

6.2.2 Matching Web Services and Goals

In order to assert a goal G and a Web service W match on a semantic level, the sets G and W describing these elements have to be interrelated somehow; specifically, we expect that some set-theoretic relationship between G and W

has to exist. The most basic set-theoretic relationships that one might consider are the following:

$G = W$ Set equality
$G \subseteq W$ Goal description is a subset of the Web service description
$W \subseteq G$ Web service description is a subset of the goal description
$G \cap W \neq \emptyset$ The goal and Web service descriptions have some elements in common
$G \cap W = \emptyset$ The goal and Web service descriptions have no elements in common

These set-theoretic relationships provide the basic means for formalizing our intuitive understanding of a match between goals and Web services. In fact, the above relationships have been considered in the context of Description Logic-based matching in [94] and [114]. The terminology for matching notions in these papers has been inspired by work done in the context of matching based on component specifications [139].

However, we have to keep in mind that in our model these sets only capture part of the semantics of goal and service descriptions, namely the relevant objects for the service requestor or service provider. The intentions of these sets in the semantic description of the goal or Web service is not considered but clearly affects whether particular set-theoretic relationships between G and W correspond to intuitive notions of matching. Hence, we have to consider the intentions of the respective sets as well. In the following we will discuss the set-theoretical relation for one notion of matching (namely, intersection match) as an example; we summarize all notions of matching in Table 6.1 on page 104.

Example: Intersection Match

We provide a detailed discussion for the case where there exist common elements in goal and Web service descriptions. In this case the set of relevant objects that are advertised by the service provider and the set of relevant objects for the requester have a non-empty intersection, i.e., there is an object that is relevant for both parties. In a sense, this criterion can be seen as the weakest possible criterion for semantic matching in the set-based modeling approach.

Let us consider the goal in Listing 6.1 and the Web service in Listing 6.2. The Web service can be used to request the price of a product as well as to buy buy a product. Recall that concepts in ontology represent sets of instances. One can verify that the sets of instances of the concepts GenericProductStore-Service and RetrievePriceInformationMedia potentially intersect, i.e., it is possible that object is an instance of both concepts. Therefore, there is an *intersection match* between the goal and the service.

We now how an intersection match should be interpreted, depending of the intentions of the goal and the Web service.

```
namespace {_"http://example.org/",
          tasks _"http://example.org/ ontologies /tasks/" }
goal GetPriceInformation
  annotations
    dc#description hasValue "Describes the desire of getting price information of any multi
        media product"
  endAnnotations
  importsOntology PriceInformation
  capability  RetrievePriceInformationMedia

ontology PriceInformation
  importsOntology {_"http://example.org/ontologies/tasks/Tasks", _"http://example.org/
        ontologies /products/MediaProducts" }
  concept RetrievePriceInformationMedia subConceptOf tasks#RetrievePriceInformation
    forProduct impliesType media#MediaProduct
```

Listing 6.1. Goal for retrieving price information

```
namespace {_"http://example.org/",
          tasks _"http://example.org/ ontologies /tasks/" }
webService GenericProductStoreService
  annotations
    dc#description hasValue "Describes a shop offering  information about products and there
        prices "
  endAnnotations
  importsOntology PriceInformation
  capability  GenericProductStore

ontology GenericProductStoreOntology
  importsOntology {_"http://example.org/ontologies/tasks/Tasks", _"http://example.org/
        ontologies /products/Products" }
  concept GenericProductStore
  axiom definedBy
    forall ?object (?object memberOf GenericProductStore equivalent
    (?object memberOf tasks#RetrievePriceInformation or ?object memberOf tasks#Buy)).
```

Listing 6.2. Web service offering price information and buying functionality

- $I_G = \forall$, $I_W = \forall$: The service requester wants to get all of the objects and the service provider claims that the Web service is able to deliver all the objects specified. In this case, the requester needs can not be fully satisfied by the service. However, the service can contribute to meeting the requirements of the client. Thus, we consider this case a *partial match*.
- $I_G = \exists$, $I_W = \forall$: The service requester wants to get some of the objects, whereas the service provider claims that the Web service is able to deliver all the objects specified. In this case, the requester needs are fully covered by the Web service. The requester might as well receive objects which are not relevant for him. We consider this case *match*.
- $I_G = \forall$, $I_W = \exists$: The service requester wants to get all of the objects, whereas the service provider claims that the Web service is able to deliver only some of the objects specified. In this case, the requester needs are not fully covered. We are even not able to determine whether the service

	$I_W = \forall$ $I_G = \forall$	$I_W = \forall$ $I_G = \exists$	$I_W = \exists$ $I_G = \forall$	$I_W = \exists$ $I_G = \exists$
$G = W$	Match	Match	Partial Match	Match
$G \subseteq W$	Match	Match	Possible Match	Possible Match
$G \supseteq W$	Partial Match	Match	Partial Match	Match
$G \cap W \neq \emptyset$	Partial Match	Match	Possible Partial Match	Possible Match
$G \cap W = \emptyset$	Non-match	Non-match	Non-match	Non-match

Table 6.1. Set-theoretic criteria, intentions, and our intuitive understanding of matching

actually can deliver any of the objects desired by the requester and hence we consider this a *possible partial match*.

- $I_G = \exists$, $I_W = \exists$: The service requester wants to get some of the objects and the service provider claims that the Web service is able to deliver some of the objects specified. In this case we have a *possible match*.

For a complete discussion of all possible matches we refer the reader to [82]. However, given the discussion for the case of an intersection match, it is straight-forward to apply it to the remaining cases. In the next subsection we give a brief summary of all possible combinations.

Summary: Understanding of Matching

Given some goal G and some Web service W, Table 6.1 summarizes the discussion and shows under which circumstances the presence of which set-theoretic relationship between G and W is considered as a match, a partial match, a possible match, a possible partial match or a non-match.

In earlier Description Logic-based approaches to service discovery (e.g., [114, 94]) the notion of "intention" was not been reflected explicitly. As we have shown above, intentions capture an important aspect of goal and Web service descriptions and affect essentially the situations in which certain set-theoretic criteria represent our intuitive understanding of matches.

We believe that certain combinations of intentions will occur more often in practice than others: Web service providers for example have a strong interest in their Web services being discovered. If we compare the number of possible matchings with a given goal under existential and universal intentions, it seems most likely that providers tend to use universal intentions, even if the description does not necessarily model the actual functionality of the service accurately and promises too much. However, if a service provider wants to be more accurate with his Web service description then in many situations he would have to use the existential intention.

For service requesters (in particular in an e-Business setting) we expect that the existential intention will suffice in many situations, however the requester has the freedom to express stronger requests than existential goals (using the universal intention) if he needs to and thus get more accurate results in these situations.

6.2.3 Consistency of Descriptions

What we have not considered so far is the possibility of inconsistent goal or Web service descriptions. In our situation, a set-based capability is inconsistent if it is necessarily interpreted as the empty set – that is, the concept representing the capability does not have instances in any model of the task ontology. Clearly such descriptions are not desirable: a requester who is asking for nothing and Web services that do not deliver anything are simply superfluous and undesired. Nonetheless, inconsistent descriptions might occur in cases where the descriptions are complex or refer to several complex ontologies which are not themselves designed by the modeler.

Additionally, when just being ignored they can have an undesired impact on matching and thus discovery: Consider for example an inconsistent goal description, i.e., $G = \emptyset$. If we check G for matching Web services using the Plugin-criterion, i.e., $G \subseteq W$, then obviously every Web service matches. For a user (who is not aware that his description is inconsistent, since otherwise he would usually not pose the query) the result would seem unintuitive and even incorrect because all checked services actually will match.

Checking for inconsistent goal and Web service descriptions is not a task that is only applicable at the design time. It is of course good practice to is allow creating an inconsistent description, but consistency does not depend exclusively on the description itself; it also depends on the ontologies the description refers to. Hence, changes to such ontologies potentially lead to inconsistent descriptions. Moreover, since Web service and goal description may refer to different ontologies, their combination (necessary when performing matchmaking) may make a previously satisfiable goal description unsatisfiable. Thus before checking for a match the satisfiability of each description involved must be checked.

6.2.4 Ranking Matches

As shown in Table 6.1, we basically have for each pair of intentions for a goal and a Web service several formal criteria that capture actual matches, partial matches, possible matches, and non-matches. According to elementary set-theory the single criteria are not completely separated, but the following interdependencies hold. Notice that in some cases we require descriptions to be non-empty as discussed before.

$$G = W \Rightarrow G \subseteq W$$
$$G = W \Rightarrow G \supseteq W$$
$$G \subseteq W, G \neq \emptyset \Rightarrow G \cap W \neq \emptyset$$
$$G \supseteq W, W \neq \emptyset \Rightarrow G \cap W \neq \emptyset$$

That means that certain formal set-theoretic criteria that we consider here are stronger notions than others: if the stronger relationship holds than the weaker relationship must hold as well. These properties induce a partial order on the set-theoretic criteria:

$$(G = W) \quad \preceq \quad (G \subseteq W), (G \supseteq W) \quad \preceq \quad (G \cap W \neq \emptyset)$$

Given a goal and a Web service description let "subsumes match" be the criterion that captures the actual match, then a weaker criterion, such as "intersection match" does also hold. However one has to note that the stronger criterion provides additional knowledge about the relationship between goal and Web service. In this particular example a "subsumes match" also guarantees that no objects are delivered besides the one requested, since this property might be important for a requestor, it does make sense to allow the use of a particular criterion for the matching between goal and Web service descriptions by the requestor. A service requester basically can exploit this property during a discovery process in order to ensure certain convenient properties from the discovered Web services.

To sum up, we have seen that there are cases where a client could benefit from exploiting the additional semantics captured by matching criteria that are stronger that the weakest match. Hence, it makes sense to not only allow a request to demand a match (i.e., at least the weakest criterion to be fullfilled), but also to allow to specify the exact criteria and thus raise the semantic requirements that are captured by the criterion. In particular this makes sense for the case that a client does not want to accept that a Web service potentially delivers objects that have not been explicitly requested (in this case a subsumes or an exact match has to be requested).

We have seen as well that in our general framework there is only one such additional property that actually can be considered as useful, namely the property of a Web service to not deliver objects that are irrelevant to the user. This leads us to allow the client to specify what particular kind of match he is accepting, by specifying the following three dimensions:

- Intention of the goal
- match, partial match, possible partial match, possible match
- within each match it can be additionally specified if a service is allowed to deliver objects that are not requested.

Partial Order on "Match"

Similar to the partial order that is defined for the basic set theoretic matching criterion, we can also define a logically order on our intuitive understanding of the matching notion.

$$\text{Match} \preceq \text{PartialMatch}, \text{PossibleMatch} \preceq \text{PossiblePartialMatch}$$

	$I_W = \forall$		$I_W = \exists$	
	additional objects	no additional objects	additional objects	no additional objects
$I_G = \forall$ Match	$G \subseteq W$	$G = W$		−
$I_G = \exists$ Match	$G \cap W \neq \emptyset$	$G \supseteq W$	$G \supseteq W$	$G \supseteq W$
$I_G = \forall$ Partial Match	$G \cap W \neq \emptyset$	$G \supseteq W$	$G \supseteq W$	$G \supseteq W$
$I_G = \exists$ Partial Match	$G \cap W \neq \emptyset$	$G \supseteq W$	$G \supseteq W$	$G \supseteq W$
$I_G = \forall$ Possible Match	$G \subseteq W$	$G = W$	$G \subseteq W$	−
$I_G = \exists$ Possible Match	$G \cap W \neq \emptyset$	$G \supseteq W$	$G \cap W \neq \emptyset$	$G \supseteq W$
$I_G = \forall$ Possible Partial Match	$G \cap W \neq \emptyset$	$G \supseteq W$	$G \cap W \neq \emptyset$	$G \supseteq W$
$I_G = \exists$ Possible Partial Match	$G \cap W \neq \emptyset$	$G \supseteq W$	$G \cap W \neq \emptyset$	$G \supseteq W$

Table 6.2. Formal criteria for checking degrees of matching

The partial ordering can be exploited during matchmaking: in order to ensure that a property is satisfied when matching (e.g., $I_G = \exists, I_W = \forall$ and additional objects might be delivered), the discovery component has to apply only the weakest criterion still fulfilling the request. In the given example it is only required to check for an intersection match $(G \cap W \neq \emptyset)$ and not for all set theoretic relation separately. Table 6.2 represents the result of this discussion for all possible combinations. Matching criteria that are colored gray in the table indicate that the criterion does in fact not check the intuitive matching criteria specified (e.g., partial match or match), but one which also satisfies the requested criteria due to the partial order on the intuitive matching notions.

Matching in the set-based framework for Web service discovery is based on rather simple semantic annotations and thus can provide only limited guarantees on the actual accuracy of the results: A detected match between a goal and a Web service actually does not ensure that the Web service can really fulfill the user requirements depicted in the goal, since important information that affects this possibility is not specified in the descriptions; e.g., the requester's ability to satisfy the requirements of the Web service when invoking and interaction with the service, namely the pre-conditions as well as a prescribed choreography. In the next section we will present a model that allows to capture the relation between pre- and post-state.

6.3 State-Based Web Service Description

This section presents a model that allows a more precise definition of the functionality of a Web service, i.e., state-based capabilities. The model itself is independent of any specific logical formalism. In general the model can be formally represented in various logics of sufficient expressivity – for example, different WSML variants – to enable reasoning with semantic descriptions of Web service capabilities. We will illustrate the model in an intuitive fashion, for the formal definitions we refer to [82].

```
  . . .
  concept CreditCard
     hasNumber ofType xsd#integer
     hasSecurityCode ofType xsd#integer
     hasExpiryDate ofType xsd#date
     hasOwner ofType Client
     hasLimit ofType xsd#decimal

  relation creditCardCharge(ofType CreditCard, ofType xsd#decimal, ofType xsd#dateTime)

  axiom noChargeBeyondLimit
     definedBy
       !− creditCardCharge(?creditCard , ?charge, ?date) and
          ?creditCard [hasLimit hasValue ?limit] memberOf CreditCard and
          ?charge>?limit.
  . . .
```

Listing 6.3. Excerpt from the commerce domain ontology

6.3.1 Abstract State Spaces

We consider the world as a set of entities that change over time. Entities that act in the world - which can be anything from a human user to some computer program - can affect how the world is perceived by themselves or other entities at some specific moment in time. At any point in time, the world is in one particular state that determines how the world is perceived by the entities acting therein. We need to consider some language for describing the properties of the world in a state. In the following we assume an arbitrary (but fixed) signature Σ that is based on some domain ontologies, and a language $\mathcal{L}(\Sigma)$.

Although the concept of ontologies has been already introduced we include a small excerpt of a commerce ontology in Listing 6.3 to illustrate a signature expressed in WSML. Within the listing we define the concept of an credit card and that no charge can be made that is beyond the credit card limit.

In the context of dynamics and properties of the world that can change, it is useful to distinguish between symbols in Σ that are supposed to have always the same, fixed meaning (e.g., $\geq$, 0) and thus can not be affected by any entity that acts in the world, and symbols that can be affected and thus can change their meaning during the execution a Web service (e.g., **memberOf**, **hasValue**). We refer to the former class of symbols as *static* (denoted by Σ_S) and the latter as *dynamic* symbols (denoted by Σ_D).

Abstract State Spaces

We consider an abstract state space $\mathcal{S}$ to represent all possible states s of the world. Each state $s \in \mathcal{S}$ completely determines how the world is perceived by each entity acting in $\mathcal{S}$. Each statement $\phi \in \mathcal{L}(\Sigma)$ of an entity about the (current state of) the world is either true or it is false. We consider classical logic (and thus only true and false as truth values) here. However, the presented model can be used as it is in the context of non-classical logics (e.g.,

```
. . .
instance myVisaCard memberOf CreditCard
    hasNumber hasValue 4444111122223333
    hasLimit hasValue 2000,00

    relationInstance creditCardCharge(myVisaCard, 100, _dateTime(2007, 1, 1, 12, 19, 10))
. . .
```

Listing 6.4. Possible state in an abstract state space

WSML-Rule) by considering a restricted class of models $\mathcal{I}$, e.g., stable models in the case of WSML-Rule. A state $s \in \mathcal{S}$ in fact defines an interpretation $\mathcal{I}$ (of some signature Σ). However, not all Σ-Interpretations $\mathcal{I}$ represent meaningful observations since $\mathcal{I}$ might not respect some "laws" that the world S underlies, e.g., that a credit card charge may not exceed the credit cards limit.

These laws are captured by a background ontology $\Omega \subseteq \mathcal{L}(\Sigma)$ as for example in Listing 6.3. Listing 6.4 illustrates some meaningful observations according to our background ontology.

Changing the World

By means of well-defined change operations, entities can affect the world through state transitions over $\mathcal{S}$. In our setting, these change operations are single concrete executions of Web services W. Following [82], a change operation is represented by a service S that is accessed via a Web service W. The transition is achieved by executing W with some given input data $i_1, \ldots, i_n$ that determine the concrete service execution S, i.e., $S \approx W(i_1, \ldots, i_n)$.

Given some input data $i_1, \ldots, i_n$, the execution of a Web service essentially causes a state transition τ in $\mathcal{S}$, transforming the current state of the world $s \in \mathcal{S}$ into a new state $s' \in \mathcal{S}$. A transition τ will in general not be an atomic transition $\tau = (s, s') \in \mathcal{S} \times \mathcal{S}$ but a sequence $\tau = (s_0, \ldots, s_n) \in \mathcal{S}^+$, where $s_0 = s$, $s_n = s'$ and $n \geq 1$. Intermediate states can be useful if it is of interest to express invariants that must hold throughout an entire execution. Similarly intermediate states might be important when describing long-lasting transactions. However, for the purpose of functional descriptions we envision that it is not necessary to model those intermediate steps, since they are generally not of interest during analysis or use of capability descriptions. In the context of our model we describe the functionality of a Web service by the pre-state (s) and the post-state (s'). More fine grained statements about a service can be described using choreographies as detailed in Chapter 7.

Outputs as Changes of an Information Space

After the execution of a Web service, it can send some information as output to the requester. We consider these outputs as updates of the so-called information space of the requester of a service. The information space is a part of the state.

```
. . .
instance myVisaCard memberOf CreditCard
    hasNumber hasValue 4444111122223333
    hasLimit hasValue 2000,00

relationInstance creditCardCharge(myVisaCard, 100, _dateTime(2007, 1, 1, 12, 19, 10))
. . .
```

Listing 6.5. Statements describing a particuar information space

Taking up our background ontology including the credit card we can model the output of an online purchase using transaction status and some id that uniquely identifies the transaction, as illustrated by the instance depicted in Listing 6.5.

Observations in Abstract States

Our aim is to describe all the effects of Web service executions for a requester. Obviously, a requester can observe in every state $s \in S$ related properties represented by statements ϕ in $\mathcal{L}(\Sigma)$ that hold in s. Additionally, he can perceive the information space, as described above. The abstract state space S in a sense "corresponds" to the observations that can be made, both in the information space and the "real world". Consequently, we represent the observations related to a state s by an observation function ω, which assigns a Σ-interpretation $\mathcal{I}$ to every state $s \in S$. We denote that part of $\mathcal{I}$ concerned with the real world by $\omega_{rw}(s)$ and the part concerned with the information space by $\omega_{is}(s)$. However, we require the observation function ω to be a (fixed) total function as it can not be arbitrary. This means that the observations $\omega(s)$ of any entity are well-defined in every abstract state s.

Web Service Executions

Given some input $i_1, \ldots, i_n$, a Web service execution induces a state transition $(\omega(s), \omega(s'))$ that can be observed by the service requester. However, not all such transitions of abstract states represent meaningful state transitions caused by a Web service execution. For a transition to faithfully represent some service execution we need to require that between the states s and s' some change can be observed by the invoker. We need to require some further constraints on the transition such that we can interpret s, s' as a possible run $W(i_1, \ldots, i_n)$ of a Web service W, as we will discuss below. We call s the pre-state of the execution and s' the post-state of the execution.

Returning to our running example we illustrate in Listing 6.6 pre- and post-states by looking at how the statements relating to a single credit card might evolve during a simple online purchase.

```
... //statments in s
instance myVisaCard memberOf CreditCard
    hasNumber hasValue 4444111122223333
    hasLimit hasValue 2000,00
...

... //statments in s'
instance myVisaCard memberOf CreditCard
    hasNumber hasValue 4444111122223333
    hasLimit hasValue 1900,00

relationInstance creditCardCharge(myVisaCard, 100, _dateTime(2007, 1, 1, 12, 19, 10))
...
```

Listing 6.6. State transition of a bank transfer Web service

Web Services

A Web service W then can be seen as a set of executions $W(i_1, \ldots, i_n)$ that can be delivered by the Web service in any given state of the world to a requester when being equipped with any kind of valid input data $i_1, \ldots, i_n$. However, in order to keep track of the input data that caused a specific execution, we need to represent a Web service in terms of a slightly richer structure than a set, namely a mapping between the provided input values $i_1, \ldots, i_n$ and the resulting execution $W(i_1, \ldots, i_n)$. This implies that we use a deterministic model for Web services here.

The corresponding Web service to our running example would be a payment service offered by a credit card company to a particular online shop that takes as input a credit card number, a expiration date and the amount to be charged. For all valid credit cards (given a sufficient initial limit) it will charge the amount requested to the card. Thus the actual Web services corresponds to a set of state transitions (and not only one), where each transition is determined by the concrete input values supplied.

Figure 6.2 illustrates the presented model. The Web service W provides three different concrete services, each of them having different pairs of input. Every single state is determined by the two components of ω - the information space and the real world. The Web service is a set of possible transitions that is denoted by a dark green area inside the abstract state space.

The model presented gives a thorough mathematical model. For the formal definitions of this model we refer to [82]. For the purpose of this book the previous intuitive description should suffice. It is important to understand that this model is defined in order to allow an unambiguous interpretation of Web service and goal descriptions, i.e., that it provides a semantic to the syntactical description within a capability. In the following we outline some basic semantic analyzes that can be performed on top of this model.

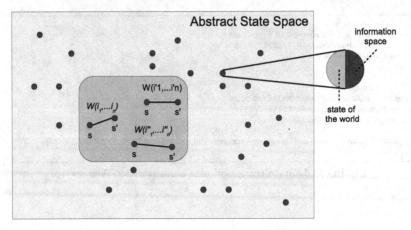

Fig. 6.2. Abstract model of Web services

```
namespace _"http://example.org/"

webService creditCardCharge
  importsOntology _"http://example.org/ontologies/commerce/Commerce"
  sharedVariables {?creditcard ,?amount}
  capability
    precondition
      definedBy
        ?amount > 0 and
        ?creditcard memberOf CreditCard
    effect
      definedBy
        creditCardCharge( ?creditcard , ?amount, ?date)
```

Listing 6.7. A non-realizable credit card payment service

6.3.2 Semantic Analysis of State-Based Web Service Descriptions

For demonstrating the suitability of the proposed model, this section shows its
beneficial application for semantic analysis of functional descriptions. Based
on our model-theoretic framework, we can carry over several semantic standard notions from mathematical logic [52, 58] that refer to formal descriptions
and are based on the model notion to our particular context in a meaningful
way.

Realizability

We can now define realizability of a description as the corresponding notion
to satisfiability in WSML ontologies. A set of formulae is satisfiable if it has
a model, i.e., if there exist an interpretation of the formulae that is true. The
very same notion can be applied to Web services. Consider Listing 6.7, which
contains the functional description of a Web service for credit card processing.

```
webService creditCardCharge
  importsOntology _"http://example.org/ontologies/commerce/Commerce"
  sharedVariables  {?creditcard ,?amount}
  capability
    precondition
      definedBy
        ?amount > 0 and
        ?creditcard [hasLimit hasValue ?limit]memberOf CreditCard and
        ?amount < ?limit.
    effect
      definedBy
        creditCardCharge( ?creditcard ,  ?amount, ?date)
```

Listing 6.8. A realizable credit card payment service

At a first glance, the given description seems to be implementable within some Web service. However, taking a closer look at the domain ontology (cf. Listing 6.3) it becomes clear that this is not the case. The ontology defines that a charge might not exceed the limit of a particular credit card. Nonetheless the pre-condition does not prevent the amount being greater the the credit card limit.

Let us assume that there is a Web service realizing this description. When considering an input binding where the amount (?amount) is greater then the limit (?creditcard[hasLimit hasValue ?limit]) then the pre-condition is satisfied and thus the post-condition should hold in the final state of the respective execution is reached. However, this is inconsistent with the domain ontology since the charge would exceed the credit card limit. This is a contradiction and shows that no Web service exist that can adhere to above descriptions for all possible input bindings. To fix the description such that it becomes realizable, we need to extend the pre-condition, as illustrated in Listing 6.8.

The example illustrates the usefulness of the notion of realizability. It provides a tool for detecting functional descriptions that contain flaws that might not be obvious to the modelers. It is shown in [82] how the problem of realizability of a Web service description $\mathcal{D} \in \mathcal{F}$ can be reduced to a well-understood problem in $\mathcal{L}$ for which algorithms already exist.

Functional Refinement

Similar to the notion of satisfiability we can look at the notion of logical entailment, which is usually defined as follows: An formula ϕ logically entails a formula ψ iff every interpretation $\mathcal{I}$ which is a model of ϕ (i.e., $\mathcal{I} \models_{\mathcal{L}} \phi$) is also a model of ψ. Substituting interpretations by Web services, formulae by functional descriptions and the satisfaction $\models_{\mathcal{L}}$ by capability satisfaction $\models_{\mathcal{F}}$. In a similar way we can define the notion of functional refinement that corresponds to the notion of logical entailment: We use $\mathcal{D}_1 \sqsubseteq \mathcal{D}_2$ to denote that description $\mathcal{D}_1$ is a functional refinement of description $\mathcal{D}_2$ in $\mathcal{A}$.

Intuitively speaking, $\mathcal{D}_1 \sqsubseteq \mathcal{D}_2$ means that $\mathcal{D}_1$ is more specific than $\mathcal{D}_2$: Every Web service (no matter which one) that provides $\mathcal{D}_1$ can also provide

```
...
precondition
  definedBy
    ...
    ?product memberOf mediaproduct#MediaProduct
    ...
effect
  definedBy
    ...
    commerce#creditCardCharge(?creditcard,?price,?date) and
    forall ?product,?entry (?products[hasEntry hasValue ?entry] and
        ?entry[hasProduct hasValue ?product] implies
        commerce#productDelivery(?product, 1, ?address,?dd)).
    ...
```

Listing 6.9. Excerpt of the mediaShoppingCapability

$\mathcal{D}_2$. In other words, $\mathcal{D}_1$ must describe some piece of functionality that always fits the requirements $\mathcal{D}_2$ as well. However, Web services that provide $\mathcal{D}_2$ do not have to satisfy $\mathcal{D}_1$ and therefore, a Web service that provides $\mathcal{D}_1$ can do something more specific than required by $\mathcal{D}_2$.

As an example, consider the excerpt of the mediaShoppingCapability in Listing 6.9. Using our formal definition we can examine another definition and check if it is a functional refinement of the previous description. Let us assume a second Web service has an identical capability, however the pre-condition is slightly broader, instead of requiring a MediaProduct the product only needs to be an instance of Product. The first Web service has a more specific pre-condition, thus every Web service fulfilling the second service automatically fulfills the first Web service.

This notion can beneficially be applied within functionality-based match-making. With the knowledge about the refinement a repository of services can be pre indexed to ease discovery at runtime.

Discovery

We can use our model for discovery through checking functional refinement by looking for Web services that guarantee certain postconditions and/or effects. For instance, let us assume that some Person wants a particular CD shipped to his home. Since a CD is a media product we can infer that he can use both Web services presented.

To conclude this chapter we briefly summarize the set-based and state-based approaches. The set-based approach has in particular the following advantages

- This modeling approach is based on a very simple and intuitive perspective of the world where everything is considered in terms of sets (or concepts)
- In opposite to other approaches we start from building a model and analyzing the intuitive understanding of a match and then try to capture the intuitive semantics of match. This results in giving the modeler more freedom to express his/her desire, e.g., through the use of intentions.

- The approach represents a general framework which does not fix the language to be used for describing goals and Web services. In particular, it allows in general description which are not possible to express using Description Logics and thus provides increased expressiveness.
- Because of the same conceptual modeling style, this approach potentially allows a seamless integration of descriptions formalized in different languages, such as present in the WSML Family of languages.

Nevertheless it has to be noted that this approach does not capture the actual relation between service input and the corresponding outputs. Thus, the semantics of a Web service is only described in a conceptual manner. In fact, this can be too coarse-grained for enabling the automation of the discovery and later execution of a service.

The state-based description of Web services a more fine grained model to describe Web service descriptions. It requires significant skills to write those descriptions, but allows to capture a great deal of the functionality of a real world Web service. Still the model has some limitations about what can be expressed or captured:

- Only finite processes can be described. A specific limitation of pre- and post-condition style descriptions is that they are based on the assumption that there will be a final state of a computation, i.e., the computation terminates. Although, this might be a valid assumption for a wide variety of Web services, it does not allow the specification of non-terminating components which nonetheless deliver meaningful functionality. An example in a technical system would be an operation system of a computer which does not terminate or a Web service that implements a clock and periodically sends a the current time to a subscribed clients.
- Statements about intermediate states. Like in common specification frameworks, our model for the semantics of Web services considers a Web service as a set of atomic state-changes, i.e., possible intermediate states during an execution of a service are invisible for an external observer and can not be referred to in a formal specifications. For planing purposes it might be relevant or useful to allow to describe services in a more detailed way, for instance as a constraint on possible execution paths. For the same reason, it is not possible to express properties which do hold during the whole execution of the service, which have been studied in Dynamic Logics in the context of throughout modalities.
- Message format and order. We do not describe interface details such as the message format or the order of messages and thus even if the model is capable of automatically determining which service does semantically match, it does not provide guarantees on the syntactic level. Those could potentially be resolved by mediators as presented for example in [106].

In this chapter we have seen two means for describing Web service functionality: set-based and state-based capabilities, and associated discovery mechanisms. In the case of set-based descriptions, discovery can be reduced to checking subsumption of concepts in an ontology (cf. Section 5.2.2). In the case of state-based descriptions, discovery can be reduced to checking logical entailment (cf. Sections 5.2.2 and 5.2.3).

A functional description is a somewhat abstract view of a Web service; it does not capture the behavior of the service. In the following chapter we describe the WSML choreography language, which allows describing such behavioral and interaction patterns.

7

Behavioral Description of Services

Functional descriptions facilitate the process of discovering Semantic Web services. As we have seen in the previous chapter, they provide a high level characterization of the underlying service by defining conditions on the input and output, as well as the state of the world before and after Web service execution. These conditions correspond to a (single) transition from the *pre-state* – the state before execution – to the *post-state* – the state after execution.

Although this is already a significant step towards automated discovery, composition and execution of Web services, more detailed descriptions are needed for the automated usage (invocation) of Web services. In fact, the typical interaction with a Web service comprises a number of steps, where each step corresponds to sending or receiving a message. Now, there are different possible interactions between a requester and a Web service. A description of all possible interactions is called the *behavioral model* of the Web service. It includes such things as the ordering of inputs and outputs and conditions governing the exchange of messages.

Behavioral models are of special significance in the context of *Business Process Integration*, which is the controlled sharing of data and business processes among connected applications and data sources within an enterprise and between trading partners [105]. Business Process Integration occurs in a number of different contexts. For example, (1) exchanging business documents, (2) integrating applications in an enterprise, and (3) establishing relations with new business partners. Behavioral models play an important role in all of these contexts, but most significantly in the latter. By checking the *compatibility* of the behavioral models of two Web services one can determine whether they can potentially interact [100, 23, 101].

Compatibility of the behavioral models of two agents (e.g., service requester and provider) implies that they can interact. However, this does not yet say how messages are sent between the agents, or how the data is formatted Specifically, when invoking a Web service it must be clear how data – that is, instances of ontological concepts and relations – are sent over the wire using, for example, XML and XML Schema. The mechanism used for encoding data as messages to be sent over the wire is called *grounding*. Before sending messages, instances of concepts and relations have to be *lowered* to XML. Conversely, when receiving messages, the enclosed XML has to be *lifted* to ontology instance data.

The behavioral model as well as the Web service grounding are found in the *behavioral description* of a Web service (cf. Section 4.1.3). Recall that in WSML a behavioral description is called a *choreography*, which can be seen as a refinement of Web service capability, exposing additional details about the Web service. In this chapter we describe the model and language for WSML choreographies, also called the *WSML choreography language*. It should be noted here that WSML also allows referring to different choreography descriptions (possibly using a different language), as described in Section 4.4.5.

The behavioral model of the WSML choreography language is based on *evolving ontologies*, where each subsequent state corresponds to a change in the instance data of an ontology. The model is inspired by evolving algebras, which are also known as Abstract State Machines [71, 24]. The behavioral model is outlined in Section 7.1.

In Section 7.2 we extend the introduction of the choreography language in Section 4.4.5 with a more detailed description of the various language constructs. We proceed with a more formal definition of the language and its semantics in Section 7.3.

As we remarked above, there is a close relationship between functional and behavioral description of the service, the latter being a refinement of the former. We describe the relationship between the functional descriptions, as described in the previous chapter, and behavioral description, as described in this chapter, in Section 7.4.

The WSML choreography language is based on the "Ontology-based Choreography of WSMO Services" [122], which was originally developed in the context of WSMO.

7.1 Behavioral Model of Choreographies

The interaction between a requester and a Web service consists of a number of *interaction steps*. These steps consist of *sequences of message exchanges* (whereby a single message exchange is normally equivalent to a single interaction step) during which the knowledge in the involved parties (i.e., the client and/or provider) is updated.

Generally, a choreography does not offer a single way on how it can be interacted with, but there are often multiple ways. Think of, for example, an online store Web service that can be used both for searching and buying products. Due to the information received by the provider from the requester, the Web service might act in different ways. For example, if a particular client has a discount voucher, this has be taken into account during the calculation of the invoice.

Deciding for one course of action (e.g., searching) or the other (e.g., selling), based on available information (e.g., input message) is called *conditional branching*: the path followed in the interaction depends on whether some condition holds. Other forms of branching typically occur during error handling procedures – for example, checking the validity of a credit card. Since we are in the Semantic Web context, in all of the above cases messages are instances of *concepts* or *relations* defined in some *ontology*. The same ontology is typically used to describe the various aspects of a Web service, including non-functional, functional, and behavioral description.

Based on the above considerations, the model underlying WSML choreographies follows the following principles:

Abstract: it hides details regarding the underly message exchange protocols and message formats

State-based: the interactions are described in the form of state transitions

Expressive: it allows describing features such as sequences of message interactions and branching

Ontology-based: ontologies are the underlying data model for message exchange

As mentioned in the introduction, the model underlying WSML choreographies is that of evolving ontologies. The state of an interaction is represented as instance information of an ontology. Transition rules govern updates of the state; such an update is a state transition.

In the following section we describe how this model is realized in the WSML choreography language.

7.2 Overview of the WSML Choreography Language

We now describe the WSML choreography language in more detail using a running example. The example illustrates a simple process of purchasing a media item from an online store. The client starts by sending a search request for the particular item. If the item is available, a confirmation is returned with details concerning the item. The client can then update the cart and finally issue an order request comprised of the item and credit card details. Once a confirmation of the transaction is sent, the client sends a shipping request with the destination address; the service returns an invoice. We show here a part of this example, namely the addition of items to a particular cart.

Recall from Chapter 4 that choreographies are part of an **interface** of a goal or Web service. See Listing 4.4 on page 51 for an example of an interface description with a choreography. Furthermore, choreographies are based on evolving ontologies, with transition rules governing state transitions. The

---

choreography buyChoreography
   annotations
      dc#title **hasValue** "Multimedia Shopping Service Choreography"
      dc#description **hasValue** "Describes the steps required for shopping multimedia items
          over this web service"
   endAnnotations

   stateSignature buyStateSignature

   transitionRules buyTransitionRules

Listing 7.1. The "Buy" choreography of the media shopping service

references to the ontologies are included in the **stateSignature**. The rules are written in a **transitionRules** block. See Listing 7.1.

The state signature declares a set of imported ontologies using the **importsOntology** keyword and a set of *modes* that are associated with concepts and/or relations. The imported ontologies contain the initial set of facts available to the choreography. The modes declare the intention of the instance data of concepts and relations, and may be of the following types:

static   meaning that the extension of the concept or relation cannot be changed; this is the default for all concepts and relations imported by the signature of the choreography,

in   meaning that the extension of the concept or relation can only be changed by the requester; a grounding mechanism for this item that implements write access for the requester must be provided,

out   meaning that the extension of the concept or relation can only be changed by the service; a grounding mechanism for this item that implements read access for the requester must be provided,

shared   meaning that the extension of the concept or relation can be changed and read by the choreography instance and the client; a grounding mechanism for this item, that implements read and write access for the requester and the service must be provided, or

controlled   meaning that the extension of the concept is changed and read only by the service.

Listing 7.2 shows part of the state signature of the buy choreography in our example. It includes the (optional) state signature identifier and a set of annotations. Following the annotations, the imported ontologies and the modes of concepts and relations are declared. In general, the state signature should at least import all the ontologies defining the concepts and relations that are assigned a mode. For conciseness, we restrict ourselves to the **in** and **out** modes in the example.

The listing shows that the AddToCart concept is assigned the **in** mode and the Cart concept is assigned to the **out** mode. Both of these concepts are defined

```
stateSignature buySignature
  annotations
    dc#title hasValue "Buy State Signature"
    dc#description hasValue "The State Signature of the buy interface for the media
            shopping service . In this case, only two types of modes are used, namely 'in'
            and 'out'. All concepts and relations that belong to these types are attached to
            a link specifying the grounding."
  endAnnotations

  importsOntology {
    _"http://example.org/ontologies/tasks/ShoppingTasks",
    _"http://example.org/ontologies/commerce/Commerce"
  }

  in
    shoptasks#AddToCart withGrounding
    _"http://example.org/webservices/shopping/mediashoppingservice#wsdl.
        interfaceMessageReference(MediaShoppingServicePortType/AddToCart/In)",

  out
    commerce#Cart withGrounding{
      _"http://example.org/webservices/shopping/mediashoppingservice#wsdl.
          interfaceMessageReference(MediaShoppingServicePortType/AddToCart/Out)",
      _"http://example.org/webservices/shopping/mediashoppingservice#wsdl.
          interfaceMessageReference(MediaShoppingServicePortType/RemoveFromCart/Out)
          "
    }
```

Listing 7.2. Excerpt from the state signature of the "Buy" choreography

in the ShoppingTasks and Commerce ontologies, respectively; observe that both ontologies are imported in the state signature. Each mode declaration of type **in** must have *exactly* one grounding information. Mode declarations of type **out** can have multiple grounding entries but must have at least one. Note that the grounding is not necessarily a direct mapping to some XML element; it might refer to any communication protocol. In the example, the AddToCart concept is linked to the input message of the WSDL operation AddToCart. The concept Cart is however attached to the output message of two operations, namely, AddToCart and RemoveFromCart. This means that the Cart object can be returned by two different operations.

Transition rules define the behavior of a choreography. Listing 7.3 shows an example of a transition rule. This transition rule fires when an instance of type AddToCart is available (the condition in the **with** part). Due to the fact that the mode of AddToCart is **in**, such an instance becoming available corresponds to receiving a message from the requester. The update part of this transition rule defines also an **if** rule. It checks whether the cart exists in the state. If this is not the case, the cart is added to the state and the updates that follow from the outer **forall** rule are performed. In this case, the updates take the form of an **add**, meaning that facts are added to the state.

The difference between an **if** and a **forall** rule, is that updates (over the bound variables) in the latter are performed in parallel. The other type of transition rule is the **choose** rule, whereby one variable binding out of all

```
forall  ?addToCart
  with
    (
      ?addToCart[
        hasCartId hasValue ?cartId ,
        hasLineItem hasValue ?lineItem
      ] memberOf shoptasks#AddToCart
      and ?lineItem memberOf commerce#LineItem
    )
  do
    if (naf ( exists  ?cart
          ( ?cart [
              hasId hasValue ?cartId
            ] memberOf commerce#Cart
          )
        )
      )
    do
      add(?cart[hasId hasValue ?cartId] memberOf commerce#Cart)
    endIf
    add(?cart[hasLineItem hasValue ?lineItem ])
endForall
```

Listing 7.3. Excerpt from the transition rules of the "Buy" choreography

possible bindings is chosen in a non-deterministic fashion. Furthermore, the
other two forms of updates are **delete** and **update**. The former, deletes facts
from the state and the latter updates old values of facts to new ones. The
update rule is a combination of both the **add** and **delete** rules.

In the following chapter we formally define WSML choreographies and their
semantics.

7.3 Formalizing WSML Choreographies

The semantics of a choreography is defined in terms of the set of possible
valid *choreography runs* that are associated with a choreography, given an
initial state. In this section we introduce the semantic notions defined by the
WSML choreography language. We will first give an intuitive description of
the notions used in the semantics definition, as well as the abstract syntax
for WSML choreographies, in Section 7.3.1. We proceed with the definition of
the semantics in Section 7.3.2.

7.3.1 Choreography Language Definition

At the heart of behavioral descriptions are ontologies. They define the basic
set of facts that are accessible by the choreography, the concepts and relations
used by the choreography, and additional constraints that must be maintained
during a choreography run. We denote the set of ontologies imported by a
choreography with **O**. The variant of **O** is the highest variant among the
variants of the ontologies in **O**.

```
instance queen_platinum memberOf mediaproduct#MediaProduct
    hasTitle hasValue "The Platinum Collection — Greatest Hits I, II & III"
    hasContributor hasValue queen
    hasId hasValue "B00004Z3AV"
    hasPrice hasValue 30.00
    hasRating hasValue 5

instance queen memberOf media#Artist
    hasStageName hasValue "Queen"
    contributorOf hasValue queen_platinum
```

Listing 7.4. Example of a choreography state

A *State* is a set of facts. A fact is simply a WSML ground atomic formula, that is, a formula with no variables. Typically these facts are instances of WSML concepts such as those in Listing 7.4. Of course, this example shows a limited number of facts. The ontologies would normally define many facts which can then be read and updated during the execution of the choreography. Note that these facts are not necessarily located in a WSML ontology, but may originate from a (corporate) database.

When one (or more) transition rule(s) fire(s), their execution typically performs updates on the current state, resulting in a new state. Formally, these updates are contained in an *update set*. An update set contains two distinct sets of updates: a set of *add* updates and a set of *delete* updates. The former contains is the set of facts that are to be added to the current state; the latter contains the set of facts that are to be removed from the current state. The two sets are required to be disjoint; i.e., the same fact may not be added and deleted at the same time. If the situation does occur, the update is said to be *inconsistent* and the choreography execution is terminated.

An *application* of an update set to a state yields the subsequent state. This new state must be consistent with the imported ontologies **O**; otherwise, the choreography execution is terminated. Update sets are inductively associated with a choreography.

A *choreography run* is defined as a sequence of states resulting from updates due to the transition rules. Each state must follow from the previous state and the application of the transition rules, which in turn depends on the imported ontologies. A run is *terminated* if one or more of the following situations occur:

- a state resulting from an update is not consistent with the imported ontologies,
- the next state is the same as the current state – in other words, the update set is empty, or
- an update set is inconsistent.

A choreography run is said to be *valid* if it is terminated and for each state in the run the following hold:

- each state is consistent with the imported ontologies
- the current state is not equal to the previous state,and
- for each state there is a consistent associated update set that leads to the next state.

The *terminating state* in a valid terminated choreography run is the last state in the run. A particular state is *reachable* in some choreography if it occurs in some valid run. Observe that the start state is always reachable as long as it is consistent.

One might be interested in verifying whether particular facts result from some choreography run or from all choreography runs, or whether particular facts do not change during a run; the latter are called *invariants*.

If there exists a choreography run with a particular start state that is valid for some choreography and also valid for another choreography, then the former choreography is said to be subsumed by the latter. Similarly, a choreography is always subsumed by another choreography if for every possible state in a choreography run with some start state is valid for both choreographies.

A choreography is said to be *consistent* if there exists at least one valid run for some consistent start state of the choreography. It is said to be *always consistent* if there exists a valid choreography run for every consistent start state of the choreography.

The semantics of a WSML choreography case is defined in terms of the WSML abstract syntax. In order to make this section self contained, we review the necessary elements in the syntax. We consider only those aspects of the definition relevant to the review of the semantics in the next section. We refer the reader to [29] for a complete definition of the WSML abstract syntax.

We start with the definition of a *WSML Choreography*, which, for our purposes, is a tuple $\langle$signature, **rule**$\rangle_{chor}$, where

- signature is a *WSML state signature*, and
- **rule** is a set of *WSML transition rules*.

A WSML choreography $\langle$signature, **rule**$\rangle$ conforms with WSML-Core (resp., Flight or Rule) if for every logical expression in every rule in **rule** holds that it does not contain the symbols $\neg$, $\supset$, and $\equiv$.[1] A WSML Choreography conforms with WSML-DL if for every logical expression in every rule in **rule** holds that it contains one free variable and its variable graph is tree-shaped.[2] Any WSML choreography conforms with WSML-Full.

For our purposes, a *WSML State Signature* is a tuple $\langle$**ontID, mode**$\rangle$, where

- **O** is a set of imported ontologies, which may be WSML, RDFS, or OWL DL ontologies and

---

[1] In fact, every such logical expression is an (FOL) query [1].

[2] In fact, every such logical expression is a tree-shaped query [39].

```
transitionRules  buyTransitions
   forall  ?search
     with
       ( ?search [
          hasTitle  hasValue  ?title
       ] memberOf shoptasks#SearchCatalog
       and exists  ?item  (
            ?item memberOf mediaproduct#MediaProduct and(
              ?item [ hasTitle  hasValue  ?title ]
       )  ) )
     do
        add( ?item memberOf mediaproduct#MediaProduct)
        delete( ?search memberOf shoptasks#SearchCatalog)
   endForall
```

Listing 7.5. A simple transition rule for searching media products

- **mode** is a set of *modes*.

The set of imported ontologies **O** is also the set of imported ontologies of the containing choreography. A *mode* is either a *concept mode* of the form ⟨type, conceptID, groundingID⟩ or *relation mode* of the form ⟨type, relationID, groundingID⟩, where

- type is one of the symbols static, in, out, shared, and controlled,
- conceptID (resp., relationID) is a concept (resp., relation) identifier, and
- groundingID is a set of grounding identifiers.

Finally, a *WSML Transition Rule* is one of:

- an *if-then rule* ⟨logExp, **rule**⟩$_{if}$,
- a *forall rule* ⟨**varID**, logExp, **rule**⟩$_{forall}$,
- a *choose rule* ⟨**varID**, logExp, **rule**⟩$_{choose}$,
- a *piped rule* ⟨**rule**⟩,
- an *add rule* ⟨α⟩$_{add}$, or
- a *delete rule* ⟨α⟩$_{delete}$,

where logExp is a WSML logical expression (cf. Section 4.4.4 and Chapter 5) such that the set of free variables in logExp correspond with **varID**; **rule** is a nonempty set of *WSML transition rules*; **varID** is a set of variable identifiers; and α is a *WSML fact* (i.e., a ground atomic formula).

7.3.2 Semantics of WSML Choreographies

This section reviews the semantics of WSML choreographies. As a running example, we will use the transition rule in Listing 7.5 and a subset of the initial set of facts available to the choreography in Listing 7.6.

```
instance queen_platinum memberOf mediaproduct#MediaProduct
    hasTitle hasValue "The Platinum Collection – Greatest Hits I, II & III"
    hasContributor hasValue queen
    hasId hasValue "B00004Z3AV"
    hasPrice hasValue 30.00
    hasRating hasValue 5

instance bohemian_rhapsody memberOf mediaproduct#MediaProduct
    hasTitle hasValue "Bohemian Rhapsody"
    hasContributor hasValue queen
    hasId hasValue "B0013AEOSU"
    hasPrice hasValue 12.00
    hasRating hasValue 5

instance queen memberOf media#Artist
    hasStageName hasValue "Queen"
    contributorOf hasValue {queen_platinum, bohemian_rhapsody}
```

Listing 7.6. Examples of facts available to the choreography

State

A *state* S of a WSML choreography C is defined as a set of facts, where a fact is a ground atomic formula. A state S is said to be consistent with a set of ontologies $\mathbf{O}$ iff $\mathbf{O} \cup S$ is satisfiable in the WSML variant of $\mathbf{O}$.

Since a state is a set of facts, any collection of WSML instances (e.g., Listing 7.4) can be seen as the description of a state.

Update Set

An update set $\mathcal{U}$ is a tuple $\mathcal{U} = \langle \mathbf{A}, \mathbf{D} \rangle$ where the add set $\mathbf{A}$ and the delete set $\mathbf{D}$ are sets of ground atoms in the variant of $\mathbf{O}$. An update set $\mathcal{U} = \langle \mathbf{A}, \mathbf{D} \rangle$ is *consistent* if $\mathbf{A} \cap \mathbf{D} = \emptyset$.

An *application* of an update set $\mathcal{U} = \langle \mathbf{A}, \mathbf{D} \rangle$ to a state S, denoted $S^{\mathcal{U}}$, is defined as: $S^{\mathcal{U}} = \mathbf{A} \cup S \setminus \mathbf{D}$. An update set $\mathcal{U}$ is consistent with the state S, with respect to a set of ontologies $\mathcal{O}$, if $\mathcal{U}$ is consistent and $S^{\mathcal{U}}$ is consistent with $\mathcal{O}$.

Example 7.1. Let us consider as an example the search transition rule in Listing 7.5 and an initial state S_0 which contains the facts in Listing 7.6 and:

$$myRequest[hasTitle \text{ hv } \text{``Bohemian Rhapsody''}] : SearchCatalog$$

which is a search request representing a title search for "Bohemian Rhapsody".

The initial state contains the facts in the background ontology and the search request. Note that the latter concept is read by the choreography through the grounding mechanism (cf. the state signature in Listing 7.2). When the request is read, it becomes part of the state. The formal model hides these communication details.

The update set of the transition rule adds the respective media products that match the title "Bohemian Rhapsody" and deletes the search catalogue

$$\pi_C(\mathbf{rule}, S) = \bigcup_{r \in \mathbf{rule}} \pi_C(\mathbf{rule}, S),$$

$$\pi_C(\langle \alpha \rangle_{add}, S) = \langle \{\alpha\}, \emptyset \rangle,$$

$$\pi_C(\langle \alpha \rangle_{delete}, S) = \langle \emptyset, \{\alpha\} \rangle,$$

$$\pi_C(\langle \mathrm{logExp}, \mathbf{rule} \rangle_{if}, S) = \begin{cases} \pi_C(\mathbf{rule}, S) & \mathbf{O} \cup S \models_x \mathrm{logExp}, \\ \emptyset & \text{otherwise}, \end{cases}$$

$$\pi_C(\langle \mathbf{varID}, \mathrm{logExp}, \mathbf{rule} \rangle_{forall}, S) = \begin{array}{l} \pi_C(\bigcup\{\mathbf{rule}\theta | \theta \text{ is a mapping from the} \\ \text{variables in } \mathbf{varID} \text{ to ground terms and} \\ \mathbf{O} \cup S \models \mathrm{logExp}\theta\}, S), \end{array}$$

$$\pi_C(\langle \mathbf{varID}, \mathrm{logExp}, \mathbf{rule} \rangle_{choose}, S) = \begin{cases} \pi_C(\mathbf{rule}\theta, S) & \begin{array}{l} \theta \text{ is a mapping from} \\ \text{the variables in } \mathbf{varID} \\ \text{to ground terms and} \\ \mathbf{O} \cup S \models \mathrm{logExp}\theta, \end{array} \\ \emptyset & \text{otherwise}, \end{cases}$$

where $\langle \mathbf{A}_1, \mathbf{D}_1 \rangle \cup \langle \mathbf{A}_2, \mathbf{D}_2 \rangle = \langle \mathbf{A}_1 \cup \mathbf{A}_2, \mathbf{D}_1 \cup \mathbf{D}_2 \rangle$, α is an atomic formula, and $\models$ is the entailment relation of the WSML variant under consideration.

Table 7.1. Definition of associated update sets

request. Although the media products already exist in the state, they are explicitly added by the rule in order for communication with the client of the choreography to take place. The *add* part of the update set consists of one fact:

$$\langle bohemian\_rhapsody : MediaProduct \rangle_{add}$$

The *delete* part likewise consists of one fact:

$$\langle myRequest : SearchCatalog \rangle_{delete}$$

Applying the update set to the state means that the set of facts in the *add* set are added to the state (unless they already exist) and the set of facts in the *delete* set are removed from the state. The resulting state contains the facts in Listing 7.6 and:

$$\langle bohemian\_rhapsody : MediaProduct \rangle$$

The update set depicted in the example is associated with the choreography and the initial state S_0. We now define formally the notion of associated update set.

An update set $\mathcal{U}$ is *associated* with a choreography $C = \langle \mathbf{O}, \text{signature}, \mathbf{rule} \rangle$ and a state S if $\mathcal{U} = \pi_C(\mathbf{rule}, S)$, where π_C is a mapping from sets of transition rules and states to update sets as defined in Table 7.1.

Choreography Run

Let $C = \langle \mathbf{O}, \text{signature}, \mathbf{rule} \rangle$ be a choreography, let S be a state, and let $\mathcal{U}$ be an update set. A *choreography run* is a sequence of states $R = \langle S_0, \dots, S_n \rangle$, with $n \geq 0$. A state S is *reachable* in R if $S = S_i$ for some $0 \leq i \leq n$. A choreography run $R = \langle S_0, \dots, S_n \rangle$ is *terminated* if there is an update set $\mathcal{U}$ associated with C and S_n such that either

- $S_n^{\mathcal{U}}$ is not consistent with $\mathbf{O}$ or
- $S_n^{\mathcal{U}} = S_n$

In this case S_n is called the terminating state of R.

Given a consistent start state S_0, a choreography run $R = \langle S_0, \dots, S_n \rangle$ is *valid* for a choreography C if S_0 is consistent with $\mathbf{O}$, R is terminated, and for each S_i, with $1 \leq i \leq n$, holds that:

- S_i is consistent with $\mathbf{O}$,
- $S_{i-1} \neq S_i$, and
- there is a consistent update set $\mathcal{U}$ that is associated with C and S_{i-1} such that $S_i = S_{i-1}^{\mathcal{U}}$.

Given a choreography C and a start state S_0, a state S_i is *terminating* if there is a valid choreography run $R = \langle S_0, \dots, S_i \rangle$ for C; S_i is *reachable* if there is a valid choreography run R for C such that S is reachable in R.

Atomic Formulas

An atomic formula α is *possible* (respectively, *guaranteed*) in C, given a start state S, if $\alpha \in S_i$ for some (respectively, every) terminating state S_i.

An atomic formula α is *always possible* (respectively, *always guaranteed*) in C if for every possible starte state S holds that $\alpha \in S_i$ for some (respectively, every) terminating state S_i.

Considering Example 7.1, the media product fact is guaranteed if the start state contains the *SearchCatalog* instance as depicted in the example.

Subsumed Choreographes

A choreography C_1 is *subsumed* by a choreography C_2, *relative to a start state* S_0, if every choreography run R with start state S_0 that is valid for C_1 is also valid for C_2. A choreography C_1 is *always subsumed by* a choreography C_2, if for every possible state S_i holds that every choreography run R with start state S_i that is valid for C_1 is also valid for C_2.

As an example, consider the transition rule in Listing 7.5 to be a separate choreography C_1, say a "Search Choreography". The same transition rule is also part of a larger choreography "Buy Choreography". We will call this choreography C_2. Considering the start state S_0 in Example 7.1, it is easy to verify that every choreography run for C_1 starting with S_0 is a valid run for

C_2, since the updates and the next state, determined by the search rule will be the same for both. However, subsumption does not hold in the converse direction: C_2 might not terminate after the search rule is applied since other transition rules might fire on the resulting set. Hence, C_1 is subsumed by C_2.

Consistent Choreographies

A choreography C is *consistent* given a state S_0 if there exists a valid run $R = \langle S_0, \ldots, S_n \rangle$ for C. C is *always consistent* if for any consistent state S, C is consistent given S.

Considering the transition rule in Listing 7.5 to be a single choreography, then it is easy to verify that the choreography is consistent given the start state S_0 from Example 7.1.

7.4 Relating Functional and Behavioral Descriptions

Although functional and behavioral descriptions are intended to be used for different purposes, they have some similarities and relationships. Recall that, in fact, the behavioral description is meant to be a refinement of a functional description. On the one hand, functional descriptions offer a high-level description of what the Web service accepts as inputs, what outputs it provides, and what real-world effects it brings about. On the other hand, a behavioral description defines the detailed direction, leading from the various inputs provided that various stages, to the output. In fact, the choreography describes the intermediate states, which are between the initial and final states of the service, thereby providing a more fine-grained description the service, from the point of view of interaction with the requester. It also provides information about communication protocols that have to be enacted during the execution of the service.

Note that choreographies, in contrast to capabilities, do not describe aspects beyond the informational world, i.e., the service inputs and outputs.

Given that functional and behavioral descriptions are meant for different purposes, it is natural that they rely on different semantics. Consequently, the formal relationship between capabilities and choreographies is at times hard, and sometimes impossible to define. Still, they need to be coherent. For example, if the functional description says that a particular object is produced by the service, then it must be ensured that the behavioral description arrives to a state where this object is actually returned by the Web service. This section describes these types of relationships and defines – where possible – mappings between the semantic notions in the functional and behavioral descriptions.

WSML allows using choreography languages other than the WSML choreography language. In such cases, it is up to the modeler to define the relationship between the model of the choreography language under consideration and WSML capabilities.

Recall the distinction between *set-based* and *state-based* capabilities. In the set-theoretic approach, a capability is defined as a set of elements; such a set is represented as a concept in a task ontology. The degree of match between the requester and the service is determined by how many of these elements they have in common and on their intentions (see Section 6.2). In the state-based approach, a capability describes simple state transitions between the pre- and post-state of the Web service; intermediate states are not considered.

7.4.1 Relationship with Set-based Capabilities

For functional descriptions based on the set-based approach, there exists little relationship with the behavioral model. One can argue that the elements that a web service can provide correspond to those elements that are marked as *shared* and *out* in the state signature of the choreography. More precisely, the union of all the facts that are added in a state during a choreography run should be a subset or equal to the set of concepts provided by the Web service. The choreography run is assumed to be valid.

Let F^{set} be a functional description (a capability) of a Web service W with a set-based semantics; let W^{set} be the set of all elements of functionality that F^{set} can provide – that is, $I_{F^{set}} = \forall$ (cf. Table 6.1 on page 104): given a valid choreography run $R = \langle S_0, \ldots, S_n \rangle$ and a set of *add* sets $\bigcup \mathbf{A}_{S_i}$, a choreography C subsumes F^{set} (denoted $C \subseteq F^{set}$) if $W^{set} \subseteq \bigcup \mathbf{A}_{S_i}$.

Although this is a limited relationship, it still helps to ensure to have coherent functional and behavioral descriptions.

7.4.2 Relationship with State-Based Capabilities

The state-based approach to capability description is closer in spirit to the behavioral model of WSML choreographies. Before describing this relationship in detail, a comment about the information space and the real world is in order.

Recall that in the state-based approach for functional descriptions (Section 6.3), a functional description is defined in terms of Abstract State Spaces. Each state in such a space comprises two main elements, namely the state of the *information space* and the state of the *real world*. In terms of a capability description, the information space is described using pre- and post-conditions and the state of the real world using assumptions and effects. The goal of behavioral descriptions is to describe the information exchange between the requester and provider. As such, real world effects are not considered in choreography descriptions. Therefore, when talking about the relationship to functional descriptions, we consider only the information space.

For our purposes, a functional description F^{state} is that there $F^{state} = (pre, post)$, where pre is the pre-condition and $post$ is the post-condition. Recall that pre is required to be satisfied by any pre-state s of the service and $post$ is required to be satisfied by any post-state s'.

One might argue that the pre-state s of a functional description F^{state} should be equivalent to the initial state S_0 of a choreography run R. Similarly, one can argue that the post-state s' of F^{state} and the final state S_n of R are equivalent. This is, however, not a realistic requirement due to the following:

1. It is assumed in functional descriptions that all input data is available prior to execution of the service. In fact, an execution is defined as $W(i_1, \ldots, i_n)$ where i_j is an input. Although the state signature of the choreography defines all possible inputs that it can handle, it is generally the case that these are received at different points in time during the execution, i.e., in different intermediate states of the choreography run. The same argument applies for the outputs.
2. A goal or a Web service includes at most one functional description, but may include several behavioral descriptions.

All that said, there is an obvious correspondence between concepts and relations used in capabilities and choreographies, on the signature level. Namely, all concepts and relations used in the pre- and post-conditions of the capability should occur in the state signature of at least one of the choreographies of the goal or Web service. Still, different types of relationships can be semi-formally defined.

As we have argued above, it is not realistic to impose strict requirements on the relationship between the functional and the behavioral description of a goal or service. Nonetheless, there are certain notions of correspondence potentially useful to authors of functional and behavioral descriptions. We describe some of these notions in the following. We are concerned with correspondence between the pre- and post-state of a capability with states in a choreography.

In what follows, we will consider the relationships between the pre-/post-state(s) of the functional description and the initial/final state(s) of the behavioral description, respectively. The following notation is used in the remainder of this section:

- A state-based functional description F^{state} is defined as $F^{state} = (pre, post)$, where pre satisfies any pre-state s and $post$ satisfies any post-state s', given the pre-state s. We refer to such a pair (s, s') as a *capability execution*.
- A valid run R of a choreography C is a sequence of states $R = \langle S_0, \ldots, S_n \rangle$, where S_0 and S_n denote the initial and final state of R, respectively.

We assume in the remainder that every choreography run under consideration is valid.

We proceed with definitions of three notions of *fulfillment*: if a choreography fulfills a capability, it is a refinement of that capability.

Partial Fulfillment

We first consider the case where the initial and final states of the choreography partially model the pre- and post-state of the functional description respectively. With *partial* we mean that there exists some valid run $R = \langle S_0, \ldots, S_n \rangle$ of the choreography C such that the initial state satisfies the precondition and the final state satisfies the postcondition. That is, at least one possible conversation leads to achieving the functionality described in the capability.

Recall that a state in a choreography is a set of ground atomic formulas and the pre- and post-condition *pre* and *post* are formulas with free variables. A choreography C *partially fulfills* a capability F^{state} if there is *some* valid run $R = \langle S_0, \ldots, S_n \rangle$ of C and some ground variable substitution θ such that $\mathbf{O} \cup S_0 \models pre\theta$ and $\mathbf{O} \cup S_n \models post\theta$, where $\models$ is the entailment relation of the variant of $\mathbf{O}$.

Complete Fulfillment

A choreography *completely* fulfills a capability if whenever the start state satisfies the precondition, the end states satisfies the post-conditions. That is, every possible conversation that meets the initial requirements leads to achieving the functionality described in the capability.

A choreography C *completely fulfills* a capability F^{state} if it partially fulfills F^{state} and for *every* valid run $R = \langle S_0, \ldots, S_n \rangle$ of C such that there is some ground variable substitution θ and $\mathbf{O} \cup S_0 \models pre\theta$, $\mathbf{O} \cup S_n \models post\theta$, where $\models$ is the entailment relation of the variant of $\mathbf{O}$.

The mentioned notions of fulfillment can be used during the development of choreography and capability descriptions, in order to ensure coherence of the goal or Web service description.

In this chapter we have defined the behavioral model for WSML choreographies. This model provides a flexible way to describe transitions between states during execution and also provides means to link to communication protocols such that the interaction between the requester and the provider can be enacted. Ontologies are directly supported and handled by the model – a pre-requisite for modeling Semantic Web services. The relationship between the behavioral and functional models have also been defined – both with the set-based and state-based approaches.

The choreography language can be used directly in goal and Web service descriptions since the entailment notions used to define the semantics of the language are directly dependent on the particular WSML variant that is used.

Part III

Enabling Technologies for WSML

8

Reasoning with WSML

In computer science, *reasoning* is commonly understood as the process of inferring "new" (i.e., not *explicitly* stated) information about some domain of discourse from a given (formal) model of that domain. This form of reasoning is usually called deductive reasoning.

A prominent example is the following: suppose we know that Socrates is a human being, and that any human being is mortal. Then we can conclude (or deduce) by logical reasoning that Socrates must be mortal. The first two statements represent a simple model of a domain (i.e., humankind). The conclusion that we derive is not part of the model itself, but instead knowledge about the domain that is only implicitly reflected in the model.

Reasoning therefore enables us to act intelligently in the following sense: given an adequate and sufficiently rich model of a domain which is not known to us, we can infer anything that we could ever observe in the domain by reasoning over the explicitly given knowledge about the domain (i.e., the model). Therefore, we are able to act in the domain, as if we would know the domain already. The *mechanization of reasoning* allows computers eventually to act in arbitrary, unknown domains in an informed manner, i.e., as if they would know and understand the domain. Instead of saying that reasoning makes computers intelligent, we prefer a more modest view and summarize that reasoning allows computers to be more *flexible*, if they face situations which are not covered literally in the control program they follow, i.e., there is no instruction matching exactly the observations of the agent.

Using a formal language for the modeling of the domain (and hence formal models) instead of informal languages and models is the key to the mechanization of reasoning. The certainly most prominent examples for formal description languages in computer science are *logics*, e.g., propositional logics, first-order logics, and modal logics [52, 58, 21]. They are usually equipped with well-understood reasoning algorithms.

WSML is a formal language specifically tailored towards a *specific* domain: the description of semantic aspects of Web services. The mechanization of reasoning with WSML therefore enables (computerized) agents to discover, invoke and execute services in an automated fashion. Thereby, it supports humans dealing with large-scale, open, and continually changing service-oriented architectures by automation of often performed, tedious, and work-intensive subtasks. Such subtask might be to discover currently available Web services that are able to achieve a certain client goal, to automatically compose a complex Web service from a set of simpler Web services which are known to a Web service repository, or to check if two or more Web services can successfully interact with each other (given knowledge about their behavior or communication model).

WSML allows describing the main conceptual components identified in WSMO, i.e., ontologies, Web services, goals, and mediators, in a formal way. Reasoning methods need to be developed for any of these elements and a variety of reasoning tasks.

In this chapter we will mainly focus on specific component in the conceptual model of WSML, namely ontologies. We discuss ontology reasoning and our enabling technologies in detail. Ontology reasoning is especially interesting because of its fundamental role in the WSML architecture: any other conceptual element makes use of ontologies to capture relevant (static) background knowledge. Reasoning with the respective descriptions therefore requires always support for ontology reasoning. Reasoning with formal description of the other conceptual elements (e.g., functional description of Web services) can sometimes even be completely reduced to ontology reasoning (See Chapter 6 and [82, 83, 12]).

The chapter is structured as follows: we discuss ontology reasoning in Section 8.1. We describe a generic framework enabling ontology reasoning in WSML in Section 8.2. The generic framework is then instantiated and considered in detail for the main ontology languages in WSML which are of practical interest, namely for rule-based WSML in Section 8.3 and for DL-based WSML in Section 8.4.

8.1 Ontology Reasoning

Ontologies [55] provide a static perspective on a world or domain under consideration. They identify the key concepts and entities within a domain, their features and their interrelation, but they are not concerned with how the domain changes.

Knowledge-based systems usually distinguish two levels of domain knowledge: factual (or assertional) knowledge describing a specific situation (such as all products that are stored at present in a warehouse), as well as schematic (or terminological) knowledge which applies not only to a specific situation and entity in the domain, but more generally to any situation that we can observe in the domain. Schematic knowledge therefore reflect general knowledge about our perception of the domain and is often expressed in terms of if-then rules, e.g., if some entity in the domain is known to be a parent of a human being, then it is also known to be a human being. Using an analogy with database systems, terminological knowledge corresponds to the database schema, whereas the assertional knowledge corresponds to a database (state). Schematic knowledge in a knowledge base (or ontology) is sometimes referred to as a so-called TBox (terminological box), whereas assertional part of a knowledge based is sometimes called an ABox.

The situation is illustrated in Figure 8.1. Ontologies capture domain models and represent them formally. The ontologies form altogether a knowledge base. Ontologies are formulated in terms of a ontology (or knowledge representation) language. A reasoning component serves for client applications as a generic interpreter of the formally represented domain models. These client applications therefore can exploit the power of knowledge and become more flexible than hard-wired solutions. In particular, the ontology can be changed without affecting the reasoning component at any point in time.

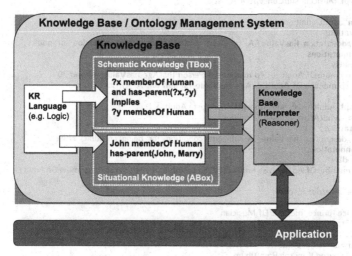

Fig. 8.1. A schematic view of knowledge-based systems

In principle, ontologies can represent both kinds of knowledge. However, they are most often used represent terminological knowledge and are enriched with situational knowledge by applications on demand, e.g., from specific datasources. This allows to reuse ontologies across various applications.

Ontology reasoning can therefore be used for two distinct purposes: on the one hand, it can be used to analyze and inspect the terminological part of an ontology (e.g., to derive schematic knowledge about the domain or to find modeling errors). On the other hand, ontology reasoning can also be used by an agent to inspect a specific situation it has to face (in regard of a domain model and schematic knowledge). The latter is similar to querying a database, whereby the terminological background knowledge is also taken into account when computing the answers to the query.

```
wsmlVariant _"http://www.wsmo.org/wsml/wsml-syntax/wsml-flight"

namespace { _"http://example.org/ontologies/Media#",
    xsd _"http://www.w3.org/2001/XMLSchema#",
    foaf _"http://xmlns.com/foaf/0.1/",
    wsml _"http://www.wsmo.org/wsml/wsml-syntax#" }

ontology _"http://example.org/ontologies/Media"
    importsOntology { _"http://xmlns.com/foaf/0.1/" }

    // The schema-level part ...

    concept MediaItem
        hasTitle ofType (1 *) xsd#string
        hasContributor impliesType (1 *) Artist

    concept Artist subConceptOf foaf#Person
        hasStageName ofType xsd#string
        contributorOf inverseOf(hasContributor) impliesType MediaItem

    concept CD subConceptOf MediaItem
    concept Musician subConceptOf Artist

    axiom adultDefinition
    annotations
        dc#description hasValue "A sufficient and necessary characterization of adults."
    endAnnotations
    definedBy
        ?p memberOf Adult :- ?p memberOf Person [hasAge hasValue ?a] and 20 < ?a.
        !- ?p memberOf Adult[hasAge hasValue ?a] and naf 20 < ?a.

    concept AdultArtist subConceptOf { Artist, Adult }
    axiom adultArtistSufficientCondition
    annotations
        dc#description hasValue "A suffcient condition for being an adult artist."
    endAnnotations
    definedBy
        ?p memberOf AdultArtist impliedBy (?p memberOf Artist and ?p memberOf Adult).

    // The assertional part ...

    instance prince memberOf Musician
        hasStageName hasValue "Prince"
        hasStageName hasValue "The Artist Formerly Known As Prince"
        foaf#name hasValue "Prince Rogers Nelson"
        contributorOf purpleRainAlbum
        hasAge hasValue 50
```

Listing 8.1. Fragment of a WSML ontology

In this chapter we will use the WSML ontology fragment shown in Figure 8.1 as a running example. One can observe that this ontology represents schema-level knowledge as well as assertional knowledge describing specific instances which are known along with their specific properties.

Reasoning over this ontology for instance allows to reveal the following implicit knowledge about the domain:

Since prince is known to be a Musician, which are known to be Artists, prince must be an instance of Artists. Similarly, we can infer further that he must be a Person too. Further, given that his age is 50, we can conclude from the first rule defined in the axiom adultDefinition, that prince is also an Adult. Hence, from axiom we can eventually infer that prince must be an AdultArtist. Hence, a query for all instances in the ontology which are known to be AdultArtists will return the instance prince eventually. From the definition of the attribute contributorOf we can derive furthermore that purpleRainAlbum is a MediaItem without having that fact explicitly mentioned.

8.2 Enabling Ontology Reasoning with WSML

WSML is a family of formal languages to describe the various elements of the WSMO conceptual model on Semantic Web services semantically and to capture the relevant aspects characterizing these elements within a specific application in a precise and well-defined way. Section 4.3 showed that WSML can be seen as a convenient uniform surface syntax to well-known knowledge representation formalisms:

- The rule-based WSML Variants (i.e., WSML-Core, WSML-Flight, and WSML-Rule) are based on the popular rule-based knowledge representation formalism investigated in the context of Logic Programming [96] and Deductive Databases [135, 136, 42], namely Datalog [1] and its various extensions.
- WSML-DL is based on a restricted subset of First-order Logic [52] which became popular during the last two decades and form the basis of other ontology languages for the Semantic Web, in particular OWL. These fragment are called Description Logics [11]. WSML-DL corresponds essentially to the expressive Description Logic $\mathcal{SHIQ}(\mathbf{D})$.

There are two extreme cases in the WSML family of languages as shown in Figure 4.3: WSML-Core can be understood conceptually as forming the intersection between these two different knowledge representation paradigms. It constitutes a *minimal* interoperation layer between both paradigms. WSML-Full on the other hand unifies both knowledge representation paradigm eventually. It provides a very expressive knowledge representation language and constitutes a *maximal* interoperation layer between both paradigms.

Since both paradigms underlying the WSML family of languages have been well-studied during the last decades, for both paradigms a wealth of algorithms has been developed to perform reasoning. Algorithms usually target at a specific reasoning task, such as query answering, checking subsumption relations between concepts, or consistency checking of ontologies.

Often they are limited to solve such a specific reasoning task only and can not necessarily be used to solve different reasoning task. Even if an algorithm can be reused in principle to solve a specific reasoning task different from the one the algorithm originally has been designed for, the result might turn out to be very inefficient and a specialized algorithm is needed to solve the reasoning task demanded by an application.

Description Logic research for instance focussed for a long while mainly on reasoning with terminologies (often called TBoxes) or data schemata. The developed algorithms were designed to perform consistency checks for terminologies very efficiently and can solve a number of terminological reasoning tasks efficiently. For other tasks such as query answering over ontologies, these systems turned out to be applicable in principle but resulted in non-efficient implementations which were not really suitable for practical applications. This triggered more recently some dedicated research activities on more efficient query answering algorithms for Description Logic knowledge bases. For Logic Programming and Deductive Database system on the other hand, implementations focussed mainly on data-intensive instance-level reasoning and not so much on schema-level reasoning. Consequently, these systems can solve query answering with data-intensive knowledge bases efficiently. However, these systems are often inadequate for performing schema-level reasoning.

Logic Programming, Deductive Database, Description Logic and First-order Logic research provided a wealth of implementations for the investigated reasoning algorithms. Each such implementations are usually complex software system themselves. They include typically sophisticated optimizations developed over years and consumed a substantial amount of development work.

Based on these observations, i.e., (i) that WSML provides a convenient uniform surface language for modelers, (ii) that numerous sophisticated implementations for various reasoning tasks for the knowledge representation paradigms underlying the different WSML variants already exist, and (iii) that it is impossible to design and implement a generic reasoning algorithm that can solve all kinds of reasoning tasks efficiently for any of the various WSML language variants, the following two-phased approach to enable ontology reasoning with WSML has been chosen:

- In a first step, a WSML ontology (and requested reasoning task in regard of the ontology) is translated into an abstract representation of the problem in the knowledge representation paradigm underlying the given ontology, e.g., a query answering request over a specific WSML-Core ontology is translated into a Datalog program and a Datalog query over this program. A detailed discussion for rule-based WSML variants can be found in Section 8.3.

  The abstract representation of the input problem which is generated follows a common *tool-independent* syntax.

- In a second step, the generated (abstract) representation of the ontology (and requested reasoning task) are converted into a tool-specific representation and fed into a dedicated reasoning component which can solve the requested reasoning task adequately and efficiently. The used reasoning component is not required to understand any of the WSML variants (and their syntax). It is integrated into the WSML reasoning system via a tool-specific adapter component, which encapsulates all tool-specific aspects (such as the required syntax or the interaction pattern with the specific reasoning component) and hides the reasoning component behind a uniform interface.

This approach allows to perform reasoning with different WSML variants based on a wide variety of existing reasoning components in a controlled way. Applications can exploit the freedom to choose the most suitable reasoning component for their purposes. At the same time, the modeling language used in the application stays the same although the input language required by the different reasoning components might differ substantially.

In other words, the two-phased approach allows modelers to leverage a uniform and convenient modeling language and to integrate reasoning components which are not WSML-aware themselves, but have been developed in a different context.

For applications working with WSML-Core ontologies the opportunities to reuse various inference systems is particularly nice: any WSML-Core ontology can be interpreted at the same time in two different ways: as a logic program or alternatively as a Description Logic knowledge base. Consequently, reasoning algorithms developed for both paradigms can be used for reasoning with WSML-Core ontologies. This is especially interesting for applications since it provides the possibility the use a wide-range of different algorithms and respective inference systems each of which usually has specific advantages and disadvantages depending on the reasoning task to be solved in regard of the given ontology.

The WSML2Reasoner[1] framework implements this two-phased approach to reasoning with WSML ontologies. The conceptual architecture of the WSML2Reasoner framework is shown in Figure 8.2. WSML2Reasoner is a generic, flexible transformational framework for reasoning with the different variants of the WSML language family. During the design phase, great importance was attached to system modularity, reuse of existing technologies, and flexibility in configuration and customization of a reasoning system for specific reasoning tasks. The WSML2Reasoner framework allows the easy integration of such external reasoning components. Consequently instead of implementing new reasoners, existing reasoner implementations can be used for WSML through an adapter that maps WSML expressions first into common (shared) knowledge representation formats (depending on the WSML variant used), and then via specific adapters into the appropriate syntaxes of concrete reasoning engines. WSML2Reasoner thus contains various validation, normalization and transformation functionalities that are reusable across different WSML variants. This generic approach allows applications to use their specific existing reasoner of choice in the WSML context, and it provides the possibility to exploit systems that are developed already for years and that are therefore well-tuned with respect to performance and stability.

---

[1] http://tools.deri.org/wsml2reasoner/

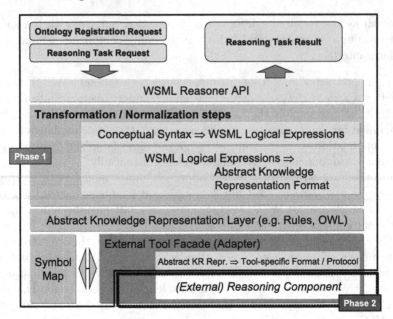

Fig. 8.2. Conceptual architecture of the WSML2Reasoner framework

8.3 Reasoning with Rule-Based Variants

In this section, we discuss a specific instantiation of the WSML2Reasoner framework. More specifically, we describe the transformation process for the rule-based WSML-variants (i.e., WSML-Core, WSML-Flight, and WSML-Rule) in detail.

The semantics of rule-based WSML can in principle be reconstructed by a mapping to Datalog [1] with support for (in)equality, default negation, function symbols, and integrity constraints. In the following, we refer to this language simply as Datalog. To make use of existing rule engines, the reasoning framework performs various syntactical transformations to convert an original ontology in WSML syntax into a semantically equivalent Datalog program. WSML reasoning tasks are then realized by means of Datalog querying via calls to an underlying Datalog inference engine fed with the rules contained in this program. The abstract knowledge representation layer shown in Figure 8.2 corresponds in this case to Datalog rules represented in a non-tool-specific manner.

8.3.1 Ontology Transformations

The transformation of a WSML ontology to Datalog rules forms a pipeline of single transformation steps that are subsequently applied, starting from the original ontology. We overview the translation steps in the following without

Expression in conceptual syntax	Resulting logical expression(s)
concept C_1 **subConceptOf** C_2	C_1 **subConceptOf** C_2.
concept C A **ofType** $(0, 1)$ T	$C[$A **ofType** $T]$. !- ?x **memberOf** C **and** ?x[A **hasValue** ?y, A **hasValue** ?z] **and** ?y != ?z.
concept C A_1 **inverseOf** A_2 **impliesType** T	$C[$A **impliesType** $T]$. (?x **memberOf** C **and** ?v **memberOf** T) **implies** (?x[A_1 **hasValue** ?v] **equivalent** ?v[A_2 **hasValue** ?x]).
relation R_1/n **subRelationOf** R_2	$R_1(?x_1, \ldots, ?x_n)$ **implies** $R_2(?x_1, \ldots, ?x_n)$.
instance I **memberOf** C A **hasValue** V	I **memberOf** C. I[A **hasValue** V].

Table 8.1. Examples for the axiomatization of conceptual ontology modeling elements

giving all details. Those can be found in [68].

Axiomatization. In a first step, the transformation τ_{axioms} is applied as a mapping $\mathcal{O} \rightarrow 2^{\mathcal{LE}}$ from the set of all valid rule-based WSML ontologies to the powerset of all logical expressions that conform to rule-based WSML. In this transformation step, all conceptual syntax elements, such as concept and attribute definitions or cardinality and type constraints, are converted into appropriate axioms specified by logical expressions. Hence, after the translation the input ontology is represented as a set of logical expression in the WSML language only. The WSML logical expression language is rich enough to represent all semantically relevant aspects of the conceptual syntax. We give the details of the conversions performed by τ_{axioms} for some representative examples in Table 8.1 to illustrate the principle (see also Table 4.2 on page 47). The WSML conceptual syntax constructs on the left-hand side are converted to the respective WSML logical expressions on the right-hand side. The meta variables C, C_i range over identifiers of WSML concepts, R_i, A_i over identifiers of WSML relations and attributes, T over identifiers of WSML concepts or datatypes and V over identifiers of WSML instances or data values. Applying the axiomatization transformation to the ontology fragment

```
concept Artist subConceptOf Person
    contributorOf inverseOf(hasContributor) impliesType MediaItem

concept Musician subConceptOf Artist

axiom adultDefinition
    annotations
        dc#description hasValue "A sufficient and necessary characterization of adults."
    endAnnotations
    definedBy
        ?p memberOf Adult :− ?p memberOf Person [hasAge hasValue ?a] and 20 < ?a.
        !− ?p memberOf Adult[hasAge hasValue ?a] and naf 20 < ?a.

concept AdultArtist subConceptOf { Artist, Adult }
```

Original expression	Normalized expression
$\tau_n(\{E_1,\ldots,E_n\})$	$\{\tau_n(E_1),\ldots,\tau_n(E_n)\}$
$\tau_n(E_x$ and $E_y.)$	$\tau_n(E_x)$ and $\tau_n(E_y)$
$\tau_n(E_x$ or $E_y.)$	$\tau_n(E_x)$ or $\tau_n(E_y)$
$\tau_n(E_x$ and $(E_y$ or $E_z).)$	$\tau_n(\tau_n(E_x)$ and $\tau_n(E_y)$ or $\tau_n(E_x)$ and $\tau_n(E_z).)$
$\tau_n((E_x$ or $E_y)$ and $E_z).)$	$\tau_n(\tau_n(E_x)$ and $\tau_n(E_z)$ or $\tau_n(E_y)$ and $\tau_n(E_z).)$
$\tau_n($ naf $(E_x$ and $E_y).)$	naf $\tau_n(E_x)$ or naf $\tau_n(E_y)$.
$\tau_n($ naf $(E_x$ or $E_y).)$	naf $\tau_n(E_x)$ and naf $\tau_n(E_y)$.
$\tau_n($ naf (naf $E_x).)$	$\tau_n(E_x)$
$\tau_n(E_x$ equivalent $E_y.)$	$\tau_n((E_x$ implies $E_y)$ and $(E_x$ impliedBy $E_y))$
$\tau_n(E_x$ implies $E_y.)$	$\tau_n(E_y) :- \tau_n(E_x)$.
$\tau_n(E_x$ impliedBy $E_y.)$	$\tau_n(E_x) :- \tau_n(E_y)$.
$\tau_n(X[Y_1,\ldots,Y_n].)$	$X[Y_1]$ and ... and $X[Y_n]$.

Table 8.2. Normalization of WSML logical expressions

```
instance prince memberOf Musician
         contributorOf hasValue purpleRainAlbum
         hasAge hasValue 50
```

therefore results in the following set of logical expressions

```
Artist subConceptOf Person.
Artist [ contributorOf impliesType MediaItem].
(?x memberOf Artist and ?v memberOf MediaItem) implies
   (?x[contributorOf hasValue ?v] equivalent ?v[hasContributor hasValue ?x]).

Musician subConceptOf Artist.
?p memberOf Adult :- ?p memberOf Person[hasAge hasValue ?a]
                 and wsml#numericLessThan(20, ?a).
!- ?p memberOf Adult[hasAge hasValue ?a] and naf wsml#numericLessThan(20, ?a).

AdultArtist subConceptOf { Artist, Adult }.

prince memberOf Musician.
prince [contributorOf hasValue purpleRainAlbum, hasAge hasValue 50].
```

Normalization. The transformation τ_n is applied as a mapping $2^{\mathcal{LE}} \rightarrow 2^{\mathcal{LE}}$ to normalize WSML logical expressions. This normalization step reduces essentially the complexity of logical expressions to bring expressions closer to the simple syntactic form of literals in Datalog rules. The reduction includes conversion to negation and disjunctive normal forms as well as decomposition of complex WSML molecules. The left part of Table 8.2 shows how the various logical expressions are normalized in detail. The meta variables E_i range over logical expressions in rule-based WSML, while X, Y_i range over parts of WSML molecules. After τ_n has been applied, the resulting expressions have the form of logic programming rules with no deep nesting of logical connectives.

Original expression	Simplified rule(s)
$\tau_{lt}(\{E_1,\ldots,E_n\})$	$\{\tau_{lt}(E_1),\ldots,\tau_{lt}(E_n)\}$
$\tau_{lt}(H_1 :- H_2 :- B.)$	$\tau_{lt}(H_1 :- H_2$ **and** $B.)$
$\tau_{lt}(H_1$ **and** $\ldots$ **and** $H_n :- B.)$	$\tau_{lt}(H_1 :- B.),\ldots,\tau_{lt}(H_n :- B.)$
$\tau_{lt}(H :- B_1$ **or** $,\ldots,$ **or** $B_n.)$	$\tau_{lt}(H :- B_1.),\ldots,\tau_{lt}(H :- B_n.)$

Table 8.3. Simplification of expressions using Llyod-Topor transformations.

Applying the normalization to the set of logical expressions that has been generated by the axiomatization transformation results in the following set of logical expressions

```
Artist subConceptOf Person.
Artist [ contributorOf impliesType MediaItem].

(?v[hasContributor hasValue ?x] :– ?x[contributorOf hasValue ?v])
and (?x[contributorOf hasValue ?v] :– ?v[hasContributor hasValue ?x])
:– ?x memberOf Artist and ?v memberOf MediaItem.

Musician subConceptOf Artist.
?p memberOf Adult :– ?p memberOf Person and ?p[hasAge hasValue ?a]
                 and wsml#numericLessThan(20, ?a]
!– ?p memberOf Adult and ?p[hasAge hasValue ?a] and naf wsml#numericLessThan(20, ?a).

AdultArtist subConceptOf Artist.
AdultArtist subConceptOf Adult.

prince memberOf Musician.
prince [ contributorOf hasValue purpleRainAlbum].
prince [hasAge hasValue 50].
```

Lloyd-Topor Transformation. The transformation τ_{lt} is applied as a mapping $2^{\mathcal{LE}} \rightarrow 2^{\mathcal{LE}}$ to flatten the complex WSML logical expressions, producing simple rules according to the Lloyd-Topor transformations [97], as shown in Table 8.3. Again, the meta variables E_i, H_i, B_i range over WSML logical expressions, while H_i and B_i match the form of valid rule head and body expressions, respectively, according to [68]. After this step, the resulting WSML expressions have the form of proper Datalog rules with a single head and conjunctive (possibly negated) body literals.

For the normalized logical expression set from above, this transformation yields eventually

```
Artist subConceptOf Person.
Artist [ contributorOf impliesType MediaItem].

?v[hasContributor hasValue ?x] :–   ?x[contributorOf hasValue ?v] and ?x memberOf Artist and
    ?v memberOf MediaItem.
?x[contributorOf hasValue ?v] :– ?v[hasContributor hasValue ?x] and ?x memberOf Artist and ?v
    memberOf MediaItem.

Musician subConceptOf Artist.
?p memberOf Adult :– ?p memberOf Person and ?p[hasAge hasValue ?a]
                 and wsml#numericLessThan(20, ?a).
!– ?p memberOf Adult and ?p[hasAge hasValue ?a] and naf wsml#numericLessThan(20, ?a).
```

Original expression	Simplified Datalog expression(s)
$\tau_{dlog}(\{E_1, \ldots, E_n\})$	$\{\tau_{dlog}(E_1), \ldots, \tau_{dlog}(E_n)\}$
$\tau_{dlog}(\ !-\ B.)$	$\square :- \tau_{dlog}(B)$
$\tau_{dlog}(H.)$	$\tau_{dlog}(H)$.
$\tau_{dlog}(H\ :-\ B.)$	$\tau_{dlog}(H) :- \tau_{dlog}(B)$
$\tau_{dlog}(E_x \textbf{ and } E_y.)$	$\tau_{dlog}(E_x) \wedge \tau_{dlog}(E_y)$
$\tau_{dlog}(\textbf{naf } E.)$	$\sim \tau_{dlog}(E)$
$\tau_{dlog}(C_x \textbf{ subConceptOf } C_y.)$	$p_{\text{sco}}(C_x, C_y)$
$\tau_{dlog}(I \textbf{ memberOf } C.)$	$p_{\text{mo}}(I, C)$
$\tau_{dlog}(I[a \textbf{ hasValue } V].)$	$p_{\text{hval}}(I, a, V)$
$\tau_{dlog}(C[a \textbf{ impliesType } T].)$	$p_{\text{itype}}(C, a, T)$
$\tau_{dlog}(C[a \textbf{ ofType } T].)$	$p_{\text{otype}}(C, a, T)$
$\tau_{dlog}(\textbf{r}(X_1, \ldots, X_n).)$	$r(X_1, \ldots, X_n)$
$\tau_{dlog}(X = Y.)$	$X = Y$
$\tau_{dlog}(X \textbf{ != } Y.)$	$X \neq Y$

Table 8.4. Translating WSML logical expressions to Datalog rules

AdultArtist **subConceptOf** Artist.
AdultArtist **subConceptOf** Adult.

prince **memberOf** Musician.
prince [contributorOf **hasValue** purpleRainAlbum].
prince [hasAge **hasValue** 50].

Datalog Rule Generation. In a final step, the transformation τ_{dlog} is applied as a mapping $2^{\mathcal{LE}} \to \mathcal{P}$ from WSML logical expressions to the set of all Datalog programs, yielding generic Datalog rules that represent the content of the original WSML ontology. Rule-style language constructs, such as rules, facts, constraints, conjunction and (default) negation, are mapped to the respective Datalog elements. All remaining WSML-specific language constructs, such as **subConceptOf** or **ofType**, are replaced by special meta-level predicates for which the semantics of the respective language construct is encoded in meta-level axioms as described in Section 8.3.2. Table 8.4 shows the mapping from WSML logical expressions to Datalog including the meta-level predicates p_{sco}, p_{mo}, p_{hval}, p_{itype} and p_{otype} that represent their respective WSML language constructs as can be seen from the mapping. The meta variables E, H, B range over WSML logical expressions with a general, a head or a body form, while C, I, a denote WSML concepts, instances and attributes. Variables T can either assume a concept or a datatype, and V stands for either an instance or a data value, accordingly.

The resulting Datalog rules are of the form $H :- B_1 \wedge \ldots \wedge B_n$, where H and B_i are literals for the head and the body of the rule, respectively. Body literals can be negated in the sense of negation-as-failure, which is denoted by $\sim B_i$. As usual, rules with an empty body represent facts, and rules with an empty head represent constraints. The latter is denoted by the head being the empty clause symbol □.

For our example from above the transformation finally yields the following Datalog rules

p_{sco}(Artist, Person)
p_{itype}(Artist, contributorOf, MediaItem)

p_{hval}(?v, hasContributor, ?x) : $-p_{hval}$(?x, contributorOf, ?v) $\wedge$ p_{mo}(?x, Artist) $\wedge$ p_{mo}(?v, MediaItem)
p_{hval}(?x, contributorOf, ?v) : $-p_{hval}$(?v, hasContributor, ?x) $\wedge$ p_{mo}(?x, Artist) $\wedge$ p_{mo}(?v, MediaItem)

p_{sco}(Musician, Artist)
p_{mo}(?p, Adult) : $-p_{mo}$(?p, Person) $\wedge$ p_{hval}(?p, hasAge, ?a) $\wedge$ wsml#numericLessThan(20, ?a)
□ : $-p_{mo}$(?p, Person) $\wedge$ p_{hval}(?p, hasAge, ?a)$\wedge$ $\sim$ wsml#numericLessThan(20, ?a)

p_{sco}(AdultArtist, Artist)
p_{sco}(AdultArtist, Adult)

p_{mo}(prince, Musician)
p_{hval}(prince, contributorOf, purpleRainAlbum)
p_{hval}(prince, hasAge, 50)

Ultimately, we define the basic transformation[2] τ for converting a rule-based WSML ontology into a Datalog program based on the single transformation steps introduced before by

$$\tau = \tau_{dlog} \circ \tau_{lt} \circ \tau_n \circ \tau_{axioms}$$

As a mapping $\tau : \mathcal{O} \to \mathcal{P}$, this composition of the single steps is applied to a WSML ontology $O \in \mathcal{O}$ to yield a semantically equivalent Datalog program $\tau(O) = P \in \mathcal{P}$ when interpreted with respect to the meta-level axioms discussed next.

8.3.2 WSML Semantics through Meta-Level Axioms

The mapping from WSML to Datalog in the reasoning framework works such that each WSML-identifiable entity, i.e. concept, instance, attribute etc., is mapped to an instance (or logical constant) in Datalog, as depicted in Figure 8.3. There, the concepts C_1, C_2, C_3 as well as the instances I_1, I_2 and the attribute a are mapped to constants such as I_{C_1}, I_{I_1} or I_a in Datalog, representing the original WSML entities on the instance level.

Accordingly, the various special-purpose relationships that hold between WSML entities such as **subConceptOf**, **memberOf** or **hasValue**, are mapped to Datalog predicates that form a meta-level vocabulary for the WSML language constructs. These are the meta-level predicates that appear in Table 8.4 for τ_{dlog}, and which are applied to the Datalog constants that represent the WSML entities. The facts listed in Figure 8.3 illustrate the use of the meta-level predicates. For example, the predicate p_{mo} takes a Datalog constant that

---

[2] Later on, the transformation pipeline is further extended to support datatypes and debugging.

represents a WSML instance and one that represents a WSML concept, to
state that the instance is in the extension of this concept.

In contrast to a direct mapping from WSML to Datalog with concepts,
attributes and instances mapping to unary predicates, binary predicates and
constants, respectively, this indirect mapping allows for the WSML metamodelling facilities. Metamodelling allows an entity to be a concept and an
instance at the same time. By representing a WSML entity as a Datalog constant, it could, for example, fill both the first as well as the second argument
of e.g. the predicate p_{mo}.

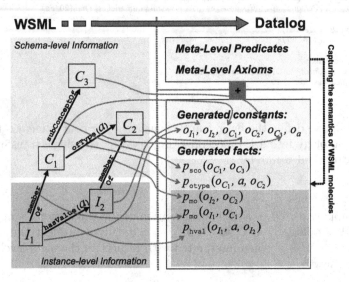

Fig. 8.3. Meta-level predicates in WSML2Reasoner

A fixed set P_{meta} of Datalog rules, shown in Figure 8.4, forms the meta-
level axioms which assure that the original WSML semantics is properly maintained. Axiom (1) realizes transitivity for the WSML **subConceptOf** construct,
while axiom (2) ensures that an instance of a subconcept is also an instance
of its superconcepts. Axiom (3) realizes the semantics for the **impliesType** construct for attribute ranges: any attribute value is concluded to be in the extension of the range type declared for the attribute. Finally, axiom (4) realizes
the semantics of the **ofType** construct by a constraint that is violated whenever
an attribute value cannot be concluded to be in the extension of the declared
range type.

8.3.3 WSML Reasoning by Datalog Queries

To perform reasoning over the original WSML ontology O with an underlying
Datalog inference engine, a Datalog program $P_O = P_{meta} \cup \tau(O)$ is built up

Meta-Level Axioms
(1) $p_{sco}(C_1, C_3) :- p_{sco}(C_1, C_2) \wedge p_{sco}(C_1, C_3) \wedge p_{sco}(C_2, C_3)$
(2) $p_{mo}(I, C_2) :- p_{mo}(I, C_1) \wedge p_{mo}(I, C_2) \wedge p_{sco}(C_1, C_2)$
(3) $p_{mo}(V, C_2) :- p_{itype}(C_1, a, C_2) \wedge p_{mo}(V, C_2) \wedge p_{mo}(I, C_1) \wedge p_{mo}(V, C_2) \wedge p_{hval}(I, a, V)$
(4) $\square :- p_{otype}(C_1, a, C_2) \wedge p_{mo}(I, C_1) \wedge p_{hval}(I, a, V) \wedge \sim p_{mo}(V, C_2)$

Fig. 8.4. Reconstructing the WSML molecule semantics in Datalog

that consists of the meta-level axioms together with the transformed ontology.
The different WSML reasoning tasks are then realized by performing Datalog
queries on P_O. Posing a query $Q(\mathbf{x})$ to a Datalog program $P \in \mathcal{P}$ is denoted
by $(P, ? - Q(\mathbf{x}))$ and yields the set of all tuples $\mathbf{t}$ of constants occuring in
P that instantiate the vector $\mathbf{x}$ of variables in the query such that $Q(\mathbf{t})$ is
satisfied in all stable models of P^3. If $Q(\mathbf{x})$ contains no variables, in fact a
boolean query Q is posed that instead evaluates either to $\{Q\}$ if Q is satisfied
in all stable models of P or $\emptyset$ otherwise.

Ontology Consistency – The task of checking a WMSL ontology for consistency is done by querying for the empty clause, as expressed by the following
equivalence: O is satisfiable $\Leftrightarrow (P_O, ? - \square) = \emptyset$. If the resulting set is empty
then the empty clause could not be derived from the program and the original
ontology is satisfiable, otherwise it is not.

Entailment – The reasoning task of ground entailment by a WSML ontology is
done by using queries that contain no variables, as expressed in the following
equivalence: $O \models \phi_g \Leftrightarrow (P_O, ? - \tau'(\phi_g))) \neq \emptyset$. The WSML ground fact
$\phi_g \in \mathcal{LE}$ is transformed to Datalog with a transformation $\tau' = \tau_{dlog} \circ \tau_{lt} \circ \tau_n$,
similar to the one that is applied to the ontology, and is evaluated together
with the Datalog program P_O. If the resulting set is non-empty then ϕ_g is
entailed by the original ontology, otherwise it is not.

Retrieval – Similarly, instance retrieval can be performed by posing a WSML
query $Q(\mathbf{x})$ with free variables $\mathbf{x}$ to the Datalog program P_O, which yields
the following set: $\{\mathbf{o} \mid O \models Q(\mathbf{o})\} = (P_O, ? - \tau'(Q(\mathbf{x})))$. The query $Q(\mathbf{x})$ is
transformed to Datalog by τ' and evaluated together with the program P_O.
The resulting set contains all object tuples $\mathbf{o}$ for which an instantiation of the
query expression is entailed by the original ontology, while the objects in $\mathbf{o}$
can be identifiable WSML entities or data values.

8.3.4 Realising Datatype Reasoning

Although most of the generic Datalog rules are understood by practically
any Datalog implementation, realizing datatype reasoning has some intricate
challenges. The main challenge is related to Axiom (4) in Figure 8.4, which
checks attribute type constraints. The crucial part of the axiom is the literal

---

[3] This criterion can be approximated efficiently by testing for satisfaction in the
(unique) well-founded model of P only.

$$\sim p_{\mathsf{mo}}(V, C_2)$$

because for datatype values no explicit membership facts are included in the ontology that could instantiate this literal. Consider, for example, the instance prince in the WSML ontology shown in Listing 8.1 – there is no fact $p_{\mathsf{mo}}(50, \_\mathsf{integer})$ for the value of the hasAge attribute. Whenever a value is defined for an attribute constrained by **ofType**, Axiom (4) would cause a constraint violation, since the semantics of an **ofType**-declared attribute requires that any value of this attribute must in fact be *known* (explicitly or by inference) as being a valid value for the corresponding type in the declaration.

To solve this problem, p_{mo} facts should be generated for all datatype constants that appear as values of attributes having **ofType** constraints in the ontology. I.e., for each such constant in the ontology, axioms of the following form should appear,

$$p_{\mathsf{mo}}(V, D) \quad :- \ typeOf(V, D_T)$$

where D denotes the WSML datatype, D_T denotes a datatype supported by the underlying Datalog implementation, which is compatible with the WSML datatype, and $typeOf$ denotes a built-in predicate implemented by the Datalog tool, which checks whether a constant value belongs to the specified datatype.

These additional meta-level axioms result in a new set of Datalog rules, denoted by P_{data}, which are no longer in generic Datalog but use tool-specific built-in predicates of the underlying inference engine. The program P_O is extended by these rules as follows.

$$P_O = P_{meta} \cup P_{data} \cup \tau(O)$$

In addition to datatypes, WSML also supports some predefined datatype predicates, such as numeric comparison (see [68] for a full list). The definition of the axiom adultDefinition in Listing 8.1, for example, uses a shortcut of the WSML wsml#numericLessThan predicate (denoted by $<$). For translation of these special predicates to the corresponding tool-specific built-in predicates supported by the underlying Datalog reasoner, we introduce a new tool-specific transformation step τ_{dpred} as a mapping $\mathcal{P} \to \mathcal{P}$. This affects the transformation pipeline τ as follows.

$$\tau = \tau_{dpred} \circ \tau_{dlog} \circ \tau_{lt} \circ \tau_n \circ \tau_{axioms}$$

In summary, the underlying Datalog implementation must fulfill the following requirements to support WSML datatype reasoning: (i) It should provide built-in datatypes that correspond to WSML datatypes. (ii) It should provide a predicate (or predicates) for checking whether a datatype covers a constant and (iii) It should provide built-in predicates that correspond to datatype-related predefined predicates in WSML.

8.3.5 Debugging Support

During the process of ontology development, an ontology engineer can easily construct an erroneous model containing contradictory information. In order to produce consistent ontologies, inconsistencies should be reported to engineers with some details about the ontological elements that cause the inconsistency.

In rule-based WSML, the source for erroneous modeling are always constraints, together with a violating situation of concrete instances related via attributes. The plain Datalog mechanisms employed in the reasoning framework as described previous sections only allow for checking whether some constraint is violated, i.e., whether the empty clause is derived from P_O indicating that the original ontology O contains errors – more detailed information about the problem is not reported. Experience shows that it is a very hard task to identify and correct errors in the ontology without such background information.

In our framework, we support debugging features that provide information about the ontology entities which are involved in a constraint violation. We achieve this by replacing constraints with appropriate rules that derive debugging-relevant information.

Identifying Constraint Violations

In case of an inconsistent ontology due to a constraint violation, two things are of interest to the ontology engineer: a) the type of constraint that is violated and b) the entities, i.e. concepts, attributes, instances, etc., that are involved in the violation.

For the various types of constraint violations, the information needed by the ontology engineer to track down the problem successfully is different from case to case:

Attribute Type Violation – An attribute type constraint of the form $C[a$ **ofType** $T]$ is violated whenever an instance of the concept C has value V for the attribute a, and it cannot be inferred that V belongs to the type T. Here, T can be either a concept or a datatype, while V is then an instance or a data value, accordingly. In such a situation, an ontology engineer is particularly interested in the instance I, in the attribute value V that caused the constraint violation, together with the attribute a and the expected type T which the value V failed to adhere to.

Minimum Cardinality Violation – A minimum cardinality constraint of the form **concept** C a $(n$ *$)$, is violated whenever the number of distinguished values of the attribute a for some instance I of the concept C is less than the specified cardinality n. In such a situation, an ontology engineer is particularly interested in the instance I that failed to have a sufficient number of attribute values, together with the actual attribute a. (Information about how many values were missing can be learned by separate querying.)

Maximum Cardinality Violation – A maximum cardinality constraint of the form **concept** C a **(0** n**)**, is violated whenever the number of distinguished values of the attribute a for some instance I of the concept C exceeds the specified cardinality n. Again, here an ontology engineer is particularly interested in the instance I for which the number of attribute values was exceeded, together with the actual attribute a.

User-Defined Constraint Violation – Not only built-in WSML constraints, but also user-defined constraints, contained in an axiom definition of the form **axiom** Ax_{ID} **definedBy** !- B., can be violated. In this case, the information which helps an ontology engineer to repair an erroneous situation is dependent on the arbitrarily complex body B and cannot be determined in advance. However, a generic framework can at least identify the violated constraint by reporting the identifier Ax_{ID} of the axiom.

Debugging by Meta-Level Reasoning

In our framework, we realize the debugging features for reporting constraint violations by replacing constraints with a special kind of rules. Instead of deriving the empty clause, as constraints do, these rules derive information about occurrences of constraint violations by instantiating debugging-specific meta-level predicates with the entities involved in a violation. In this way, information about constraint violations can be queried for by means of Datalog inferencing.

The replacement of constraints for debugging is included in the transformation

$$\tau = \tau_{dpred} \circ \tau_{dlog} \circ \tau_{lt} \circ \tau_n \circ \tau_{debug} \circ \tau_{axioms}$$

where the additional transformation step τ_{debug} is applied after the WSML conceptual syntax has been resolved, replacing constraints on the level of WSML logical expressions. Table 8.5 shows the detailed replacements performed by τ_{debug} for the different kinds of constraints.

Minimal cardinality constraints (with bodies $B_{mincard}$) and maximal cardinality constraints (with bodies $B_{maxcard}$) are transformed to rules by keeping their respective bodies and adding a head that instantiates one of the predicates $p_{\text{v\_mincard}}$ and $p_{\text{v\_maxcard}}$ to indicate the respective cardinality violation. The variables for the involved attribute a and instance I are the ones that occur in the respective constraint body B.

Similarly, a user-defined constraint is turned into a rule by keeping the predefined body B_{user} and including a head that instantiates the predicate $p_{\text{v\_user}}$ to indicate a user-defined violation. The only argument for the predicate $p_{\text{v\_user}}$ is the identifier Ax_{ID} of the axiom, by which the constraint has been named.

Constraints on attribute types are handled differently because these constraints are not expanded during the transformation τ_{axioms}; they are rather represented by WSML **ofType**-molecules for which the semantics is encoded

Constraint	Rule
$\tau_{debug}(\{E_1,\ldots,E_n\})$	$\{\tau_{debug}(E_1),\ldots,\tau_{debug}(E_n)\}$
$\tau_{debug}(\;!\!-\;B_{mincard}.)$	$p_{\text{v\_mincard}}(a,I):-\;B_{mincard}.$
$\tau_{debug}(\;!\!-\;B_{maxcard}.)$	$p_{\text{v\_maxcard}}(a,I):-\;B_{maxcard}.$
$\tau_{debug}(\;!\!-\;B_{user}.)$	$p_{\text{v\_user}}(Ax_{ID}):-\;B_{user}.$
$\tau_{debug}(C[a\;\textbf{ofType}\;T].)$	$p_{\text{v\_otype}}(a,T,I,V):-$
	$C[a\;\textbf{ofType}\;T]\;\textbf{and}\;I\;\textbf{memberOf}\;C\;\textbf{and}$
	$I[a\;\textbf{hasValue}\;V]\;\textbf{and}\;\textbf{naf}\;V\textbf{memberOf}\;T.$

Table 8.5. Replacing constraints by rules

in the meta-level axioms P_{meta}. In order to avoid the modification of P_{meta} in the reasoning framework, such molecules are expanded by τ_{debug}, as shown in Table 8.5.[4]

To maintain the semantics of the replaced constraints, an additional set of meta-level axioms $P_{debug} \subseteq \mathcal{P}$ is included for reasoning. The rules in P_{debug} have the form $\square\;:-p_v$ and derive the empty clause for any type and occurrence of a constraint violation.

Including the debugging features, the Datalog program for reasoning about the original ontology then turns to

$$P_O = P_{meta} \cup P_{data} \cup P_{debug} \cup \tau(O)\;\;.$$

Occurrences of constraint violations can be recognized by querying P_O for instantiations of the various debugging-specific meta-level predicates $p_{\text{v\_otype}}$, $p_{\text{v\_mincard}}$, $p_{\text{v\_maxcard}}$ and $p_{\text{v\_user}}$. For example, the set

$$(P_O,\;?-\;p_{\text{v\_otype}}(a,T,I,V))$$

contains tuples for all occurrences of attribute type violations in P_O, identifying the respective attribute a, expected type T, involved instance I and violating value V for each violation. This set is empty no attribute types are violated.

8.3.6 Fitting the Transformation into WSML2Reasoner

The design goals of our framework are modularity for the transformation steps and flexibility with respect to the underlying inference engine. High modularity allows to reuse transformation functionality across different WSML variants and reduces the effort for accomplishing other reasoning tasks. By realizing WSML on top of a generic Datalog layer, we have also reduced the effort of integrating other reasoners to a minimum.

The presented framework has been fully implemented in Java and can be downloaded and tested online[5].

---

[4] After this expansion of **ofType** molecules, the respective axiom (4) in P_{meta} for realising the semantics of attribute type constraints does not apply anymore.

[5] http://tools.deri.at/wsml2reasoner

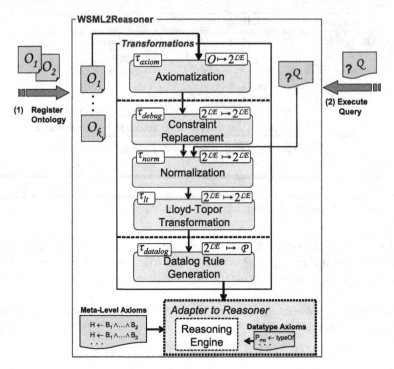

Fig. 8.5. Transformation pipeline for rule-based variants

Architecture and Internal Layering.

Figure 8.5 shows the internal architecture of the framework as well as the data flow during a prototypical usage scenario. The outer box outlines a WSML reasoner component that allows a user to register WSML ontologies and to pose queries on them. The inner box illustrates the transformation pipeline introduced in Sections 8.3.1 – 8.3.4 and shows its subsequent steps in a layering scheme.

Registered ontologies go through all the transformation steps, whereas user queries are injected at a later stage, skipping the non-applicable axiomatization and constraint replacement steps. Here, the internal layering scheme allows for an easy reorganization and reuse of the transformation steps on demand, assuring high flexibility and modularity. A good example for this is the constraint replacement transformation τ_{debug}: if included in the pipeline, it produces the rules that activate the debugging features according to Section 8.3.5; if excluded, the constraints remain in the resulting Datalog program and are mapped to native constraints of the underlying reasoning engine.

The core component of the framework is an exchangeable Datalog inference engine wrapped by a reasoner adapter which embeds it in the framework infrastructure. This adapter component mediates between the generic Datalog program produced in the transformations and the external engine's tool-specific Datalog implementation and built-in predicates. The adapter bridges syntax-related as well as interaction-protocol related heterogeneities between the WSML2Reasoner framework and the native reasoning component.

Interface and Integration with Existing Technology.

Our framework is based on the WSMO4J [6] project, which provides an API for the programmatic handling of WSML documents. WSMO4J performs the task of parsing and validating WSML ontologies and provides the source object model for our translations. For a reasoner to be connected to the framework, a small adapter class needs to be written, that translates generic Datalog elements to their equivalent constructs within the internal representation layer of the underlying reasoner. Our framework currently comes with facades for two built-in reasoners: KAON2[7] and IRIS[8]. The initial development was done with the KAON2 inference engine that, with respect to the challenges for datatype reasoning, provides a very flexible type system that allows for user-defined datatypes, together with predicates on these datatypes, including type checking predicates. However, KAON2 cannot be used for reasoning in WSML-Rule as it does not support function symbols and unsafe rules. The second reasoner, IRIS is currently under development. IRIS can be used for the WSML-Flight variant and is currently being extended to support WSML-Rule.

8.4 Reasoning with WSML-DL

In addition to the rule-based reasoning support, the WSML2Reasoner framework also supports Description Logic-based reasoning for WSML-DL. Analogously to rule-based WSML, WSML2Reasoner implements a a semantics-preserving syntactic transformation of WSML-DL ontologies to a suitable abstract knowledge representation format which can be mapped to various Description Logic reasoning systems. More specifically, OWL-DL has been selected as the abstract representation. The WSML reasoning tasks of checking ontology consistency, entailment and instance retrieval can then be performed by means of OWL DL reasoning applied on a transformed ontology. Thus, the framework directly builds on top of existing OWL-DL or DL reasoning engines. Besides the reasoning tasks, the framework provides validation of WSML-DL ontologies, as well as the serialization of the latter to OWL-DL. The full details of the transformation pipeline which has been developed to deal with WSML-DL ontologies can be found in [130].

---

[6] http://wsmo4j.sourceforge.net
[7] http://kaon2.semanticweb.org
[8] http://iris-reasoner.org/

Ontology Transformation

The transformation of a WSML-DL ontology to an OWL DL ontology is done in a sequence of single transformation steps that are applied one after another.

- **Relations to Attributes.** Replace relations, subrelations and relation instances by attributes and axioms, according to the preprocessing steps described in [130].
- **Axiomatization.** All conceptual elements are converted into appropriate axioms specified by logical expressions, according to [130]. The resulting set of logical expressions is semantically equivalent to the original WSML ontology.
- **Implication Reduction Rules.** Replace equivalences and right-implications in logical expressions by left-implications.
- **Inverse-Implication Reduction Rules.** Replace conjunctions on the left side and disjunctions on the right side of an inverse implication by left implications.
- **Molecule Decomposition Rules.** Replace complex molecules inside a logical expression by conjunctions of simple ones.
- **OWL API Transformation.** All logical expressions that are resulting from the transformation and normalization steps described above, are processed one by one. Each logical expression is translated into the corresponding OWL Description, according to the mapping described in [130].

Architecture and Internal Layering

Figure 8.6 shows the internal architecture of the WSML2Reasoner framework that is related to WSML-DL, as well as the data flow during a prototypical usage scenario. The outer box outlines a WSML reasoner component that allows a user to register WSML-DL ontologies and to reason over them. The inner box illustrates the transformation pipeline and shows its subsequent steps in a layering scheme. Registered ontologies go through all the transformation steps, whereas the user reasoning tasks are injected at a later stage, skipping the non-applicable axiomatization and normalization steps. Here, the internal layering scheme allows for an easy reorganization and reuse of the transformation steps on demand, assuring high flexibility and modularity. The core component of the framework is an exchangeable Description Logic or OWL DL inference engine wrapped by a reasoner facade which embeds it in the framework infrastructure. This facade mediates between the OWL DL ontology produced in the transformations and the tool-specific implementation used by the external inference engine.

Supported Reasoning Tasks

The following reasoning tasks are supported by a WSML-DL Reasoner within the WSML2Reasoner framework:

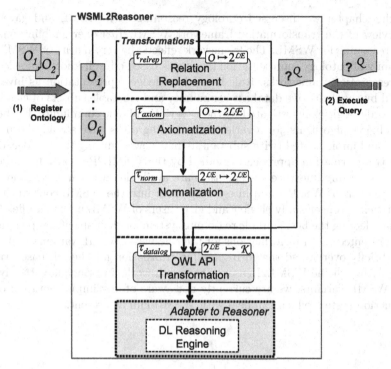

Fig. 8.6. Transformation pipeline for WSML-DL

- **Knowledge Base Consistency.** This task checks a WSML-DL ontology for consistency and verifies that the ontology does not contain any contradictory facts. It checks whether the TBox and ABox of the knowledge base do have a common, non-empty, model.
- **Concept Satisfiability.** This task checks whether there exists a model of the knowledge base in which a given concept is interpreted non-empty.
- **Concept Subsumption.** This tasks checks whether a concept A is more general than a concept B, i.e., whether B denotes a subset of the set denoted by A. This task can also be used to check for Concept Equivalence or Disjointness.
- **Instance Checking.** This tasks checks whether a given instance is member of a given concept.
- **Realization.** This task determines the direct concept that a given instance is member of.
- **Instance Retrieval.** This tasks is about retrieving all instances of a given concept. It also allows to retrieve tuples of instances that satisfy certain conditions.

In this chapter we discussed ontology reasoning with WSML and gave an overview of the transformation framework WSML2Reasoner enabling ontology reasoning for WSML. The framework reflects the very nature of WSML as a family of ontology representation languages based on well-known knowledge representation frameworks: Rule-based knowledge representation as investigated by the deductive database community and tractable subsets of classical first-order logic as investigated by the Description Logic community. For both paradigms, algorithms for a variety of reasoning tasks have already been defined and implemented (with substantial man-power) during the last decades. The transformation approach embodied by the WSML2Reasoner framework aims at reusing inference systems that are available on the market (and are independent of WSML) and integrating them into the WSML context. This approach is conceptually elegant and gives users of WSML maximum flexibility in selecting the best suitable reasoning system for their specific application. We presented the transformations for the rule-based WSML variants in detail and briefly overviewed the corresponding translation for the DL-based variant. Although the WSML2Reasoner approach works in principle with any of the WSML variants, we are currently not aware of any implementation of a deduction system which can deal with WSML-Full at present.

9

Creating and Managing WSML Descriptions

Throughout this book we have seen many examples of the usefulness of describing Web services semantically through the WSMO conceptual model and the WSML language. Using these additional semantic descriptions of Web services it is possible for many parts of the process of building Service Oriented Architectures to be automated. Most importantly service providers and service requesters can be dynamically bound together at runtime, rather than hardwired to one another at application design time. Such runtime binding involves tasks like service *discovery, selection, composition, adaptation, mediation* of both data and process, and *invocation*, with these tasks taking place within a Semantic Execution Environment (SEE) like the Web Service Execution Environment (WSMX) [72] or IRS-III [38]. A Semantic Execution Environment acts a broker between the service requester and the many services available on the web, ensuring that the right service is chosen for the requester that can solve the user's problem and that interoperability problems between the requester and the service can be automatically resolved.

However the process of creating the necessary semantic descriptions in WSML for a SEE to function is not a trivial task and without tool support many of the tasks that need to be performed by the engineer can be lengthy and involved, essentially discouraging the adoption of Semantic Web service technology by industry. In this chapter we describe the Web Service Modeling Toolkit (WSMT)[1] [85, 86], an Integrated Development Environment for Semantic Web services that supports the engineer through the full life cycle of their semantic descriptions in WSML, from creation, through validation and testing, to deployment on a Semantic Execution Environment.

An Integrated Development Environment (IDE) is defined as a type of computer software that assists computer programmers to develop software. The main aim of an IDE is to improve the productivity of the developer by seamlessly integrating tools for tasks like editing, file management, compilation, debugging and execution. Before the creation of the WSMT, developers

---

[1] Available for download from http://wsmt.sourceforge.net

of semantic descriptions using the WSMO paradigm and the WSML Language were forced to create their ontologies, web services, goals and mediators by hand in a text editor. This has many inherent problems as, due to the lack of validation and testing support, it is very easy for errors to creep into these semantic descriptions, which go unnoticed by the developer until run-time. Many other tasks that are very easy in an IDE can be hugely time consuming without one, for example registering a semantic description with an execution environment. Providing a fully integrated suite of tools for Semantic Web services, that supports the Semantic Web service engineer through the full development life cycle will improve that engineer's productivity, reduce the overall of cost of creating and maintaining Semantic Web services and aid in the adoption of the WSML langauge.

The WSMT is implemented as a collection of plug-ins for the Eclipse framework. Eclipse[2] is a rich-client platform that enables the development of rich-client applications on top of it through the creation of plug-ins for the framework. A huge advantage of the Eclipse platform is the ability to combine different sets of plug-ins together dynamically within one application. This means that the WSMT is not only an Integrated Development Environment for Semantic Web services, but can be combined with for example an IDE for Web services to support the engineer through more of the day to day tasks that he must perform. This sort of combination allows engineers to do their work in one application with a consistent predictable tool suite, and removes the necessity to constantly switch back and forth between different applications. Eclipse also has the huge advantage of being written in java and thus multi platform. Rich client applications can be written once and deployed to different desktop operating systems like Windows, Linux and Mac OSX with little to no effort.

The Web Service Modeling Toolkit currently focuses on four main categories of tools in order to support the engineer in the creation of WSML descriptions and the structure of this chapter revolves around these categories. Initially tools for editing and browsing WSML descriptions are introduced, focusing on the fact that different methods for displaying semantic descriptions to the engineer have different advantages depending on the task being performed. Following this the validation tools for WSML within the WSMT are presented, showing that notifying the engineer of errors made as they are made can reduce the time spent debugging semantic descriptions later in the development process. Tools for testing valid semantic descriptions are then introduced that allow the engineer to ensure that the semantic descriptions created behave as expected in their intended deployment environment prior to deploying them. Finally tools for actually deploying the semantic descriptions in WSML to Semantic Execution Environments like WSMX and IRS-III are described.

---

[2] http://www.eclipse.org

9.1 Editing and Browsing WSML Descriptions

As introduced in Chapter 4 the WSML surface syntax offers the engineer a very light language for creating WSMO ontologies, Web services, goals and mediators in WSML. However even with this language, which has only a small amount of syntactic sugar, it is still quite difficult for an engineer to create descriptions. Editing tools can aid the engineer in focusing on the conceptual modeling tasks at hand and minimizing tasks that do not directly impact the result, i.e., ensuring that the description being created is syntactically correct, manually entering complex IRIs etc. Thus by abstracting the engineer from the underlying syntax of the document he can focus on ensuring that his descriptions are modeled in the way that he wants and so produce better descriptions. The tools can also enable the engineer to better understand the descriptions being created, for example it can be hard to see the hierarchical structure of the concepts in an ontology within a textual representation; however this structure becomes clearer when a tree or graph is displayed to the user within an IDE.

The Web Service Modeling Toolkit (WSMT) provides tools at different levels of abstraction with the aim of aiding engineers with tasks that involve different types of tool support. The WSML Text Editor can be very useful to those engineers already familiar and comfortable with the WSML service syntax, while the WSML Form based Editor allows the engineer to forget about the syntax of the document and use a form-filling approach to create semantic descriptions. The WSML Visualizer is a graph based approach to editing semantic descriptions and allows the engineer to see the complexities that exist within the semantic description as that description is being modified. Alongside these three editors the WSMT also provides a number of views that can be used in parallel with these editors to help the engineer to better understand the semantic description being edited. For example the engineer may use the WSML Text Editor, as he is familiar and comfortable with the syntax, alongside the WSML Outline view that provides an overview of the hierarchy of the document. In the following sections these editors and views are described in more detail.

9.1.1 Editing WSML Descriptions through the Surface Syntax

As already described, by abstracting the engineer from the syntax of the document he is editing can help to better focus him on the conceptual modeling task that he is working on; however prior to the existence of any tool support for WSML such engineers were creating these descriptions by hand and are now familiar and comfortable working with the WSML syntax. Therefore it is important that an IDE for Semantic Web services through WSML should also support these experienced engineers as much as trying to support new WSML users.

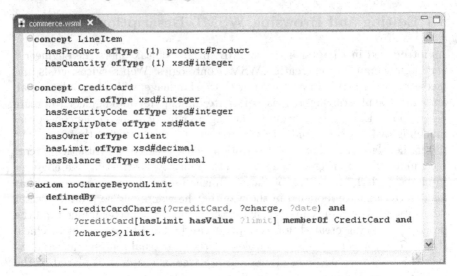

Fig. 9.1. WSML text editor showing an ontology

The WSML Text Editor in the WSMT is designed as such a tool for supporting users who are more experienced with WSML, providing these users with enhanced editing support for the WSML surface syntax. The features supported by the WSML Text Editor include:

- **Syntax Highlighting:** This feature allows the engineer to easily identify the parts of the text that are structural parts of the semantic description. This is done by displaying WSML keywords, strings and IRIs in different colors. the colors that are used for the different types of things can be configured from the WSMT preference dialog.
- **Syntax and Content Auto-completion:** One inherent issue with text based editing is that the user needs to type every character of the description. Auto-completion allows the user to perform some key combination and then receive suggestions regarding the sorts of things they could type here. Auto-completion in the WSML Text Editor suggests WSML Keywords and relevant IRIs based on the users location in the document.
- **Error Notification:** The text editor takes advantage of the validation support within the WSMT (described in more detail in Section 9.2). Errors are displayed, both syntactic and semantic, within the text as the user types. This is achieved by underlining erroneous parts of the text in red.
- **Content Folding:** For large semantic descriptions the surface syntax of WSML can create quite large documents. These documents can become unwieldy to manage and navigate. Code folding is a feature introduced in the Java Development Toolkit[3] that allows certain methods, comments

---

[3] An Integrated Development Environment for the Java programming language developed within the Eclipse framework

etc. to be 'folded' away so that they are removed from the view of the user (the top line of the folded section remains visible). This folding technique has been implemented in the WSML Text Editor for WSML constructs. Folding elements allows the user to configure the current view of the text of the semantic description to that which makes them most productive.

- **Bracket Highlighting:** WSML descriptions can contain many brackets that make up the syntactic sugar of the description. These brackets can be angle, round, square or curly brackets. Errors in the syntax are prevented by highlighting the location of a closing bracket when the user places the cursor beside an opening bracket and vice versa.

9.1.2 Form-Based Management of WSML Descriptions

One step up from the WSML Text Editor is the WSML Form based Editor, which abstracts the engineer from the underlying WSML syntax by providing a structured form to complete. The content entered into the form can be serialized to the WSML surface syntax whenever the engineer desires, thus allowing the engineer to focus on the conceptual modeling task at hand and not having to manually manage the syntactical structure of the WSML document. Not only does this abstraction result in a benefit in terms of focus it also brings a benefit of time, firstly it reduces the number of key strokes that the user must make and secondly it removes the time that the user would have spent debugging problems with the syntax and structure of the document containing the WSML semantic description.

The forms displayed to the engineer are made up of text fields, lists and tables. Commonly with a form based approach the engineer would be required to view the information on the form and then edit the information in the form via some form of popup menus, this is especially true when dealing with tables. Within the WSML Form based Editor all of the fields are directly editable by the engineer to further reduce the number of key strokes or clicks that the engineer must make in order to create a valid semantic description.

To ensure that the size of the forms presented to the engineer do not become too large and difficult to use the WSML Form based Editor is broken up into a number of different tabs, with each tab focusing on a different part of the WSML semantic description being created or edited. For example when working with a Web service in WSML there are three tabs available to the engineer, namely the Header, Web service and capability tabs as can be seen in Figure 9.2.

There are certain parts of a description that are easier to create by textual means, for example when specifying the logical expression belonging to the pre-condition of the capability of a Web service. in these cases the user is presented with a text area into which the logical expression can be input. To improve the productivity of the engineer in these text areas they have been enhanced with relevant features from the WSML Text Editor, for example

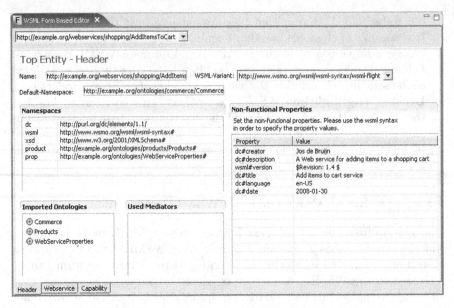

Fig. 9.2. WSML form-based editor showing a service description

syntax highlighting, syntax and content auto-completion, error notification and bracket highlighting.

9.1.3 Graph-Based Description Engineering and Browsing

As described in [84] the WSML Visualizer is a graph based editing and browsing tool for WSMO ontologies, Web services, goals and mediators expressed through WSML. The advantage of using a graph based approach for representing semantic descriptions is that the complexities of the semantic description that are usually hidden in a text based approach or hard to represent in a form based approach, are easily displayed to the user. The WSML Visualizer is based upon the JPowerGraph[4] graphing library, that was also developed by the WSMT team. The editor is relatively unique in that most visualization tools for semantic descriptions are bolted on top of existing editing tools, such that the engineer needs to constantly switch back and forth between the editing and visualizing tool in order to understand the effects of changes that are being made, while this tool provides editing support directly within the visualization such that the engineer can immediately see the effects of making a change to the semantic description.

As can be seen in Figure 9.3 semantic descriptions within the visualizer are represented as nodes and edges of a graph, and are laid out using the spring layout algorithm from JPowerGraph. In a spring layout the nodes in

---

[4] Available for download from http://jpowergraph.sourceforge.net

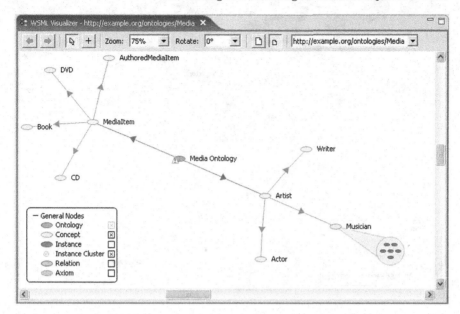

Fig. 9.3. WSML visualizer showing an ontology

the graph repel one another, while edges between nodes attract nodes to one another. The result of this layout is that semantically related things (denoted as related due to the edges between them) are displayed in groups close to each other. Within the graph a number of primitive manipulation techniques are available that users are familiar with from web browsers, word processing and image manipulation applications. Using controls that users are familiar with sets the user at ease as they immediately understand how these controls work, emphasizing the predictability of the GUI. The primitive manipulation tools include Zoom, Rotate, Drag and Drop (for manually positioning the graph) and the ability to change the node size from large to small.

Many visualization solutions for semantic descriptions do not scale as the size of the semantic description increases. Within the WSML Visualizer a number of mechanisms are provided that aim to improve the quality of the visualization as the complexity and size of the semantic description being visualized increases:

- **Filtering:** There are a finite number of types of nodes that can appear within the visualization of WSML semantic description, thus it is possible to provide a mechanism allowing the engineer to filter the types of nodes which should be displayed within the graph. The legend within the WSML Visualizer, which can be seen in Figure 9.3, is interactive and allows the engineer to modify the state of the filter and change the contents of the visualization. Such a filtering allows the engineer to focus on those

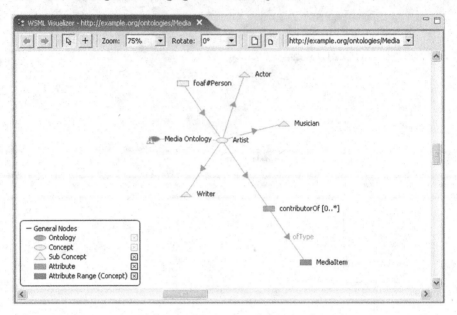

Fig. 9.4. WSML visualizer showing an ontology concept

elements of interest within a semantic description and remove those that are currently not of interest.

- **Semantic Levels:** One common approach to resolving the graph complexity issue is to remove certain types of complexities from the graph, i.e., not to represent certain relationships between elements in the semantic description. For example OWLViz[5], a visualization tool for OWL, does not show the properties of classes in an OWL ontology. However this approach inevitably results in an incomplete solution, where many functions required by the engineer are not available. The WSML Visualizer approaches the problem in a different manner; complexities are grouped together into Semantic Levels with each of these levels being associated with a given entity type in WSMO. Thus at any semantic level all the complexities needed by the user are visible. If the user wishes to see more detail about a given entity they can double click on it; this will change the focus of the visualization onto this entity and more detail of this entity can be seen.

An example of two semantic levels can be seen in Figure 9.4, at the ontology semantic level the instances, relations, relation instances and axioms of the ontology are displayed. At this level the user can gain information about the structure of the ontology, with respect to the subConceptOf, subRelationOf and memberOf relationships in a WSMO ontology. By double clicking on a given concept the user can switch to the concept semantic level. At this level the selected concept is displayed along with all of its

---

[5] http://www.co-ode.org/downloads/owlviz/

super concepts, direct sub concepts and instances. Also at this level all the attributes of the concept can be seen along with their ranges, thus allowing the user to see more information about the concept and to see more clearly the relationship that this concept has with other entities in the ontology.

- **Instance Clustering:** When dealing with ontologies there can exist cases where a large number of instances, which are used in the modeling process, are present within an ontological description. These large numbers of instances can make the graph very cluttered and hard to understand. Within the WSML Visualizer the approach described in [60], which introduces the concept of a cluster map for visualizing light-weight ontologies, is implemented. This allows large numbers of instances in an ontology to be grouped together in clusters. These clusters give the engineer an understanding of the relative number of instances within an ontology for different concepts.

The combination of all these features within the WSML Visualizer provides a visualization solution for ontologies, Web services, goals and mediators expressed in WSML that scales to a better degree than any other existing visualization approaches.

9.1.4 Additional browsing tools

The different layers of editing support provided by the WSML Text Editor, WSML Form Based Editor and WSML Visualizer described in the previous sections gives the engineer a suite of tools that can be useful for editing semantic descriptions in WSML and can each be employed separately for the most appropriate editing tasks; However it is possible to enhance the function of these editors by providing additional tools that operate in parallel with each of these editors. These tools, referred to as Eclipse views, provide the engineer with different views over the data currently being edited allowing the engineer to see the data from another angle.

Within the WSMT there are a number of views relevant for the engineer when editing a WSML description. The WSML Outline View provides an outline of the structure of the file that is currently open in a given editor. This is especially useful when editing WSML descriptions using the WSML Text Editor as the outline view provides an overview of all the elements contained within the structure. By selecting an element, for example a concept in an Ontology or the capability of a Web service, in the outline view this element is then selected in the editor currently being used, thus providing an additional mechanism for browsing a semantic description while editing it, as can be seen in Figure 9.5. The WSML Hierarchy View provides the engineer with more information on the hierarchy that the currently selected entity belongs too. This view is used primarily with elements of an WSML ontology to better understand the subConceptOf, subRelationOf, and memberOf relationships

Fig. 9.5. Outline view with WSML text editor showing an ontology

that a given concept, relation, instance or relationInstance is part of. The user can select any of these entities within an editor and by pressing the F4 key the hierarchy for that element is displayed within the hierarchy view.

9.2 Validating WSML Descriptions

One of the most common and costly problems when creating semantic descriptions is incorrect modeling and human input errors. Without the benefit of tool support it is very easy for the engineer to make mistakes in the syntax and semantics of the WSML description being created. Providing embedded validation support within the development environment being used by the engineer at both the syntactic and semantic levels can vastly reduce the time an engineer spends debugging a semantic description.

The Web Service Modeling Toolkit (WSMT) uses functionality embedded within the WSMO4J library, which provides an object model for WSMO that comes bundled with a parser and serializer for the WSML surface syntax, to perform both syntactic and semantic validation on WSML documents within the workspace of the engineer. From the perspective of ensuring that the syntax of the document is correct, the WSMT uses the WSMO4J parser to parse any file within the workspace that changes, i.e., when the engineer saves a given document the WSMT will ensure that it parses correctly. Having ensured that the file parses correctly the WSMT then puts the ontologies, Web services, goals and mediators parsed from the changed file into the WSMO4J validator to ensure that the top entities are valid.

This validation consists of checking whether the conceptual and the logical-expression definitions within a WSML file are compliant to the WSML variant specified in the header of the document. The validator starts by checking the

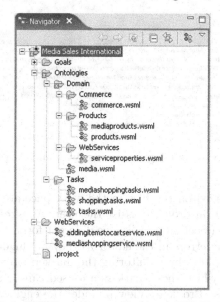

Fig. 9.6. WSML navigator showing a WSML project

correct usage of unnumbered anonymous identifiers in a WSML file, as an object with an unnumbered anonymous identifier must never be referenced. Then it goes on to check which features are used, e.g., attribute cardinality, impliesType, ofType, etc., and whether they are allowed in the variant specified within the header of the given WSML document, for example cardinality constraints are not allowed in the WSML-Core or WSML-DL variants and would thus result in a validation error. Next the validator checks whether the logical expressions in each of the axioms in the file conform to the WSML variant used. The WSMO4J Validator does not only check for errors, but also produces warnings. While an error always indicating an incorrect usage of WSML features with respect to a given WSML variant, a warning is meant to point out unrecommended usages of WSML, and with them suggest an alternate "clean" usage of WSML, for example in WSML-DL the validator checks whether all entities are explicitly defined, and produces warnings if not.

Issues that result either from being unable to parse a given document in the workspace or errors and warnings resulting from the validation process are collated and placed as markers on the WSML file that was validated. If there exists any error on a given file then this file will be graphically marked as having an error within the WSML Navigator. If no errors exist but some warnings are present then the file will be graphically marked as having a warning within the WSML Navigator. Files with no errors or warnings are unmarked. These three states within the WSML Navigator can be seen within Figure 9.6.

Description	Resource	Location
Attribute 'hasTitle' on Concept 'MediaItem' - Attribute Cardinality Error: Attributes may not contain cardinality constraints	media.wsml	line 26
Attribute 'hasTitle' on Concept 'MediaItem' - Attribute Constraint Error: The attribute type 'ofType' is not allowed, other than for dat...	media.wsml	line 26
Attribute 'hasContributor' on Concept 'MediaItem' - Attribute Cardinality Error: Attributes may not contain cardinality constraints	media.wsml	line 27
Attribute 'hasContributor' on Concept 'MediaItem' - Attribute Constraint Error: The attribute type 'ofType' is not allowed, other than...	media.wsml	line 27
Attribute 'contributorOf' on Concept 'Artist' - Attribute Constraint Error: The attribute type 'ofType' is not allowed, other than for dat...	media.wsml	line 29
Attribute 'contributorOf' on Concept 'Artist' - Attribute Feature Error: Attributes may not contain the attribute feature 'inverseOf'	media.wsml	line 29
Relation 'stageNameContributor' - Relation Arity Error: The arity of relations is restricted to 2	media.wsml	line 40
Axiom 'stageNameContributorAxiom' - Inadmissible formula	media.wsml	line 51
Axiom 'stageNameContributorAxiom' - Inadmissible formula: A LogicProgrammingRule is not a valid formula	media.wsml	line 51

Fig. 9.7. Problem view showing an ontology with an incorrect WSML variant

The markers placed on the files in the workspace are used in two other ways by the WSMT in order to assist the user. As already mentioned the editors introduced in Section 9.1 all have different forms of error notification facilities that display errors in the editor as they are made. These errors are shown within the editors by monitoring the markers on the respective files. The second way in which these markers are used can be seen in Figure 9.7. The standard Eclipse Problems View provides the engineer with a list of all the errors and warnings within the workspace, within a specific project, or in a specific file. The engineer can use this list to track down all the problems within the workspace and repair them.

9.3 Testing WSML Ontologies, Web Services and Goals

Once the validity of semantic descriptions has been established the next step is usually to deploy these descriptions to the application in which they will be used. In many industrial scenarios this will be some form of test environment where the new descriptions can be tested for a period of time prior to making the changes live on a live server. At this point the engineer enters an iterative process that involves deploying the description to the test environment, performing some testing on the system, making modifications and then redeploying for further testing. Such a process can be very costly if the number of redeployments required, before a satisfactory result is achieved, is high. As mentioned in the previous section, the WSMT checks the syntactic and semantic validity of the WSML descriptions in the workspace; however such validity does not ensure that the descriptions created actually match what the engineer was attempting to model in the first place.

The WSMT aims to reduce the number of redeployments that the engineer needs to make by providing functionality within the development environment that enables the engineer to test that the semantic descriptions behave as expected in an environment similar to that in which they will eventually be used. By performing this testing within the development environment itself the engineer removes the overhead of having to setup and configure a deployment environment for each test run and can quickly make changes to the semantic description open in the current editor and see how the changes that he makes effect the behavior of the semantic description. It should of course be noted that this form of testing does not replace the necessity to test the description in a testing environment identical to the deployment environment prior to actual deployment, but provides a mechanism for the engineer to quickly debug problems within the development environment and improve his overall productivity in the test cycle. In the rest of this section we describe the testing support within the WSMT that helps the engineer to test the behavior of WSML ontologies, Web services and goals in the environments in which they will be used.

9.3.1 Testing WSML Ontologies Using the WSML2Reasoner Framework

Ontologies act as the data model for all descriptions in WSML and an engineer should test each of the ontologies that he has created to ensure that the ontology behaves as expected before he bases other descriptions on the ontology. The deployment environments for a WSML ontology is generally a reasoner within with reasoning tasks over the ontology can be performed. In the WSMT we use the WSML2 Reasoner framework to perform testing of WSML ontologies in a variety of reasoners. The WSML2 Reasoner[6] framework (see the previous chapter) provides normalization and transformation functions that allow translation of ontology descriptions in WSML to the appropriate underlying syntax of a number of underlying reasoners. Thus allowing users of different WSML variants to perform their reasoning through the same framework. The functionality of the WSML2 Reasoner framework is exposed to the engineer in the form of the WSML Reasoning View. This view, as can be seen in Figure 9.8 allows the engineer to perform reasoning functions over the ontology that is visible in the currently open editor (plus any ontologies that this ontology imports) and to view the results of that reasoning task.

The types of reasoning tasks that can be performed in the WSML Reasoner View depends upon the variant of the ontology open in the current editor. For WSML-Flight and WSML-Rule, access is provided to the IRIS, MINS and KAON2 reasoners which provide query answering support. The engineer can enter a query that is to be posed to the current ontology and the results of executing this query are displayed to the user in a table. For WSML-DL, access is provided to the Pellet reasoner, which can perform consistency checking and a selection of predefined queries over description logic ontologies. By providing access to these reasoning functions the engineer can test that the reasoning functions, that will be used in the deployment environment, behave as expected and return the expected answer. In cases where this does not occur the engineer can be sure that some form of remodeling within his ontologies is

---

[6] http://tools.deri.org/wsml2reasoner/

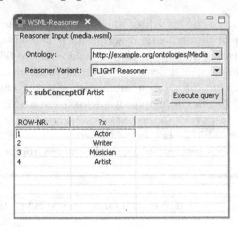

Fig. 9.8. Reasoner view with resources in the workspace

required in order to get the correct behavior for the current ontology within the desired reasoner.

The WSML Reasoner View is also connected to all the editors in the WSMT, so not only can it retrieve the ontology that is currently being edited but can also change the current visible entity within a given editor when the user double clicks that entity in the table of results. This functionality allows the results of a query to act as a mechanism for browsing entities in the workspace.

9.3.2 Testing WSML Web Services and Goals Using Discovery Engines

A crucial point when created Semantic Web services is to ensure that users can find them. Any service created by an engineer that cannot be found by any discovery engine is useless for an open and distributed environment like the Web. As described in Chapter 6, discovery is the process of matching the user's goal against the available Semantic Web services to find the most appropriate functional match. To enable the engineer to test that the WSML Web services that he has created do indeed match the expected WSML goals the WSMT provides the WSML Discovery view.

The WSML Discovery View, as can be seen in Figure 9.9, allows the engineer to select a WSML goal and a collection of WSML Web services from the workspace and execute the matching process between them, from this the engineer can determine if the selected goal finds the expected Web services or not. The view functions by invoking the discovery engines from the Web Service Execution Environment (WSMX), which have been embedded within the WSMT in a similar manner as with the WSML2Reasoner framework.

One crucial point that should be noted is that the engineer will not necessarily know all of the WSML goals that will be provided by end users.

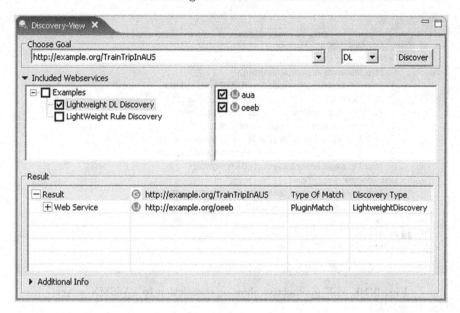

Fig. 9.9. Discovery view showing matching goal and Web service descriptions

Therefore he can realistically only test what he believes are good examples of end user goals. Towards these ends many service providers may offer sample goals that end users can use in order to find their services. These sample goals can play a crucial role in the competitiveness of a given company, in that if it can ensure that its Semantic Web services match the sample goals of competing companies it can ensure that end-users of its competitors services will also see their services. The WSML Discovery View gives the engineers of such services the ability to quickly perform these tests and ensure that the services he creates match with the desired goals.

9.4 Interfacing with Semantic Execution Environments

Ultimately the purpose of creating WSMO ontologies, Web services, goals and mediators in the WSML language is to allow the automation of the process of using Web services and building Service Oriented Architectures, by making the descriptions of Web services processable and understandable by machines. An environment that performs automation of tasks within the process of using Web services, like service *discovery, selection, composition, adaptation, mediation* of both data and process, and *invocation* is referred to as a Semantic Execution Environment (SEE). Such a SEE is essentially responsible for binding service requesters and service providers at runtime through the interaction of the requesters goal description and the providers Web service description.

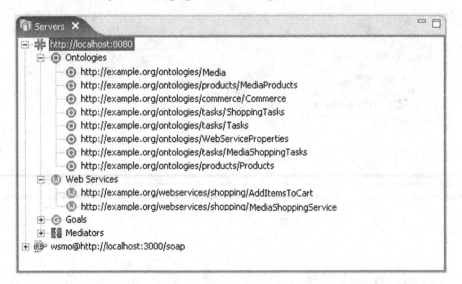

Fig. 9.10. SEE perspective showing connection to a WSMX server

However in order for the functionality of the SEE to be realized the relevant Web services and goals need to be available to the SEE along with any ontologies that these Web services and goals import or mediators that they use. Without the availability of tool support, the process of deploying WSMO semantic descriptions expressed in WSML to a Semantic Execution Environment would be complex and would involve either interfacing manually with the management Web services of the SEE or manually placing the relevant WSML documents into the SEEs repositories by hand.

The Web Service Modeling Toolkit makes it easy for the engineer to interface with a Semantic Execution Environment in order to deploy relevant WSML descriptions. The WSMT allows the engineer to configure multiple Semantic Execution Environments in order to :

- **Browse** the ontologies, Web services, goals and mediators already present on a SEE. As can be seen in Figure 9.10 the SEE Servers view provides the user with an overview of the contents of the internal repositories of a given SEE.
- **Store** WSML descriptions from the WSMT workspace into a SEE. Within the WSML Navigator, as already seen in Figure 9.6, the engineer can right click on one or more WSML files and store the contents of these files to a given SEE.
- **Retrieve** existing descriptions from a SEE in order to edit them. By right clicking on an ontology, Web service, goal or mediator in the SEE Servers view this element can be stored into the local workspace for editing and then later stored back into the SEE repository.

- **Invoke** an entrypoint of the SEE in order to test that created descriptions behave as expected on the SEE. Again by right clicking on one or more WSML files in the workspace different entry points of the WSMT can be invoked. For example, if the files selected contain a WSML goal then the achieveGoal entrypoint is available to the engineer. These entrypoints allow the engineer to do further testing of the semantic descriptions that they have created in a runtime scenario.

At the time of writing, the WSMT supported two Semantic Execution Environments, namely the Web Service Execution Environment (WSMX) [72] and IRS-III [38]. Both of these environments expose a set of Web services that provide access to the functionality of the SEE, allowing the engineer to browse, store and retrieve WSML descriptions and invoke entrypoints of the SEE. One interesting difference between WSMX and IRS-III is that all data within IRS-III is described in terms of the OCML format [110], and the WSMT must translate to and from WSML and this format when sending data to or retrieving data from IRS-III.

In this chapter we have seen how an integrated development environment can be used to assist the authors with the task of writing goal and Web service descriptions. The Web Service Modeling Toolkit not only provides graphical support for modeling various aspects of ontologies, goals, and Web services, but also makes use of reasoning and discovery tools for checking consistency of descriptions and allowing authors to make sure their descriptions meet their expectations.

10

Conclusions and Outlook

Throughout this book we have described the WSML language in detail, we have shown how the language can be used for describing the various aspects of Web services, and we have shown how WSML descriptions can be managed and processed. In this chapter we summarize the content of the book and give an overview of the ongoing research standardization efforts in the area of Semantic Web service description.

10.1 Semantic Web Service Description with WSML

While the Web Service Modeling Ontology WSMO [57] identifies and describes the elements that are important for the semantic description of Web services, it does not provide a concrete language for writing such descriptions, nor does it provide means for processing such descriptions. The Web Service Modeling Language WSML fills these gaps by providing a language for the description of goals, Web services, mediators, and ontologies, and by providing means for matching goals and services, processing service interfaces (choreographies), and reasoning with ontologies.

We have seen that WSML consists of three sub-languages: the WSML *ontology language*, the WSML *capability language*, and the WSML *choreography language*. The ontology language is used for the description of terminologies and background knowledge, and can be combined with RDFS and OWL DL, thereby enabling the use of ontologies written using these languages for Web service description. The capability language introduces two notions: (a) set-based capabilities, which correspond to Description Logic concepts – essentially, ontologies are used for capability description; the capability corresponds to a concept in a task ontology – and (b) state-based capabilities, which extend the ontology language with a notion of pre- and post-state – a Web service execution is seen as a state transition and the capability defines conditions on the state before and after execution; ontologies are used to define the format of inputs and outputs, as well as background knowledge.

The choreography language is used for the description of client interfaces – choreographies – of Web services. The interaction between the client and the service typically involves a number of messages sent back and forth between the requester and provider. The content of the messages is described by ontology concepts; the rules governing the interaction itself are captured using *transition rules*. Essentially, given a state of the interaction, the transition rules determine whether a state transition will take place, and which state will be next in the interaction.

We have also seen that, orthogonal to the mentioned sub-languages, WSML contains a number of *language variants*, which are based on different knowledge representation paradigms. Notably, WSML-DL corresponds to the Description Logics (DL) paradigm, specifically the Description Logic $\mathcal{SHIQ}$ [78], and WSML-Rule corresponds to the Logic Programming (LP) paradigm, specifically the Stable Model Semantics for normal logic programs [62].[1] Then, WSML-Flight is the function-free, locally stratified subset of WSML-Rule, WSML-Core is the intersection of Flight and DL, and WSML-Full extends both the Rule and DL variants. Thus, WSML gives the user a choice the DL and LP paradigms for ontology and Web service modeling, and allows interaction between the paradigms through a common subset (WSML-Core). As there is currently no widespread consensus about the best way of combining the DL and LP paradigms, and since the problem of reasoning with such combinations using the existing approaches has not been investigated as much as the DL and LP paradigms, and suffers from problems of tractability and undecidability, it was decided not to define a normative semantics for WSML-Full. However, there is a proposal [32] for using an expressive nonmonotonic logic as the underlying paradigm for WSML-Full.

Finally, we have seen two tools for processing and managing WSML descriptions, namely the WSML2Reasoner and the Web Service Modeling Toolkit (WSMT). The former exploits the correspondence between the respective WSML variants and the DL and LP paradigms; it uses existing DL and LP reasoners to process WSML descriptions. The WSMT is an Integrated Development Environment for Semantic Web services that supports the engineer in editing, browsing, testing, and validating WSML descriptions. The WSMT not only allows users to manage WSML descriptions, but also enables interfacing with Semantic Execution Environments [56] for storing and retrieving descriptions and for invoking services.

---

[1] Recall that the Well-Founded Semantics [61] may be used to approximate the Stable Model Semantics for query answering.

10.2 Ongoing Standardization Efforts

Semantic Web Services

Recall that WSDL [2] is concerned with the format of messages and communication protocols, whereas WSML is concerned with the meaning of messages and the functionality and behavior of services; therefore, WSML and WSDL address orthogonal aspects of Web service descriptions. SAWSDL [54] is a recent W3C recommendation concerned with modeling Semantic Web services. It defines a simple extension of WSDL, allowing referring to ontologies and Semantic Web service descriptions from a WSDL Web service description. Since such references are IRIs, and WSML elements are identified using IRIs, SAWSDL may be used to connect WSDL descriptions and WSML descriptions.

The OASIS Semantic Execution Environment Technical Committee (SEE-TC)[2] aims to provide a standardized description of the interfaces and behavior of the services that make up a Semantic Execution Environment for Semantic Web services, along with a description of how these services should interact with each other. The services within a SEE are broken up into two main categories namely *broker services* and *base services*. Broker services provide high-level functionality such as service discovery and data mediation, while base services perform a supporting role, offering services such as reasoning for semantic descriptions and resource management and storage. The OASIS SEE-TC also provides a reference ontology for Service Oriented Architectures that is based on a abstraction from WSMO and thus WSMO and WSML can be used to realize concrete implementations of the services standardized in the SEE-TC.

The Object Management Group (OMG) standardization body recently issued a Request For Proposals (RFP) for a UML Profile and Metamodel for Web services. The RFP solicits those working in the field of modeling Web services to submit proposals for a services metamodel and profile for extending UML with capabilities for modeling services using SOA. A solid proposal is currently being drafted by a number of research and industry partners both in the US and in Europe aimed to address this RFP from OMG; these partners include members of the Semantic Web service community. The intention of the proposal is to provide a UML Profile and Metamodel that considers how the services will be realized, allowing services created with UML to be grounded to Web services using technologies like grid, Semantic Web services and P2P. The proposal considers semantics as a core solution to resolving heterogeneity issues between services in an SOA and as part of the proposal extensions to the existing Ontology Definition Metamodel (ODM) standard from OMG will be made. ODM provides a Metamodel based on the Meta-Object Facility (MOF) enabling the transformation of models for different ontology languages. As already mentioned WSMO is also defined using MOF

---

[2] http://www.oasis-open.org/committees/semantic-ex/

and ongoing work will enable the use of WSMO with the ODM standard to enable the exchange of WSMO models through the ODM standard. This research will enable further adoption of WSMO and as such will see further adoption of the WSML language.

Semantic Web

Related, and to some extent orthogonal to Semantic Web service description efforts are the Semantic Web efforts. Recall that ontologies form the basic vocabulary for service descriptions, and Semantic Web technologies such as RDFS and OWL may be used for describing these ontologies.

In 2007 an effort has been started by the W3C OWL Working Group[3] to define a new version of the Web Ontology Language OWL – dubbed OWL 1.1. At the time of writing, the working group is still in early stages. However, if, as expected, OWL DL 1.1 will be based on the standard Description Logic technology, there should be no problem to use it in Web service descriptions with the DL variant of WSML.

When the WSML effort started there was no standard rules language for the Semantic Web. In fact, WSML-Flight and WSML-Rule can be seen as efforts to define rules languages for the Web and they have been proposed for standardization [35, 7]. In 2005 the W3C Rule Interchange Format (RIF) working group[4] set out to standardize a Web rules language. At the time of writing, there preliminary versions of the RIF language specification and the RIF RDF and OWL compatibility [22, 43] have been published. Since RIF is a logical rule-based language, we expect there will be no problem in using RIF with the rule-based variants of WSML.

[3] http://www.w3.org/2007/OWL/
[4] http://www.w3.org/2005/rules/

References

1. Serge Abiteboul, Richard Hull, and Victor Vianu. *Foundations of Databases*. Addison-Wesley, 1995.
2. Rama Akkiraju, Joel Farrell, John Miller, Meenakshi Nagarajan, Marc-Thomas Schmidt, Amit Sheth, and Kunal Verma. Web service semantics - WSDL-S. W3C Member Submission, November 2005. Available from: http://www.w3.org/Submission/WSDL-S/.
3. H. Peter Alesso and Craig F. Smith. *Developing Semantic Web services*. AK Peters, 2004.
4. Gustavo Alonso, Fabio Casati, Harumi Kuno, and Vijay Machiraju. *Web services*. Springer-Verlag, Berlin Heidelberg, 2004.
5. Anastasia Analyti, Grigoris Antoniou, Carlos Viegas Damásio, and Gerd Wagner. Stable model theory for extended RDF ontologies. In *Proceedings of the 4th International Semantic Web Conference (ISWC2005)*, pages 21–36. Springer, 2005.
6. Tony Andrews et al. Business process execution language for web services version 1.1. Technical report, BEA, IBM, Microsoft, SAP, Siebel, 2003. Available from: http://www-106.ibm.com/developerworks/webservices/library/ws-bpel/.
7. Jürgen Angele, Harold Boley, Jos de Bruijn, Dieter Fensel, Pascal Hitzler, Michael Kifer, Reto Krummenacher, Holger Lausen, Axel Polleres, and Rudi Studer. Web rule language (WRL). W3C Member Submission 09 September 2005, 2005. Available from: http://www.w3.org/Submission/WRL/.
8. Anupriya Ankolekar et al. OWL-S 1.1 release, 2004. Available from: http://www.daml.org/services/owl-s/1.1/.
9. Grigoris Antoniou and Frank van Harmelen. *A Semantic Web Primer*. MIT Press, 2004.
10. Daniel Austin, Abbie Barbir, Christopher Ferris, and Sharad Garg. Web services architecture requirements. Working Group Note 11 February 2004, W3C, 2004. Available from: http://www.w3.org/TR/wsa-reqs/.
11. Franz Baader, Diego Calvanese, Deborah L. McGuinness, Daniele Nardi, and Peter F. Patel-Schneider, editors. *The Description Logic Handbook*. Cambridge University Press, 2003.
12. Franz Baader, Carsten Lutz, Maja Milicic, Ulrike Sattler, and Frank Wolter. Integrating description logics and action formalisms: First results. In *Proceedings*

of the 20th National Conference on Artificial Intelligence (AAAI2005), Pittsburgh, PA, USA, 2005.

13. Chitta Baral. *Knowledge Representation, Reasoning and Declarative Problem Solving*. Cambridge University Press, 2003.

14. Dave Beckett. RDF/XML syntax specification (revised). Recommendation 10 February 2004, W3C, 2004. Available from: http://www.w3.org/TR/rdf-syntax-grammar/.

15. David Beckett and Tim Berners-Lee. Turtle – terse RDF triple language. W3C Team Submission 14 January 2008, 2008. Available from: http://www.w3.org/TeamSubmission/turtle/.

16. Tom Bellwood et al. *UDDI* version 3.0, July 2002. Available from: http://uddi.org/pubs/uddi-v3.00-published-20020719.htm.

17. Tim Berners-Lee, Roy Fielding, and Larry Masinter. Uniform resource identifiers (URI): Generic syntax. Standard RFC 3986, Internet Engineering Task Force, 2005.

18. Tim Berners-Lee, James Hendler, and Ora Lassila. The semantic web. *Scientific American*, 284(5):34–43, May 2001.

19. Piergiorgio Bertoli, Jörg Hoffmann, Freddy Lécué, and Marco Pistore. Integrating discovery and automated composition: from semantic requirements to executable code. In *Proceedings of the 2007 IEEE International Conference on Web services (ICWS 2007)*, pages 815–822. IEEE Computer Society, 2007.

20. Paul V. Biron and Ashok Malhotra. XML schema part 2: Datatypes second edition. Recommendation 28 October 2004, W3C, 2004. Available from: http://www.w3.org/TR/xmlschema-2/.

21. Patrick Blackburn, Maarten de Rijke, and Yde Venema. *Modal Logic*. Cambridge Tracts in Theoretical Computer Science (No. 53). Cambridge University Press, 2003.

22. Harold Boley and Michael Kifer. RIF basic logic dialect. Working Draft 30 October 2007, W3C, 2007. Available from: http://www.w3.org/TR/rif-bld/.

23. Lucas Bordeaux, Gwen Salaün, Daniela Berardi, and Massimo Mecella. When are two web services compatible? In Ming-Chien Shan, Umeshwar Dayal, and Meichun Hsu, editors, *Technologies for E-Services*, volume 3324 of *Lecture Notes in Computer Science*, pages 15–28. Springer, 2004.

24. Egon Börger and Robert Stärk. *Abstract State Machines: A Method for High-Level System Design and Analysis*. Springer, 2003.

25. Alex Borgida. On the relative expressiveness of description logics and predicate logics. *Artificial Intelligence*, 82(1–2):353–367, 1996.

26. Tim Bray, Dave Hollander, Andrew Layman, and Richard Tobin. Namespaces in XML 1.1 (second edition). Recommendation 16 August 2006, W3C, 2006. Available from: http://www.w3.org/TR/xml-names11/.

27. Tim Bray, Jean Paoli, C. M. Sperberg-McQueen, Eve Maler, Franois Yergeau, and John Cowan. Extensible markup language (XML) 1.1 (second edition). Recommendation 16 August 2006, W3C, 2006. Available from: http://www.w3.org/TR/xml11/.

28. Dan Brickley and Ramanathan V. Guha. RDF vocabulary description language 1.0: RDF schema. Recommendation 10 February 2004, W3C, 2004. Available from: http://www.w3.org/TR/rdf-schema/.

29. Jos de Bruijn. WSML abstract syntax and semantics. Working Draft D16.3 v0.3, WSML, 2007. Available from: http://www.wsmo.org/TR/d16/d16.3/v0.3/.

30. Jos de Bruijn, Thomas Eiter, Axel Polleres, and Hans Tompits. On representational issues about combinations of classical theories with nonmonotonic rules. In *Proceedings of the 1st International Conference on Knowledge Science, Engineering and Management (KSEM2006)*, pages 1–22. Springer, 2006.

31. Jos de Bruijn, Thomas Eiter, Axel Polleres, and Hans Tompits. Embedding non-ground logic programs into autoepistemic logic for knowledge-base combination. In *Proceedings of the 20th International Joint Conference on Artificial Intelligence (IJCAI2007)*, pages 304–309, Hyderabad, India, January 6–12 2007. AAAI Press.

32. Jos de Bruijn and Stijn Heymans. A semantic framework for language layering in WSML. In *Proceedings of the First International Conference on Web Reasoning and Rule Systems (RR2007)*, pages 103–117, Innsbruck, Austria, June 7–8 2007. Springer.

33. Jos de Bruijn and Stijn Heymans. WSML ontology semantics. Working Draft d28.3, WSML Working Group, 2007. Available from: http://www.wsmo.org/TR/d28/d28.3/v0.2/.

34. Jos de Bruijn and Stijn Heymans. On the relationship between description logic-based and f-logic-based ontologies. *Fundamenta Informaticae*, 82(3):213–236, 2008.

35. Jos de Bruijn, Holger Lausen, Axel Polleres, and Dieter Fensel. The WSML rule languages for the semantic web. In *Proceedings of the W3C Workshop on Rule Languages for Interoperability*, Washington DC, USA, April 2005. Position paper.

36. Jos de Bruijn, David Pearce, Axel Polleres, and Agustín Valverde. Quantified equilibrium logic and hybrid rules. In *Proceedings of the 1st International Conference on Web Reasoning and Rule Systems (RR2007)*, pages 58–72, Innsbruck, Austria, June 7–8 2007. Springer.

37. Jos de Bruijn, Axel Polleres, Rubén Lara, and Dieter Fensel. OWL DL vs. OWL Flight: Conceptual modeling and reasoning on the semantic web. In *Proceedings of the 14th International World Wide Web Conference (WWW2005)*, pages 623–632, Chiba, Japan, 2005. ACM.

38. Liliana Cabral, John Domingue, Stefania Galizia, Alessio Gugliotta, Barry Norton, Vlad Tanasescu, and Carlos Pedrinaci. IRS-III: A broker for semantic web services based applications. In *Proceedings of the 5th International Semantic Web Conference (ISWC2006)*, Athens, Georgia, USA, Nov 2006.

39. Diego Calvanese, Giuseppe De Giacomo, and Maurizio Lenzerini. Conjunctive query containment and answering under description logics constraints. *Transactions on Computational Logic (ToCL)*, 9(3), 2008. To be published.

40. Roberto Chinnici, Jean-Jacques Moreau, Arthur Ryman, and Sanjiva Weerawarana. Web services description language (WSDL) version 2.0 part 1: Core language. Recommendation 26 June 2007, W3C, 2007. Available from: http://www.w3.org/TR/wsdl20.

41. Kendall Grant Clark, Lee Feigenbaum, and Elias Torres. SPARQL protocol RDF. Recommendation 15 January 2008, W3C, 2008. Available from: http://www.w3.org/TR/rdf-sparql-protocol/.

42. Michael Dahr. *Deductive Databases: Theory and Applications*. International Thomson Publishing, December 1996.

43. Jos de Bruijn. RIF RDF and OWL compatibility. Working Draft 30 October 2007, W3C, 2007. Available from: http://www.w3.org/TR/rif-rdf-owl/.

44. Jos de Bruijn. *Semantic Web Language Layering with Ontologies, Rules and, Meta-Modeling*. PhD thesis, Faculty of Mathematics, Computer Science and Physics of the University of Innsbruck, Innsbruck, Austria, 2008. Available from: `http://www.debruijn.net/publications/debruijn-thesis-final.pdf`.
45. Jos de Bruijn. WSML/RDF. Working Draft D32v0.2, WSML Working Group, 2008. Available from: `http://www.wsmo.org/TR/d32/v0.2/`.
46. Mike Dean and Guus Schreiber. OWL web ontology language reference. Recommendation 10 February 2004, W3C, 2004. Available from: `http://www.w3.org/TR/owl-ref/`.
47. Xin Dong, Alon Y. Halevy, Jayant Madhavan, Ema Nemes, and Jun Zhang. Similarity search for web services. In *Proceedings of the 13th International Conference on Very Large Data Bases (VLDB2004)*, pages 372–383, 2004.
48. Francesco M. Donini, Maurizio Lenzerini, Daniele Nardi, and Andrea Schaerf. AL-log: integrating datalog and description logics. *Journal of Intelligent Information Systems*, 10:227–252, 1998.
49. M. Duerst and M. Suignard. Internationalized resource identifiers (iris). Proposed standard RFC 3987, Internet Engineering Task Force, 2005.
50. Thomas Eiter, Giovambattista Ianni, Roman Schindlauer, and Hans Tompits. A uniform integration of higher-order reasoning and external evaluations in answer-set programming. In *IJCAI 2005*, pages 90–96, 2005.
51. Thomas Eiter, Thomas Lukasiewicz, Roman Schindlauer, and Hans Tompits. Combining answer set programming with description logics for the semantic web. In *Proceedings of the 9th International Conference on Principles of Knowledge Representation and Reasoning (KR2004)*. AAAI Press, 2004.
52. Hebert B. Enderton. *A Mathematical Introduction to Logic*. Academic Press, second edition edition, 2000.
53. David C. Fallside and Priscilla Walmsley. XML schema part 0: Primer second edition. Recommendation 28 October 2004, W3C, 2004. Available from: `http://www.w3.org/TR/xmlschema-0/`.
54. Joel Farrell and Holger Lausen. Semantic annotations for WSDL and XML schema. Recommendation 28 August 2007, W3C, 2007. Available from: `http://www.w3.org/TR/sawsdl/`.
55. Dieter Fensel. *Ontologies: Silver Bullet for Knowledge Management and Electronic Commerce, 2nd edition*. Springer-Verlag, Berlin, 2003.
56. Dieter Fensel, Mick Kerrigan, and Michal Zaremba, editors. *Implementing Semantic Web services: The SESA Framework*. Springer, 2008.
57. Dieter Fensel, Holger Lausen, Axel Polleres, Jos de Bruijn, Michael Stollberg, Dumitru Roman, and John Domingue. *Enabling Semantic Web services – The Web service Modeling Ontology*. Springer, 2006.
58. Melvin Fitting. *First-Order Logic and Automated Theorem Proving*. Springer-Verlag, second edition edition, 1996.
59. Melvin Fitting. *First Order Logic and Automated Theorem Proving (second edition)*. Springer Verlag, 1996.
60. Christiaan Fluit, Marta Sabou, and Frank van Harmelen. Supporting user tasks through visualisation of light-weight ontologies. In Stefan Staab and Rudi Studer, editors, *Handbook on Ontologies in Information Systems*, pages 415–434. Springer-Verlag, 2003.
61. Allen Van Gelder, Kenneth Ross, and John S. Schlipf. The well-founded semantics for general logic programs. *Journal of the ACM*, 38(3):620–650, 1991.

62. Michael Gelfond and Vladimir Lifschitz. The stable model semantics for logic programming. In Robert A. Kowalski and Kenneth Bowen, editors, *Proceedings of the Fifth International Conference on Logic Programming*, pages 1070–1080, Cambridge, Massachusetts, 1988. The MIT Press.

63. Michael Gelfond and Vladimir Lifschitz. Classical negation in logic programs and disjunctive databases. *New Generation Computing*, 9(3/4):365–386, 1991.

64. J. Gettys, J. Mogul, H. Frystyk, L. Masinter, P. Leach, and Tim Berners-Lee. Hypertext transfer protocol - http/1.1. Draft standard RFC 2616, Internet Engineering Task Force, 1999.

65. Jan Grant and Dave Beckett. Rdf test cases. Recommendation, W3C, 2004. Available from: http://www.w3.org/TR/rdf-testcases/.

66. Benjamin N. Grosof, Ian Horrocks, Raphael Volz, and Stefan Decker. Description logic programs: Combining logic programs with description logic. In *Proc. Intl. Conf. on the World Wide Web (WWW-2003)*, Budapest, Hungary, 2003.

67. W3C HTML Working Group. XHTML 1.0 the extensible hypertext markup language (second edition). Recommendation 26 January 2000, revised 1 August 2002, W3C, 2002. Available from: http://www.w3.org/TR/xhtml1.

68. WSML Working Group. WSML language reference. Working Draft D16.1 v0.3, WSML, 2008. Available from: http://www.wsmo.org/TR/d16/d16.1/v0.3/.

69. Martin Gudgin, Marc Hadley, Noah Mendelsohn, Jean-Jacques Moreau, Henrik Frystyk Nielsen, Anish Karmarkar, and Yves Lafon. Soap version 1.2 part 1: Messaging framework (second edition). Recommendation 27 April 2007, W3C, 2007. Available from: http://www.w3.org/TR/soap12-part1/.

70. Martin Gudgin, Marc Hadley, Noah Mendelsohn, Jean-Jacques Moreau, Henrik Frystyk Nielsen, Anish Karmarkar, and Yves Lafon. Soap version 1.2 part 2: Adjuncts (second edition). Recommendation 27 April 2007, W3C, 2007. Available from: http://www.w3.org/TR/soap12-part2/.

71. Yuri Gurevich. Evolving algebras 1993: Lipari Guide. In Egon Börger, editor, *Specification and Validation Methods*, pages 9–37. Oxford University Press, 1994.

72. Armin Haller, Emilia Cimpian, Adrian Mocan, Eyal Oren, and Christoph Bussler. Wsmx - a semantic service-oriented architecture. In *Proceedings of the International Conference on Web services (ICWS2005)*, Orlando, Florida, USA, July 2005.

73. Patrick Hayes. RDF semantics. Technical report, W3C, 2004. W3C Recommendation 10 February 2004. Available from: http://www.w3.org/TR/rdf-mt/.

74. Jörg Hoffmann, Piergiorgio Bertoli, and Marco Pistore. Web service composition as planning, revisited: In between background theories and initial state uncertainty. In *Proceedings of the 22nd National Conference on Artificial Intelligence (AAAI2007)*, pages 1013–1018, Vancouver, BC, Canada, 2007.

75. Matthew Horridge, Nick Drummond, John Goodwin, Alan Rector, Robert Stevens, and Hai Wang. The manchester OWL syntax. In *Proceedings of the workshop OWL: Experiences and Directions 2006*, Athens, GA, USA, 2006.

76. Ian Horrocks and Peter F. Patel-Schneider. A proposal for an OWL rules language. In *Proc. of the Thirteenth International World Wide Web Conference (WWW 2004)*, pages 723–731. ACM, 2004.

77. Ian Horrocks, Peter F. Patel-Schneider, and Frank van Harmelen. From SHIQ and RDF to OWL: The making of a web ontology language. *Journal of Web Semantics*, 1(1):7–26, 2003.

78. Ian Horrocks, Ulrike Sattler, and Stephan Tobies. Practical reasoning for very expressive description logics. *Logic Journal of the IGPL*, 8(3):239–264, May 2000.
79. Herman J. ter Horst. Combining RDF and part of OWL with rules: Semantics, decidability, complexity. In *Proceedings of the 4th International Semantic Web Conference (ISWC 2005)*, Galway, Ireland, 2005.
80. Ian Jacobs. Architecture of the world wide web, volume one. Recommendation 15 December 2004, W3C, 2004. Available from: http://www.w3.org/TR/webarch/.
81. Michael Kay. XSL transformations (XSLT) version 2.0. Recommendation 23 January 2007, W3C, 2007.
82. Uwe Keller, Rubén Lara, Holger Lausen, Axel Polleres, and Dieter Fensel. Automatic location of services. In *Proceedings of the 2nd European Semantic Web Conference (ESWC2005)*, pages 1–16. Springer-Verlag, 2005.
83. Uwe Keller, Holger Lausen, and Michael Stollberg. On the semantics of functional descriptions of web services. In *Proceedings of the 3rd European Semantic Web Conference (ESWC2006)*, pages 605–619, Budva, Montenegro, 2006. Springer-Verlag.
84. Mick Kerrigan. Wsmoviz: An ontology visualization approach for wsmo. In *Proceedings of the 10th International Conference on Information Visualization (IV06)*, London, England, July 2006.
85. Mick Kerrigan, Adrian Mocan, Martin Tanler, and Werner Bliem. Creating semantic web services with the web service modeling toolkit (wsmt). In *Proceedings of the workshop on Making Semantics Work For Business (MSWFB2007) at the 1st European Semantic Technology Conference (ESTC2007)*, Vienna, Austria, May 2007.
86. Mick Kerrigan, Adrian Mocan, Martin Tanler, and Dieter Fensel. The web service modeling toolkit - an integrated development environment for semantic web services (system description). In *Proceedings of the 4th European Semantic Web Conference (ESWC2007)*, Innsbruck, Austria, June 2007.
87. Michael Kifer, Jos de Bruijn, Harold Boley, and Dieter Fensel. A realistic architecture for the semantic web. In *Proceedings of the International Conference on Rules and Rule Markup Languages for the Semantic Web (RuleML-2005)*, number 3791 in Lecture Notes in Computer Science, pages 17–29, Ireland, Galway, November 2005. Springer.
88. Michael Kifer, Georg Lausen, and James Wu. Logical foundations of object-oriented and frame-based languages. *JACM*, 42(4):741–843, 1995.
89. Michel C. A. Klein, Jeen Broekstra, Dieter Fensel, Frank van Harmelen, and I. Horrocks. Ontologies and schema languages on the web. In D. Fensel, J. Hendler, H. Lieberman, and W. Wahlster, editors, *Spinning the Semantic Web: Bringing the World Wide Web to Its Full Potential*, pages 95–139. MIT Press, Cambridge, MA, USA, 2003.
90. Graham Klyne and Jeremy J. Carroll. Resource description framework (RDF): Concepts and abstract syntax. Recommendation 10 February 2004, W3C, 2004.
91. Rubén Lara, Dumitru Roman, Axel Polleres, and Dieter Fensel. A conceptual comparison of WSMO and OWL-S. In *European Conference on Web services (ECOWS 2004)*, Erfurt, Germany, 2004.
92. Holger Lausen and Thomas Haselwanter. Finding web services. In *1st European Semantic Technology Conference*, Vienna, Austria, June 2007.

93. Alon Y. Levy and Marie-Christine Rousset. Combining horn rules and description logics in CARIN. *Artificial Intelligence*, 104:165 – 209, 1998.

94. Lei Li and Ian Horrocks. A software framework for matchmaking based on semantic web technology. In *Proceedings of the 12th International Conference on the World Wide Web*, pages 331–339, Budapest, Hungary, 2003.

95. Zhen Liu, Anand Ranganathan, and Anton Riabov. A planning approach for message-oriented semantic web service composition. In *Proceedings of the 22nd National Conference on Artificial Intelligence (AAAI2007)*, pages 1389–1394, Vancouver, BC, Canada, 2007.

96. John W. Lloyd. *Foundations of Logic Programming (2nd edition)*. Springer-Verlag, 1987.

97. John W. Lloyd and Rodney W. Topor. Making prolog more expressive. *Journal of Logic Programming*, 1(3):225–240, 1984.

98. Ashok Malhotra, Jim Melon, and Norman Walsh. Xquery 1.0 and xpath 2.0 functions and operators. Working draft, W3C, 2005. http://www.w3.org/TR/xpath-functions/.

99. V. Wiktor Marek and Miroslaw Truszczynski. Stable semantics for logic programs and default theories. In *Proceedings of the North American Conference on Logic Programming*, pages 243–256, Cleveland, Ohio, USA, 1989. MIT Press.

100. A. Martens. On compatibility of web services. *Petri Net Newsletter*, 65:12–20, 2003.

101. A. Martens. Simulation and equivalence between bpel process models, 2005.

102. Dean Martin et al. Owl-s: Semantic markup for web services. W3C Member Submission, November 2004. Available from: http://www.w3.org/Submission/OWL-S/.

103. Deborah L. McGuinness and Frank van Harmelen. OWL web ontology language overview. Recommendation 10 February 2004, W3C, 2004. Available from http://www.w3.org/TR/owl-features/.

104. Sheila McIlraith, Tran Cao Son, and Honglei Zeng. Semantic web services. *IEEE Intelligent Systems, Special Issue on the Semantic Web*, 16(2):46–53, 2001.

105. Sun Microsystems. *Sun ONE Architecture Guide*. Sun, 2002.

106. Adrian Mocan and Emilia Cimpian. An ontology-based data mediation framework for semantic environments. *International Journal on Semantic Web and Information Systems (IJSWIS)*, 3(2):66–95, 2007.

107. Boris Motik, Ian Horrocks, Riccardo Rosati, and Ulrike Sattler. Can owl and logic programming live together happily ever after? In *Proc. of the 5th Int. Semantic Web Conf. (ISWC 2006)*, Athens, GA, USA, November 5 – 9 2006.

108. Boris Motik and Riccardo Rosati. A faithful integration of description logics with logic programming. In *Proceedings of the Twentieth International Joint Conference on Artificial Intelligence (IJCAI-07)*, Hyderabad, India, January 6–12 2007.

109. Boris Motik, Ulrike Sattler, and Rudi Studer. Query answering for OWL-DL with rules. In *Proceedings of 3rd International Semantic Web Conference (ISWC2004)*, Hiroshima, Japan, November 2004.

110. Enrico Motta. *Reusable Components for Knowledge Modelling. Case Studies in Parametric Design Problem Solving*, volume 53 of *Frontiers in Artificial Intelligence and Applications*. IOS Press, 1999.

111. Anthony Nadalin, Chris Kaler, Phillip Hallam-Baker, and Ronald Monzillo. Web services security: SOAP message security 1.0 (WS-Security 2004). Standard 200401, OASIS, 2004. Available from: http://docs.oasis-open.org/ wss/2004/01/oasis-200401-wss-soap-message-security-1.0.pdf.

112. Srini Narayanan and Sheila A. McIlraith. Analysis and simulation of web services. *Computer Networks*, 42(5):675–693, 2003.

113. Justin O'Sullivan, David Edmond, and Arthur H.M. ter Hofstede. Formal description of non-functional service properties. Technical report, Queensland University of Technology, Brisbane, 2005. Available from: http://www. service-description.com/.

114. M. Paolucci, T. Kawamura, T.R. Payne, and K. Sycara. Semantic matching of web services capabilities. In *Proceeding of The First International Semantic Web Conference (ISWC2002)*, Sardinia, Italy, 2002.

115. Peter F. Patel-Schneider, Patrick Hayes, and Ian Horrocks. OWL web ontology language semantics and abstract syntax. Recommendation 10 February 2004, W3C, 2004.

116. Axel Polleres, François Scharffe, and Roman Schindlauer. SPARQL++ for mapping between RDF vocabularies. In *OTM 2007, Part I : Proceedings of the 6th International Conference on Ontologies, DataBases, and Applications of Semantics (ODBASE 2007)*, pages 878–896, Vilamoura, Algarve, Portugal, 2007. Springer.

117. Eric Prud'hommeaux and Andy Seaborne. SPARQL query language for RDF. Recommendation 15 January 2008, W3C, 2008. Available from: http://www. w3.org/TR/rdf-sparql-query/.

118. Teodor C. Przymusinski. On the declarative and procedural semantics of logic programs. *Journal of Automated Reasoning*, 5(2):167–205, 1989.

119. Alan Rector, Chris Welty, Natasha Noy, and Evan Wallace. Simple part-whole relations in owl ontologies. Editor's Draft 11 Aug 2005, W3C, 2005. Available from: http://www.w3.org/2001/sw/BestPractices/OEP/SimplePartWhole/.

120. Raymond Reiter. A logic for default reasoning. In Matthew L. Ginsberg, editor, *Readings in nonmonotonic reasoning*, pages 68–93. Morgan Kaufmann Publishers Inc., San Francisco, CA, USA, 1987.

121. Dumitru Roman, Holger Lausen, and Uwe Keller. Web service modeling ontology (WSMO). Final Draft D2v1.3, WSMO, 2006. Available from: http://www.wsmo.org/TR/d2/v1.3/.

122. Dumitru Roman and James Scicluna. Ontology-based choreography of WSMO services. Final Draft D14v0.3, WSMO, 2006. Available from: http://www. wsmo.org/TR/d14/v0.3/.

123. Riccardo Rosati. Towards expressive KR systems integrating datalog and description logics: A preliminary report. In *Proc. of the 1999 International Description Logics workshop (DL99)*, pages 160–164, 1999.

124. Riccardo Rosati. On the decidability and complexity of integrating ontologies and rules. *Journal of Web Semantics*, 3(1):61–73, 2005.

125. Riccardo Rosati. Semantic and computational advantages of the safe integration of ontologies and rules. In *Proceedings of PPSWR2005*, pages 50–64. Springer-Verlag, 2005.

126. Riccardo Rosati. $\mathcal{DL}+log$: Tight integration of description logics and disjunctive datalog. In *KR2006*, 2006.

127. François Scharffe and Jos de Bruijn. A language to specify mappings between ontologies. In *Proceedings of the 1st International Conference on Signal-Image Technology and Internet-Based Systems (SITIS2005)*, Yandoué, Cameroon, November 2005. Dicolor Press.

128. Nigel Shadbolt, Tim Berners-Lee, and Wendy Hall. The semantic web revisited. *IEEE Intelligent Systems*, 21(3):96–101, May/June 2006.

129. Evren Sirin, Bijan Parsia, Dan Wu, James A. Hendler, and Dana S. Nau. HTN planning for web service composition using SHOP2. *Journal of Web Semantics*, 1(4):377–396, 2004.

130. Nathalie Steinmetz. WSML-DL reasoner. Bachelor thesis, Digital Enterprise Research Institute (DERI), University of Innsbruck, Austria., August 2006. Available from: http://www.sti-innsbruck.at/teaching/theses/completed/details/?uid=78.

131. Katia Sycara, Massimo Paolucci, Anupriya Ankolekar, and Naveen Srinivasan. Automated discovery, interaction and composition of semantic web services. *Journal of Web Semantics*, 1(1):27–46, 2003.

132. Henry S. Thompson, David Beech, Murray Maloney, and Noah Mendelsohn. XML schema part 1: Structures second edition. Recommendation 28 October 2004, W3C, 2004. Available from: http://www.w3.org/TR/xmlschema-1/.

133. Ioan Toma. WSML/XML. Working Draft D36 v0.1, WSML, 2008. Available from: http://www.wsmo.org/TR/d36/v0.1/.

134. Ioan Toma, Douglas Foxvog, and Michael C. Jaeger. Modeling QoS characteristics in WSMO. In *Proceedings of the 1st workshop on Middleware for Service Oriented Computing (MW4SOC 2006)*, pages 42–47, Melbourne, Australia, 2006.

135. Jeffrey D. Ullman. *Principles of Database and Knowledge-Base Systems, Volume I.* Computer Science Press, 1988.

136. Jeffrey D. Ullman. *Principles of Database and Knowledge-Base Systems, Volume II.* Computer Science Press, 1989.

137. Stuart Weibel, John Kunze, Carl Lagoze, and Misha Wolf. Dublin core metadata for resource discovery. RFC 2413, IETF, 1998.

138. Gio Wiederhold. Mediators in the architecture of future information systems. *IEEE Computer*, 25(3):38–49, March 1992.

139. Amy Moormann Zaremski and Jeannette M. Wing. Specification matching of software components. *ACM Transactions on Software Engineering and Methodology (TOSEM)*, 6(4):333–369, 1997.

Index